(continued from front flap)

tion of words in the reading vocabulary.
She also discusses visual and auditory discrimination, the significance of contextual
clues in independent word perception,
and the appropriate techniques for word
identification while reading.

PHONICS

FOR THE READING TEACHER

Anna D. Cordts

PHONICS

FOR THE READING TEACHER

Holt, Rinehart and Winston, Inc.

NEW YORK
CHICAGO
SAN FRANCISCO
TORONTO
LONDON

FOREWORD

The value of phonics as an aid to reading is recognized by school administrators, classroom teachers, and specialists in the field of reading. Whether the school's approach to reading is phonetic, linguistic, individualized reading, or the whole-word method of instruction, phonics is almost certain to be included in the total reading program.

Along with the growing interest in phonetic instruction in the schools, the teacher's need for a scientific background in phonics has become increasingly clear. It is particularly significant, therefore, that *Phonics for the Reading Teacher* has brought the science of phonetics to bear on the teaching of phonics. This book is a unique contribution to reading instruction in the nation's schools.

The book is distinguished for its scientific study of the sounds of English in the children's reading vocabulary in relation to phonics; for the phonetic principle on which the auditory discrimination of sounds is based; and the effective techniques for children's independent word perception in reading.

The author's treatment of the problem of pronunciation in our country, and the chapter on syllabication of words in the reading vocabulary are equally noteworthy. The history of phonetic instruction in the schools of our land from the days of

v

41155

Noah Webster to the present is an interesting story, exceedingly well told in the book.

The informal tests at the close of the chapters provide a convenient means of enabling the reader of the book to discover how well the information in the chapter has been learned and retained.

College professors of education, teachers of reading and the language arts, elementary supervisors, directors of teachers' workshops, clinicians, and other specialists in the field of reading will find in the rich offerings of this book the answer to a long-felt need.

The author is to be congratulated on the clear and scholarly presentation of a technical subject in a book that is both readable and exceedingly instructive.

Henry C. Herge
Dean, School of Education
Rutgers—The State University

PREFACE

   With the upsurge of interest in the teaching of reading in
the nation's schools, "phonetic" instruction has come into promi-
nence. After having so long been held in ill-repute, phonics has
regained respectability.

   Whatever brand of phonics is used or whatever role phonics
is playing in a given school system, whether as *the* method of beginning reading or as part of the total reading program, teachers
by their own admission find their knowledge of phonics inade-
quate to give them confidence and joy in their teaching.

   While not all upper-grade instructors in our elementary
schools are as badly off as the fourth-grade teacher who confessed
that he did not know one phonic from another, few teachers have
more than a superficial knowledge of phonics or have had any
training in the science of speech sounds. Older teachers continue
to rely on the methods with which they are familiar, and younger
teachers depend largely on the manuals that accompany the basic
reading systems.

   Research and educational experiment have pointed the way
to more effective methods of teaching phonics, from the child's
first experiences in listening to speech sounds straight through to
the point where the youngster achieves independence in reading.
These improved methods unfortunately are not yet generally in

use in the classrooms of our elementary schools. How often have teachers asked, "Why is it that so many children in school are tone deaf? They seem unable to hear when words begin alike, even the most familiar words like *big, boys, bears, beetles, bananas;* or words like *milk, mouse, mice, music,* and *monkeys.*"

Should anyone be expected to *hear* that because words start with the same consonant they all begin with the same sounds? Why must auditory discrimination still be made as difficult and confusing today as it always has been? It will no longer be so when children are given the opportunity to hear likenesses in sounds that are identical. Auditory discrimination will then be a delightful experience for the beginner in school and at the same time lay the groundwork for his growing into reading.

Again one sees how deeply rooted are the traditional methods of teaching in the way the vowels and consonants are being taught. Rather than to tell pupils the sounds and drill them in isolation, how exciting it is for children to *discover* the sounds in words they have already learned to recognize in reading; and having learned the sounds, to associate them with the letters in working out the new words in reading or the unfamiliar components in the words. Then how gratifying it is to have identified the word without "sounding it out" and checking it against the context "to see that it fits the sentence," as the children say.

It is the pioneer task of this book to provide the teacher with a background in the science of phonetics as a crucial foundation for effective instruction on all levels in reading and the language arts. It attempts to build not only a knowledge of the speech sounds but also that clear understanding of sound-to-letter and letter-to-sound relationships of vowels and consonants that is essential to effective teaching. Tables showing these relationships amplify the discussion in the text and serve as a ready reference for the teacher.

With a knowledge of the science of phonetics it is reasonable to assume that the sounds of the letters will be correctly taught. Mispronunciation of the consonants, particularly the troublesome plosives; confusion of single sounds in the children's reading vocabulary with blends, and of one-letter blends with single sounds; and the confusion of diphthongs with the so-called digraphs, and digraphs with diphthongs, will be a thing of the past.

The author hopes that the book will clarify the function of phonics in the reading program and illustrate the flexibility of phonics in relation to and in conjunction with other ways of identifying unfamiliar words in reading; and that it will help the teacher to become a critical judge of the validity of "phonetic" instruction provided in the reading materials she is now using. For by no means are all exercises dealing with sounds, in fact, reliable phonics.

As teachers become more fully aware of the value of effective instruction in phonics, the author believes they will find new confidence, hence greater joy, in teaching reading, and through more meaningful teaching they will heighten the pleasure that children find in one of the most rewarding experiences of childhood—the achievement of independence in reading.

The author is indebted to Elizabeth M. Jenkins for her able and untiring assistance in research and in organizing material throughout the book.

A. D. C.

New York
November 1964

CONTENTS

PHONICS

FOR THE READING TEACHER

1

INTRODUCTION

Since the beginning of the twentieth century theory and classroom procedures in word perception in reading have swayed from one extreme to another. We have gone from the practice of "sounding out" the new words in reading (with its overemphasis on the form of the words) to guessing from the context, with little or no attention given to the visual form of words. We have moved from a revolt against phonics to a powerful swing back to "phonetic" instruction in the schools.

Phonics has played a dramatic role in American education since the time of its advent in the nation's schools. It has been in good and ill repute, in and out of the schools, and now in again, and in unquestionably good standing. The problem is no longer whether or not phonics should be taught. The question now is, How effectively is phonics being taught as a means of independent word perception in reading?

There is probably no area of instruction in the elementary schools today about which there are so many conflicting theories and about which teachers have so much to learn as in the field of phonics. One bright young teacher in commenting on her inability to teach phonics intelligently was speaking not only for herself when she said, "I've never had a course in the science of phonetics; and we didn't even have phonics when I was in the grades; but we have to teach it as part of the reading program, so I go ahead and do the best I can."

The late William S. Gray described the situation in this way:

Unfortunately, during the past twenty years teachers have had very little preparation for teaching of word perception and especially of phonetic analysis. Older teachers know only the old methods and younger teachers have never been taught newer and better techniques of teaching phonetics. What the younger teachers know about the teaching of phonetics consists almost entirely of what they were taught as children and of what they have learned from reading manuals. Many of these manuals do little more than suggest the teaching of phonetic elements and do not attempt to develop understandings and skills which both teacher and pupils need as helps to word analysis.[1]

Observations of classroom instruction in phonics show the teachers' need of a knowledge of the science of phonetics and an adequate knowledge of the subject matter of phonics, and the techniques for effective functioning of phonics in word perception in reading.

CONFUSION BETWEEN SOUNDS AND LETTERS

It is understandable that without a knowledge of the science of phonetics one would have difficulty in distinguishing between the sounds in a word and the letters that stand for the sounds in the English language. If every sound were always represented by the same letter, and every letter consistently stood for the same sound, and for that sound only, there would be no confusion between sounds and letters in a given word. But when the same sound, like the vowel in *food,* for example, is spelled seventeen different ways, and the same symbol, like the letter *o,* which, with the letters that are associated with it, has twenty-six different spellings to represent its various vowel sounds, the relationship between sounds and letters may indeed be perplexing.

It is not surprising to see a letter in a word that is not pronounced when the word is spoken, like the letter *b* in *lamb* and *debt,* for example. But when one hears a speech sound in a word

1 Reprinted from *On Their Own in Reading* by William S. Gray, copyright © 1948 by Scott, Foresman and Company, Chicago.

for which there is no letter, as in the case of the word *one* or *once* in which the (w) is missing, that can indeed be confusing.

Many teachers of reading have not learned to hear speech sounds irrespective of the letters that represent the sounds. Mrs. Brown, an otherwise able teacher, presents a case in point. Wishing to share with a visitor her pleasure in the children's progress in phonics, Mrs. Brown pointed out their responses to an assignment in their workbooks.

"Look," she exclaimed, "what nice work these little ones can do!"

The children were to draw a circle around every word that had the same vowel sounds as in *owl*. Nearly everyone in the group had encircled all the words having the letters *ow*. Not only the words having the diphthong as in *owl*, but the words *snow, grown, low, blow,* and *flown* as well!

"Oh dear," the teacher sighed, as her pupils' errors were pointed out to her. "Of course, I see it now. But I know so little about phonetics or phonics, I shouldn't be trying to teach it!"

Letters that look alike seem to sound alike; and not having learned to hear the sounds in words regardless of the letters that represent the sounds, Mrs. Brown, as she rightly said later, was hearing the words with her eyes.

Because the vowels in the words *few* and *flew*, in *tune* and *June*, and in *cue* and *true* look alike, many teachers have difficulty in distinguishing between the sounds of the vowels that are heard and the letters that are seen in each pair of words; and that too is understandable, without a knowledge of phonetics.

In pronouncing the words in the following list, one hears that they all have the same vowel sound, although the spelling does not show it.

| sigh | buy | choir | isle | right |
| sides | type | guide | aisle | height |

Not only the vowels but the consonants too are often misleading. By listening as you pronounce each of the following words, you will hear four different pronunciations for the letters *ng*.

| long | congress | longitude | congratulate |

One needs only to observe the discrepancies between sounds and letters to realize how difficult it is for the untrained ear to hear the sounds in a word regardless of the spelling of the word. Many otherwise able teachers fail to hear the differences between the voiceless sound of *th* as in *thin* and its voiced counterpart as in the word *this;* between the sound of the letter *s* as in *sure* and the sound of the same letter as in *usual.*

Similar difficulty is experienced in trying to hear that (d) is the first sound in the word *jumped;* that (t) is the first sound that is heard in the word *chick;* and that the sound of the letter *z* in *seizure* and the letter *s* in *pleasure* is the same sound that one hears at the end of the words *rouge* and *garage.*

Failure to assign the correct sounds to the letters that represent the sounds in words is not peculiar to classroom teachers. Those who write the children's textbooks are often at fault. In one of their workbooks the children were directed to find the following little words in the bigger words:

in in think and drink	*of* in often and soft
an in thank and bang	*ball* in balloon

Having taken their cue from the workbook assignment, the children were misled into making discoveries on their own. They were finding the following little words in the bigger words:

all in shall	*is* in island
bat in bath	*table* in comfortable
be in better	*was* in washing
ear in heard	*hand* in handkerchief

One ambtious little girl announced gleefully that she had found the little word *he* in *the; yes* in *eyes;* and *on* in *millions;* "and what's more," she added, "I found *on* two times in *onions!*"

Further confusion between letters and sounds is shown by the following quotations from classroom teachers in our elementary schools.

"What 'long' vowel sound (meaning letter) do you see in the word *sleep,* children?"

"Pronounce the word *recognize* again; and this time let me hear every letter [meaning every sound] in the word."

"Point to the last sound [meaning letter] in the word *train,* George."

"What letter [meaning sound] do you hear in *cup* that is not in *cap?*"

"What two consonant sounds do you see [meaning hear] at the end of *must?*"

"We didn't hear the letter *d* [meaning the sound (t)] at the end of the word *jumped.*"

"Remember to put a *g* at the end of *look'un*" (meaning to substitute *ing* for *un* at the end of *look'un,* there being no sound of (g) at the end of the word *looking*).

PRONUNCIATIONS OF SPEECH SOUNDS

The sounds of English are often incorrectly pronounced in teaching phonics, the consonants being more likely to be distorted than the vowels.

The voiceless sounds (k), (f), (h), (wh), (p), and (t) are usually voiced. The voiced consonants too are likely to be mispronounced. The sound (b) is heard as (bŭ), (d) as (dŭ), (g) as (gŭ), (v) as (vŭ), and (w) as (wŭ).

For the correct utterance of the consonant sounds, see "The Phonetic Study of the Consonants," Chapter 6.

PREVAILING METHODS OF WORD PERCEPTION

It has been found that teachers of reading need to become familiar with more effective techniques for word perception in reading. To illustrate: A first-grade group was gathered for reading. The children were seated around their teacher with their readers opened in their laps. Barbara had her finger on the word *then.* "I don't know that word," she said.

"Well," Miss Corwin said, "let's find out what it is," as she wrote the word *then* on the chalkboard. "Now what does this little word say?" the teacher asked, as she pointed to the letters *h-e-n* in the word *then.* "You know that little word. You saw it in one of your stories. What does it say?"

"Hen!" Barbara answered.

"That's right!" her teacher agreed. "You can see *hen* in *then*."

But does one hear the word *hen* in *then*, since the letters *th* are inseparable and stand for neither (t) nor (h)? Is there, then, a *hen* in *then*, a *hat* in *that*, a *hose* in *those*, or an *heir* in *their?*

For the true nature of the sounds for the letters *th*, see "The Phonetic Study of the Consonants," Chapter 6.

In another classroom George was "stuck," as he said, on the word *do* in the sentence he was trying to read.

"You should know that little word," the teacher said. "It begins like *Dick* and it ends like *to*. Just put the beginning sound of *Dick* with the ending in *to* and you'll have it."

"I was surprised," the teacher later explained to the visitors, "that George couldn't get the little word *do*, because he knows *Dick* and *to* from his reading. But I saw that I was at fault, when George got the word easily enough from the context and by comparing it with the word *to*."

In another school, the word *how* was being attacked for identification. The teacher wrote the words *he* and *cow* on the chalkboard beside the word *how*. "Now think the beginning sound in *he*," the teacher advised, "and then put it with the vowel sound in *cow*, and what do you get?"

"*He-ow!*" the little fellow replied.

"I know what the word is," one of the girls in the group volunteered. "It's *how*."

In an adjoining school district, the children were being drilled on the sounds of the letters of the alphabet from *a* to *z*, in preparation for reading.

"The letter is *a* and the sound is (ă); the letter is *b* and the sound is (bŭ); the letter is *c* and the sound is (kŭ)," the children recited in unison to the end of the alphabet.

"Later the sounds are put into words," the teacher explained, "and the children sound out the words in reading. They call this the phonetic approach to reading. This is certainly not the way we were taught in our education courses in college; but this is the method used here and this is my first year of teaching."

If you are a teacher of reading who can identify the speech sounds in words irrespective of the letters that represent the sounds; if you know how the sounds are correctly pronounced; if you can distinguish between single sounds and blends and between diphthongs and the so-called digraphs; and if you are familiar with the techniques for independent word perception by means of which the reader identifies the new words or the unfamiliar components in the words without interrupting his thinking while reading, then you are among the minority of those who are teaching reading in the schools today. But if you number among those who are inadequately prepared to teach phonics as an effective means of word perception, however talented you may be in other areas of instruction, then this is your book, which it is hoped will be a source of useful information for you and your pupils.

2

INDEPENDENT WORD

PERCEPTION IN READING

Before we begin our study of the subject matter of
phonics and the phonetic study of the speech sounds, let us
evaluate phonics—the association of the sounds with their letters—
as a means of word perception in reading. The exact extent to
which phonics functions in children's reading is subject to considerable variation, as we shall see later in the chapter.

Upon meeting a new word in the course of his reading, a
youngster may identify the word entirely by means of phonics or
he may employ little or none of his "phonetic" skill and ability
in identifying the word. He may recognize the word by its form,
by the way the word looks, and by its meaning in the sentence.
Or the reader may identify the new word by the whole-word
method in conjunction with phonics and the contextual clue.
Or he may identify a new word by its known components, as in
the recognition of *or* and *bit* in the word *orbit* or the known
words *count* and *down* in the new word *countdown*. Or a known
component at the beginning of a new word may give the reader
the clue to the word's identity, like *sat* in *satellite* or *ox* in
oxygen, for example.

A new word may be identified by means of comparison in
conjunction with phonics and the contextual clue, as illustrated
by the reader who identified the word *Saturn* in the sentence:

People are trying to find out if there are any living things on Saturn. "I thought it was *Saturn*," the child said, "because it looked like *Saturday,* except for the (n) at the end, and *Saturn* looks right."

One nine-year-old lad who lived on the "other side of the tracks" and who in all probability had not even heard of the planet Saturn, succeeded with his assignment in reading and by the same means the child who read about the living things on Saturn had employed; namely, by phonics in conjunction with the contextual clue. This little fellow was to read the label *hot dog stand.*

"I know *dog!*" he said; and having learned the "short o" from the known word *cop,* and because he had also learned the consonant sounds, he worked out the word *hot.*

"Oh, boy!" he shouted, "hot dog!" Then pointing to the word *and* in *stand,* he announced, "I know that word. I got it! *Hot dog sand!* Nope, that's not it! I got it! *Hot dog stand!* That's it! It's got to be it! I bet it's a hot dog stand!"

And indeed, it was!

Experience has demonstrated that the particular way in which phonics functions in a child's reading varies with the individual, his social and language background, his intelligence, and with the type of word to be identified.

EARLY STAGES IN READING

It is an established principle in education that when children first learn to read they have no need for phonics. Indeed, any atttempt at word analysis could only interfere with the beginner's experience in finding out what the sentences are telling him and direct his attention to the letters and their sounds before he has learned to look for the meaning of what he is reading.

The beginner in reading learns to identify the words he sees by the way the words look, that is, by their form or configuration. By seeing the same word over and over again and in different situations, the young reader learns to recognize and recall the word on sight.

"I know that word," he will tell you. "That's *mother,* and that's *grandfather!* It's a lot bigger than *father,* and it looks like *grandfather.*"

Not all children, of course, know the word *grandfather,* or even the word *mother.*

The pupils' reading matter in the beginning must be determined by the words the pupils know when they hear the words spoken. The widening of horizons through the enrichment of the reading vocabulary comes later, after the youngster has learned to communicate his ideas and to interpret the symbols of those ideas on the printed page.

One little so-called underprivileged child in telling how he always knew the difference between the words *cat* and *coat* in the piece he was reading said, "cat is littler than *coat,* 'cause it don't have no *o* in it; and my cat," he went on to say, "can ketch a rat, 'cause I saw him do it, the way it says here. I got a coat too, but I like my cat."

Another child pointed out that *ball* looks different from *baby* because of the tall letters at the end of *ball;* "and," he added, "they don't mean the same either."

In the beginning, the whole-word method of recognition is adequate as a means of word perception in reading. *Dog, cat, coat, ball, baby, horse, lion, school, cowboys, Indians, is, are, was, the, a, have, want, and, where, rattlesnakes, raccoons,* each is taken in stride by the young reader, provided he has the words in his reading or speaking vocabulary—not because of the sounds of the letters in the word but because of the way the word looks and its meaning in the sentence.

There comes a time, however, when the whole-word method of recognition alone, even with an obliging context, may not be adequate. It is then that the various techniques for independent word perception in reading come into focus.

NEED FOR WORD PERCEPTION TECHNIQUES

During their first year in school, while the reading vocabulary is still sufficiently limited to be recognized and recalled on sight, children normally have no need for word-analysis techniques. But in the second year, when the number of different words children encounter in reading has more than doubled, and when in the fourth year it is five times as great as it was in the child's first year in school, and when on the higher levels of learning the primer words *horse, sheep, lion,* and *raccoon,* for example, have been replaced by such scientific terms as *equine quadruped, herbivorous ruminant, carnivorous feline,* and *nocturnal aboreal omnivorous mammal,* and each school subject—history, geography, health and hygiene, literature, mathematics, and all the sciences, botany, biology, geology, physics, chemistry—and all the new terms that have come into use with the space age have added their particular terminology to the total vocabulary load, there are far too many unfamiliar words to be recognized and recalled on sight, except perhaps by the ablest students and that rare individual, the gifted reader.

It is then that the reader needs to know *how to identify* the unfamiliar words by the most appropriate means and to do it so quickly that he remains in communication with the author of the text while he works out the new word.

In "Phonics Study and Word Analysis," Paul Witty reports on the recommendation of Arthur I. Gates that instruction be given the children to enable them to "exercise judgment in using the technique (in word perception in reading) best suited to an individual word."[1]

It might be useful at this time to observe how two children, John and George, exercised their judgment in attacking and identifying the new words *capsule, orbited, atmosphere,* and *government* independently of each other in an article they had chosen to read. The boys were seven years and eight months of age; their IQ's were each 105.

DEMONSTRATING THE TECHNIQUE

In showing how he had identified the word *capsule,* John said, "Well, I saw right away that it started with *cap;* but then I had to work out the rest of it. I gave the *u* the long sound on

---

[1] *Elementary English,* May 1953 and October 1953.

account of the *e* at the end; and I got *su* and then *sule;* and then I put the two parts together and I was pretty sure *cap-sule* was right, because it says here, *The capsule orbited the earth three times."*

In telling how he had identified the word, George said, "As soon as I gave the word the once over, I saw right away how it started and then I knew it was *capsule* because that fit the sentence. I didn't work it out, because I didn't have to."

When John was asked how he had identified the word *orbited,* he said, "That was easy. I saw *or* and *bit* in it, and that added up to *orbit;* and then I knew it was *orbited,* because that fit the sentence."

George reported that he had gotten *orbited* the same way that John had. He then told how he had identified the word *atmosphere.* "When I got as far as *at-mos,"* he said, "I guessed what it was because the sentence says, *John Glenn told how it felt when he hit the atmosphere coming back to earth."*

When asked how he knew the syllable *mos* in *atmosphere,* George replied, "I knew the sounds of the letters; and I just put them together like *mo-s* and that said *mos."*

Unlike George, John had to work out all the components in *atmosphere* with the exception of the beginning *at.* "I gave the *o* the short sound," he said, "and I got *mo-s;* and I gave the *e* the long sound on account of the *e* at the end and I got *phere;* and then I had *at mo-s phere,* and I knew that was right, because *atmosphere* fit the sentence."

When asked how he knew that the letters *ph* in *phere* had the sound of (f), John said, "we learned that from *elephant."*

Interestingly enough, both boys made wrong starts in attacking the word *government,* but each erred in a different way. John reported that he had "latched on" to the word *go.* "Then," he said, "I looked ahead and worked out *ver-n* and I knew *men-t;* and so I got *go-vern-ment.* But then I changed it to *gov-ern-ment,* because the sentence says, *Our government helps people in many lands to get ahead."*

George explained that he had made the mistake of "latching on" to the little word *over* in *government.* "And that's how I got the wrong word," he said; "but then I guessed it was *government* because that made sense."

It is reasonable to assume that the boys had the word *government* in their hearing, if not in their speaking, vocabularies and thus recognized the word in spite of their errors at the outset.

George then showed how he had just worked out another new word. To prove that he now knew the word *circumnavigate,* he read the sentence *A long time ago people wanted to circumnavigate the earth, and now they are talking about orbiting the moon.*

In showing how he had worked out *circumnavigate,* George said, "I saw the vowel we learned from *bird,* and that helped me to get *cir;* and then I worked out *cu-m na-v i;* and then when I put the parts together and I had *cir-cum-nav-i.* I guessed it was *circumnavigate* and it was!"

"But how did you know that all the vowels up to *gate* had their short sounds?" George was asked, to which he replied, "They looked as if they had to be short and I took a chance on it."

"But what about the sounds of all the other letters, the vowel and consonant sounds?" George was asked. "I knew them too," he said.

In telling how he knew that the letter *c* had the sound of (s) in *cir,* George said, "on account of the *i.* There's a rule about that. It says when *c* comes in front of *i* it says (s)."

It is significant to note that although the boys had been instructed in the same word-perception techniques, each had adapted the method to suit his own particular needs. Although George did not need to use his "phonetic" skill in identifying the word *capsule,* he did need it in working out the word *circumnavigate.*

ANALYSIS OF THE TECHNIQUE

In identifying an unfamiliar word the reader glances first at the word *as a whole* with the sentence in mind. This may be all that is needed for the reader to identify the word. "When it works," a teacher once said, "the whole word with the context in mind is an excellent means of identifying a new word, because it functions so intimately with comprehension in reading."

When a quick glance at the word as a whole does not at once lead to identification, the reader looks to the component at the beginning of the word, since the beginning of the word may give him the clue to the word. It was the beginning *cap* in *capsule* that gave George the clue to the word. The known syllable *sat* in *satellite* enabled another child to identify the word in the sentence *The satellite is a man-made moon.*

If the beginning of the word does not at once reveal the word's identity, the reader works out the word or the unfamiliar parts of the word by associating the sounds with their letters; then by blending the sounds, he identifies the word and checks it against the context to see if it fits the sense of the sentence. If it does, well and good. If it does not, but if the reader came close enough to the word's identity, he has a good chance with the aid of the context of being able to guess the word.

It is significant to note that the technique of associating the sounds with their letters is quite different from "sounding out" the new word. When the reader associates the sounds with their letters he interprets the letters in terms of their sounds as he works out the new word or the unfamiliar parts of the word, as the case may be. It has long been known that sounding out a word is not only a boresome and laborious task but it is incompatible with comprehension in reading. By the time he has sounded out the new word, the reader has forgotten what the author of the sentence was telling him. He then looks back to the beginning of the sentence to pick up the thread of the thought, only to lose it again upon meeting the next new word in his reading. Although the practice of sounding out the new words children met in reading was a contributing factor in the revolt against phonics a generation ago, it is still prevalent in schools today.

Effective Functioning of Phonics

Phonics may be said to function effectively in word perception in reading when it enables the reader to come so close to the word's identity that with the aid of the context he can guess the word. We just observed how John and George by means of their "phonetic" skill and ability had approximated the identity of the word *government* so closely that they were able to guess the word. When he had gotten as far as *circumnavi* by associating the sounds with their letters and then blending them, and with the sense of the sentence in mind, George was able to guess that the word was *circumnavigate*.

Value of Known Components in New Words

We observed that George's recognition of the word *cap* in *capsule* provided the clue to the word's identity; and although John's recognition of the same component did not do as much for him, it relieved him of having to work out the entire word. The recognition of the syllable *gate* in *circumnavigate* reduced the number of syllables the reader had to work out in order to identify the word.

The little girl who complained that she had to work out the entire word *Nickerruckerrubblegrubb* in the story she was reading, "because," she said, "there wasn't a single part in the whole word that I knew," was not unmindful of the value of a known component in a new word.

It must not be assumed that a component is always a whole word. It might be a syllable of a word like *tel* in *telstar, mos* in *atmosphere,* or even a part of the syllable like *mo* in *mos.* It may be a prefix like *ex* in *expect, re* in *return, con* in *connect,* or a suffix like *ness* in *kindness* or *tion* in *attention.*

A component, then, is an integral part of a word that may occur at the beginning or at the end of a word or in any other part of a word or syllable, the ready recognition of which is a significant factor in word perception in reading.

Although any known component in a new word may be useful to the reader in identifying the word, the known component at the beginning of the new word is by far the most helpful. The known word *den* is more useful to the reader in identifying the word *denticle* than the same component in *identical;* and the prefix *con* may be of more value in identifying the word *controlled* than the same component in the word *uncontrolled.*

Looking for a known component in an unknown word is not an unmitigated good. It can be misleading as we observed when

John "latched on" to the little word *go* in *government* or when George thought he saw the word *over* in *government*. Teachers too have been misled, as Miss Corwin was (Chapter 1) when she pointed out the little word *hen* in *then*. One ambitious youngster reported that she had found the word *yes* in *eyes, he* in *the,* and *bat* in *bathroom.* The English language is something to conjure with!

Importance of the Contextual Clue

It has been noted that the context alone may give a child all the help he needs in order to identify a new word in reading. We have also learned that phonics depends upon the context for its successful functioning in word perception in reading. The reader must check the word he worked out against the context to "see if it makes sense," as the children say. It was the context that showed a little girl that she had associated the wrong sounds with the vowels in the word *meant.* "I called it *mean-t,*" she said, "but that didn't make sense; so I changed it to *meant* and that was right."

Indeed, it is easy enough to associate the wrong sounds with the letters in an English word and thus go astray in working out the new word. The vowels are likely to be particularly misleading, since the same letter stands for so many different sounds, and the same sound is represented by many different letters and letter combinations, as we shall see in Chapter 9. But the context is always there and oftener than not it can give the reader the help he needs in identifying a new word.

It was the context that came to the rescue of the little boy who in reading about life on the farm had pronounced the word *bushel* as *bus'hel.* "But then," he said, "I changed it to *bushel,* because it told about a bushel of ripe apples. I had to change another word, too," he went on to say. "I called it *gat'her,* but I knew that couldn't be right, because it said the children on the farm went out to gather the eggs the hens had laid in the barn."

It would be difficult to overestimate the value of the context in children's word perception in reading. Some words in the English language depend entirely for their identification upon the meaning of the words in the sentence—words like *row, bow, read, lead,* and *live.* Furthermore, how would the reader know, without benefit of the context, that *naïve* is not (nāv); that *create* is not (krēt); that *idea* is not (i·dē′); and, as Ernest Horn has pointed out, that *altogether* is not (al·to·get′her)?

However, the context is not always this obliging. Horn found that numerical concepts like *few, many,* and *average* are often so difficult contextually that the sense of the sentence is of little help to the reader in identifying the words. It has also been found that the extent to which the context can be helpful to the reader depends not only on the type of word to be identified but upon the ability of the individual as well. Not every child has the intelligence and the language facility to make the maximum use of the context in reading. Not every child has the ability that intelligent, or what is known as "educated," guessing requires in word perception in reading. Then, too, children who have been conditioned to rely solely on the sounds of the letters in word identification are not likely to make the best use of the context and thereby fail to profit by an invaluable aid to reading.

WORD PERCEPTION AN INDIVIDUAL MATTER

It has been found that the means employed in identifying an unfamiliar word in reading varies (a) with the indivdual who is identifying the word and (b) with the word itself.

Individual Differences

Given the same word to be identified in reading, no two children are likely to achieve their objective in precisely the same way. While one child may need only the context to aid him in identifying the word, another may also need his "phonetic" skill and ability in order to succeed.

Upon meeting the word *submarine* in his reading, one boy said that he knew the word as soon as he saw it in the sentence. Another boy in the same reading group reported that he knew the word as soon as he had gotten as far as *sub·mar.* One of the girls explained that she had worked out the word as *sub·ma·rīn′*

and had then changed it to *sub·ma·rēn'* "because, that," she said, "fit the sentence."

It is not surprising to find that children differ in the means they employ in identifying an unfamiliar word in reading, even though they have been taught the same techniques for independent word perception. Children vary in degrees of intelligence, in backgrounds of experience, in language ability and training, and in emotional maturity and interest in reading, all factors that play their part in determining the kind of people they are and, hence, their ways and means of attacking and identifying the reading vocabulary. Reading and all the factors associated with it is by no means the same kind of activity for all children.

Differences in Words

The unfamiliar words children encounter in reading vary greatly in kind; thus the word itself may also determine the means by which the reader attacks and identifies the word. Compare, for example, the words *Skybolt, missiles, Saturn, radiation,* and *anxious.* The word *Skybolt,* being a compound word, is the type to be identified as a word whole, or by means of its simple words, *sky* and *bolt. Missiles* is the kind of word whose beginning, *mis* or *miss,* may provide the clue to the word's identity. The word *Saturn* may yield its identity by means of its similarity to the familiar word *Saturday.* In the word *radiation* the letters have the sounds usually associated with them (except for the suffix *tion,* which may be recognized as a familiar component in the word). The unknown syllables in *radiation,* then, may be identified by means of phonics. The word *anxious* differs from each of the other words. One sees neither a known component in the word, nor does the word conform to the rules of pronunciation (see Chapter 3). The first syllable in the word *anxious* may even be misleading, since it is not pronounced (an) as the spelling would indicate, but (ang) or (angk)! Unless with the help of an obliging context the reader is able to guess the word, it may need to be respelled for him or he may go to the dictionary for the respelling of the word. The respelled word (ang'shəs) or (angk'shəs) can then be identified very nicely by means of phonics.

Thus the ways and means employed in independent word perception in reading vary not only with the individual who encounters the unfamiliar word in reading but with the type of word to be identified.

TWO CLASSIFICATIONS OF WORDS

It has been found expedient in teaching reading to consider the vocabulary as consisting of two types of words, one known as sight words and the other as phonetic words. Such a classification, however convenient, is not scientific. Exactly what is a phonetic word and what is a sight word?

A phonetic word has been defined as a word that is spelled as it is pronounced, and pronounced as it is spelled. In his article on pronunciation in the Introduction to *Webster's New International Dictionary,* Second Edition, John S. Kenyon points out, "It has been said and it is probably true that one cannot be entirely certain of the pronunciation of any English word solely from its spelling."

A phonetic word has also been defined as a word in which the sounds can be spelled in only one way, and the letters can be pronounced in only one way. Consider the words *sat, saw, say, sail, safe.* Can the letters in these words be pronounced in only one way? Take the letter *s.* It is pronounced (s) in *sat,* (z) in *is,* (sh) in *sure,* (zh) in *pleasure,* and it has no sound at all in *isle* or *island.* The vowels in *sat, saw, sail, say,* and *safe* are even more irregular. The letter *a,* which is pronounced (ă) in *sat,* is pronounced (ô) in *ball,* (ā) in *safe,* (ä) in *car,* (âr) in *care,* (i) in *senate,* and (ə) in *about.*

According to definition, then, neither *sat, saw, say, sail,* or *safe* is a phonetic word. But are not these words usually considered as being phonetic? (For the various pronunciations of the letters *aw, ai,* and *ay,* see the Table 4 in Chapter 9.)

Take the words *tune, rude, true, due, grew, juice, few, fuel, duty, fruit,* and *suit.* Every vowel in these words stands for more than one sound or it may have no sound at all in the word in which it occurs. According to definition, then, none of these is a phonetic word. But because words like these as well as the words *sat, saw, say, safe,* and *sail* conform to the rules of phonics, they are usually regarded as phonetic words in reading.

The term "phonetic," then, is used as an adjective to describe those words in the children's reading vocabulary that conform to the established rules of pronunciation. When used in this sense of the term, the word *"phonetic"* is enclosed in quotation marks; and the term *phonetic* is used to designate the science of phonetics throughout the book.

"Phonetic" Words

A study of the children's reading vocabulary shows that with each successive level of reading the relative number of "phonetic" words increases.[2] On the preprimer level about 20 percent of the basic words in the children's readers are "phonetic." On the sixth-year level the percentage is reversed. Then more than four-fifths of the words children meet in their readers and textbooks are regarded as being "phonetic."

It is significant to note that the subject-matter vocabulary in the students' textbooks in the social studies, history, geography, health and hygiene, mathematics, and in all the sciences, biology, botany, geology, chemistry, and physics, as well as the terms that have come into use with the space age, are almost entirely "phonetic." Hence the unfamiliar terminology in the children's textbooks and in the students' current reading of scientific matter can readily be identified by the reader whose knowledge and skill in phonics are adequate to meet the need.

This is not to say that every child upon meeting an unfamiliar word in his textbooks or current literature will need to work out the word. It does mean that the subject-matter terms are the kind that lend themselves nicely to "phonetic" analysis, in the sense that the words conform to the rules of phonics.

The following lists of phrases chosen at random (1) from magazine articles on the adventures into space and (2) from textbooks

2 "An Analysis and Classification of the Sounds in the Children's Reading Vocabulary in Grades 1–3"; unpublished dissertation, University of Iowa, Iowa City, Iowa; and a subsequent "Study of the Reading Vocabulary, Grades 4–6."

in United States history, geography, science, and in health and hygiene currently in use in the elementary grades and high school show the "phonetic" vocabulary in the subject-matter areas. With the exception of a very few syllables, all the words are "phonetic" in the sense that they conform to the rules of pronunciation.

From Articles on Adventures into Space

Redstone Booster Rockets	re-entry into the atmosphere
Project Mercury	radiation hazards
antimissile missiles	weightlessness in space
astronauts rocketed into space	effect of gravitation
countdown before take-off	circumnavigating the moon
manually manipulated capsules	interplanetary explorers
automatic control capsule	aircraft carrier *Trepid*
intercontinental missiles	U.S. satellite in orbit
messages via Telstar	microwave radio relay
U.S. aircraft carrier *Kearsarge*	Astronaut Cooper's *Faith 7* capsule

These expressions, all of which are currently in use, will be found in the textbooks of tomorrow. Even though the words in these lines conform to the rules in phonics, some children will identify some of the words, and perhaps all of them, on sight with only the context to aid them. Others will need their "phonetic" skill and ability in order to identify the words. Still others may find in the word's familiar components like *rock* in *rockets* and *rocketed, sub* in *submarine, miss* in *missiles, cap* in *capsules, at* in *atmosphere, man* in *manually,* and not unlikely, in *manipulated* as well, the clue to the word's identity. Recognition of the simple words *Red* and *stone* in *Redstone* and *count* and *down* in *countdown* may reveal the identity of the compound words. The prefix *inter* and the word *continent* may give the reader the clue to *intercontinental;* and the same prefix with *planet* may lead to the identification of *interplanetary.*

However, the same individual who may have identified these particular words on sight, or by recognizing their components, may need his "phonetic" skill to identify the words *astronauts, project, re-entry, radiation,* and *circumnavigating,* among others in the list. Although the first syllable in *weightlessness* does not conform to the rules of pronunciation, recognition of the word *eight* in *weight* may lead at once to the word's identity.

From the Vocabulary in Social Studies

UNITED STATES HISTORY

thirteen colonies	presidents of the United States
Articles of Confederation	political parties
Committees of Correspondence	House of Representatives
American Revolution	United States Senate
treaty of peace	Justice of the Supreme Court
disarmament conference	policy of coexistence
United Nations' Charter	nonviolent resistance
opposition to communism	underdeveloped nations
Continental Congress	republican government
Declaration of Independence	democratic principles
Constitutional amendments	Emancipation Proclamation
immigration laws	transcontinental railways
European Common Market	confrontation with Cuba
ratified test ban treaty	Monroe Doctrine

This sampling of phrases is typical of the vocabulary children meet in their study of United States history. Since nearly all of these terms, too, like those in the foregoing list, conform to the rules of phonics, they can readily be identified by the reader whose skill in independent word perception is adequate to meet the need.

A comparison of this list with that pertaining to the space age shows a slight difference in the characteristics of the words. For example, we do not find so many words in the history vocabulary whose *beginning* component—like *cap* in *capsule, Red* in *Redstone, man* in *manually,* or *sat* in *satellite*—could give the reader the clue to the word's identity. Assuming that the reader recognizes the components *fed* and *tion* in *confederation, men* or *mend* in *amendments, pen* or *depend* in *independence,* and *den* or *dents* in *presidents,* it can hardly be expected that these components could give the reader the clue to the identity of the words in which they occur. Well-known components in the middle or at the end of an unfamiliar word, although useful in identifying the word, would hardly serve as the means of revealing the word to the reader. It is the beginning of the word, as we have already observed, that is most likely to give the reader the clue to the word's identity.

The words in the foregoing list are the kind that, unless the reader identifies them on sight, will yield their identity readily by means of phonics plus the use of appropriate rules of pronunciation and, of course, the ever-needed contextual clues.

Geography

topography	Atlantic and Pacific oceans
climactic conditions	Arctic Circle
average annual precipitation	Antarctica
equatorial belt	Mediterranean Sea
latitude and longitude	Caspian Sea
municipalities	exports and imports
occupations	volcanic eruptions
population centers	radius and circumference
natural resources	subterranean deposits
International Dateline	continental divide
eastern and western hemispheres	atmospheric disturbances

This sampling of terms, however limited, serves to illustrate the type of words children meet in their study of geography; and like the other subject-matter terms, the geographic vocabulary too is almost entirely "phonetic." The names of the continents, states, cities, counties, townships, seas, rivers, lakes, parks, canals, canyons, the planets, and the like are all largely "phonetic," in that they conform to the rules of phonics.

Recognition of the components *pop* and *tion* should aid in the ready identification of *population*. The reader who sees the little word *top* in *to·pog′ra·phy* will likely correct his mistake, as did George and John in their misidentification of the word *government,* provided he has the sense of the sentence in mind as he identifies the word and is familiar with the word when he hears it spoken.

The familiar syllables *hem* and *is* should lead to the identity of the new word *hemisphere*. In the event that the reader sees these components as *he-mis* instead of *hem-is,* he can correct his error if he has the word in his hearing or speaking vocabulary.

The ready recognition of the prefixes *ex* in *exports, im* in *imports, sub* in *subterranean, Inter* in *International,* and the suffix *tion* are definite aids in identifying the words in which these components occur.

The geographic terms resemble the history vocabulary in that they yield their identity readily by means of phonics and the contextual clue.

From the Vocabulary in Science

laboratory	evaporation
experiments in science	condensation of vapor
scientific data	saturation point
a structural formula	results of investigations
elements and compounds	the study of electronics
positive reaction	electromagnetic energy
negative reaction	catalytic agents
atomic energy	evidences of humidity
thermometer, barometer	microscope, telescope
barometric pressure	oxygen, hydrogen, nitrogen
microscopic matter	atomic fission and fusion
radioactive strontium 90	atmospheric phenomena
nuclear engineering	radioactivity
the electron microscope	geophysical year

This sampling of terms, although limited, serves to illustrate the expressions the student meets in his textbooks in science. It is significant to note that these terms, too, like those in the other subject-matter areas, are largely "phonetic." The names of the sciences themselves conform to the rules of phonics: botany, biology, zoology, physics, chemistry, biochemistry, anthropology, and geology, for example.

Some students will, of course, identify these terms on sight, with only the context to aid them. Others will be aided by the familiar component at the beginning of the word, like *for* or *form* in the word *formula, sat* in *saturation, cat* in *catalytic,* or *tel* in *telescope.* It is to be expected that some children will try to identify *barometer* as *bar′o·me·ter,* and *atomic* as *at′o·mic,* and *humidity* as *hum′i·di·ty.* Mistaken identities like these may be promptly corrected by the youngster who has auditory knowledge of the word and the sense of the sentence in mind—all of which again points up the value of a rich background of experience and language facility as an aid to reading!

Some children may want to give the letter *i* its "long" sound in the syllable *tive* in *positive* and *negative*. They may not yet have learned that the letter *i* has its "short" sound when the syllable *tive* is unaccented, as in the words *positive* and *negative*. But here again the reader who has auditory perception of the words *positive* and *negative,* and certainly if he has approximated the word's identity, can readily correct whatever mistake he may have made in working out the word.

The little boy who was reading about life on the farm, you may recall, promptly changed his mistaken identity of *bus'hels* to *bush'els* and *gat'her* to *gather*. Jane likewise changed *mean-t* to *meant,* "because," as she said, *"meant* made sense and *mean-t* didn't!"

From the Textbooks on Health and Hygiene

medicare	stimulants
contagious diseases	sedatives
secondary meningitis	anesthetic
hypodermic needles	dental hygiene
bacteria	protein foods
vaccination	carbohydrates
injections of serum	unsaturated fats
viruses	respiratory diseases
antidotes	artificial respiration
radioactive fall-out	cardiogram
hypersensitivity	stethoscope, hemostat
antiseptics	poliomyelitis
germicides and antibiotics	booster shots

A close look at this sampling of terms shows how nicely these words too can be identified by phonics in conjunction with the other well-known means of independent word perception in reading. Recognition of the known components *sat* and *rate* enabled one reader to identify the word *saturated* in *unsaturated fats* without further ado. Recognition of the little word *car* got another youngster off to a good start in identifying the words *carbohydrates* and *cardiogram*. Ready recognition of the prefix *un* in *unsaturated* or *anti* in *antidotes, antiseptics,* and *antibiotics* quickens the speed in identifying the words in which the prefixes occur and thereby helps the youngster to remain in contact with the author as he reads. The syllable *tion* should be recognized as a known component in *vaccination* and *respiration,* thereby shortening the time required to identify the words in reading.

Sight Words

After having observed the discrepancy between the scientific and the pedagogical description of a "phonetic" word, we shall now see why it is no less baffling to define a sight word than it was to define a "phonetic word." The term *sight word* is used to designate two different and unrelated categories of words in the children's reading vocabulary.

In one sense of the term, a sight word is an "unphonetic" or irregular word that does not conform to the rules of pronunciation. Because of its "unphonetic" characteristics, children are usually taught to identify a word of this type as a whole, on sight, or at sight in reading. Hence the term *sight word.* This group of so-called sight words, then, consists solely of those words that are classified as being "unphonetic" in that they do not conform to the rules of pronunciation.

The other classification of sight words includes both "phonetic" and "unphonetic" words. It constitutes what is known as a "basic stock of sight words"—the words that children learn to recognize on sight during the beginning stages of learning to read. It is understandable, then, that these words too should be known as sight words.

This group of sight words includes "phonetic" words like *dog, cat, kitten, baby, run, jump, like, make, see, can;* and "unphonetic" words like *a, the, was, were, are, come, have, mother, said, one, once, want, what, where, they* and *you,* for example.

The term *sight word,* then is an ambiguous term. A sight word may be one of a basic stock of words that a child is taught to recognize *on sight* before instruction in phonics begins; or it may be a word, which because of its "unphonetic" spelling may always be recognized and recalled *on sight* in reading.

GROUP 1

Under this heading you will find two representative lists of "unphonetic" words known as *sight words* in reading. The first of these lists is from children's preprimers, primers, and Book 1 currently in use in the schools.

The rating indicates whether the word is of preprimer, primer, or Book 1 rank.

A close look at these words shows how they differ from the "phonetic" words we studied earlier in the chapter in their sound-to-letter and letter-to-sound relationships.

"Unphonetic" Words from Preprimers–Book 1

Word	Rating	Word	Rating	Word	Rating
a	pp	guess	p	talk	1
again	p	have	pp	the	pp
another	1	heard	1	their	1
any	1	high	1	there	p
are	pp	into	1	they	pp
bear	1	kind	1	thought	1
beautiful	1	knew	1	through	1
been	1	laugh	p	to	pp
breakfast	1	light	1	told	1
brother	1	love	1	too	pp
brought	1	many	1	two	p
buy	1	money	1	walk	p
caught	1	monkey	1	want	pp
Christmas	1	mother	pp	warm	1
climb	1	move	1	was	p
clothes	1	night	p	wash	1
color	1	of	p	watch	1
come	pp	oh	p	water	p
could	p	once	1	wear	1
country	1	one	pp	were	p
cover	1	only	1	what	pp
do	p	other	1	where	pp
does	1	pull	1	who	p
don't	1	put	p	woman	1
eye	1	said	pp	word	1
find	pp	school	p	work	p
for	1	shoe	1	worm	1
give	p	should	1	would	1
gone	1	sign	1	you	pp
great	1	some	p	your	p

"Unphonetic" Words from Readers Books 2 and 3

above	daughter	island	question	war
against	delicious	journey	reindeer	warn
although	discover	knee	rough	weigh
among	doesn't	knelt	search	we've
answer	donkey	knife	should	whole
anyone	dozen	knit	shovel	whom
anywhere	earn	knives	sign	whose
apron	earth	knock	soldier	wolf
aren't	eight	knot	someone	women
beautiful	England	known	son	won
beauty	English	learn	soup	wonder
become	enough	limb	special	worker
bought	fierce	measure	stalk	world
break	folk	million	stomach	worry
brood	forward	Monday	straight	worse
build	fought	month	sugar	worth
bush	friendly	neighbor	sure	wouldn't
business	gnaw	none	sword	wound
busy	group	obey	taught	wrap
chief	guard	ocean	though	wren
child	guest	onion	thoughtful	wrinkle
comb	guide	ought	tomorrow	write
comfort	half	oven	tongue	written
comfortable	handkerchief	pear	tonight	wrong
command	handsome	piece	touch	wrote
company	heart	prayer	toward	you'll
cornfield	honey	precious	treasure	young
couldn't	honor	prove	trouble	you're
cousin	hurrah	pudding	usual	yourself
cupboard	idea	push	wander	zoo
cushion	iron	pussy		

GROUP 2

Under this heading you will find what is known as a basic stock of sight words in primary reading. In this list of so-called sight words, fifty-six of the words may be classified as being "phonetic" in that they conform to the rules of pronunciation. These words are indicated by the asterisk.

a	father	I	one	too
*am	find	*in	*play	two
*and	*for	*is	pretty	*up
are	*found	*it	*ran	*very
*away	*funny	*jump	*run	want
*baby	*gave	*kitten	said	was
ball	*get	*like	*saw	*we
*big	*girl	*little	*see	*went
*bird	*go	look	*she	were
*box	good	*make	*that	what
*boy	good-by	*me	the	where
*can	have	*milk	*them	who
come	*he	mother	there	*will
*did	*her	*my	they	*with
do	*here	*no	*this	*yes
*dog	*his	*not	*time	you
*down	*house	*on	to	your

AN INFORMAL TEST*

WHICH ONE IS IT?

1. A child's skill in independent word perception in reading is a matter of knowing (a) how to sound out the unfamiliar word; (b) how to identify the word while at the same time keeping the sense of the sentence in mind.

2. When a quick glance at the new word does not at once reveal the word's identity, the reader should (a) look to the components in the word; (b) start at once to sound out the word letter by letter.

3. The sense of the sentence is (a) a useless consideration in trying to identify an unfamiliar word; (b) an essential aid in identifying the word.

4. Phonics serves the reader adequately when it enables him to (a) come so close to the word's identity that with the help of the context he can guess the word; (b) succeed in identifying a new word even though he loses contact with the author of the sentence while he works out the word.

5. Sounding out an unfamiliar word while reading (a) is a decided aid to comprehension in reading; (b) interferes with the reader's comprehension.

* Answers are listed under the appropriate chapter number in the Appendix.

6. The means employed in word perception in reading should (a) vary with the individual who is identifying the word; (b) be the same for all children of the same mental and chronological age.

7. The means used to identify an unfamiliar word should (a) be the same for all "phonetic" words in the reading vocabulary; (b) vary with the composition of the word to be identified.

8. In identifying a new word, if the reader knows the beginning component of the word, he knows the (a) least helpful part of the word; (b) most useful part of the word.

9. All known components in an unfamiliar word are (a) equally helpful to every child in identifying the word; (b) not equally useful to every child.

10. The "phonetic" words in the reading vocabulary are (a) always most readily identified by means of phonics; (b) very often most easily identified by means of phonics.

11. In identifying an unfamiliar word, the able reader looks first to (a) the word as a whole; (b) every individual letter in the word.

12. In classifying the words in the reading vocabulary, the term *phonetic* is (a) scientific in its implication; (b) pedagogical in its application to reading.

13. A so-called "sight" word (a) is always an "unphonetic" word; (b) may be an "unphonetic" word.

14. The terminology that is peculiar to the study of history, geography, and science (a) is strictly phonetic; (b) usually conforms to the rules of pronunciation.

15. The relative number of "phonetic" words in the children's reading vocabulary (a) increases with each succeeding level of reading; (b) decreases progressively.

16. Phonics is (a) the only successful means of identifying an unfamiliar word in reading; (b) one of several means of independent word perception in reading.

17. Phonics functions (a) more effectively in a child's reading with the aid of the context; (b) equally well without the help of the context.

18. In independent word perception children should (a) always use the same technique; (b) adapt the technique according to their particular needs in reading.

3

PHONICS FOR WORD
PERCEPTION IN READING

We learned in Chapter 2 that when a quick glance at the new word as a whole or at the beginning of the word (with the sense of the sentence in mind) does not at once reveal the word's identity, the reader works out the new word. In doing so, he must be able to remain in communication with the author of the sentence. If the reader because of his ineptitude loses the thread of the thought, little if anything has been accomplished, even though the reader finally succeeds in identifying the new word.

In the present chapter we shall see what skills and abilities are required for effective functioning of phonics in word perception in reading. We shall begin our study by observing how children grow into phonics before instruction in phonics begins. Getting ready for phonics is comparable to readiness for reading. Although readiness for phonics may begin simultaneously with readiness for reading, the program for readiness in phonics may extend well beyond the early stages of learning to read. (See "Criteria for Readiness in Phonics" later in this chapter.)

EXPERIENCES IN READINESS
FOR PHONICS

Learning to listen is first in importance in readiness for phonics. Children learn to listen to the sounds that can be heard round about them, indoors and out, and to the speech sounds in conversation. By listening the beginner in school learns to hear the sounds in familiar words; to hear the sounds at the beginning and at the end of a spoken word and to identify the sounds that are heard at the beginning of a spoken word; to tell when words begin alike and to name words that begin with the same sounds; to tell when words end with the same sound; and to tell when words rhyme or do not rhyme.

Experiences in listening and in auditory discrimination provide a useful background for visual discrimination and later on for effective functioning of phonics in reading and in learning to spell, as well as for improvement in speech.

Listening to Sounds Indoors and Out

Children learn to identify the sounds they hear by listening to the wind in the trees, the rustle of leaves in the branches, the song of a bird, the whirr of the wings of an airplane, the honking of a horn, the sound of a gong or whistle, a dog's bark, the footsteps of people on the street or in the house, the ringing of the telephone, the strains of music in the air, and many other sounds. It is fun to learn to listen, especially to nature's sounds.

Listening to Speech Sounds

Children themselves find it profitable to listen to the sounds in spoken words when they can build on their past experiences in hearing the sounds in the words. Children of English-speaking parents who have since their infancy heard (mŭ) in *mummy* and *mother,* (dă) in *daddy,* and (bŏ) in *bottle* are ready upon entering school to broaden their experiences by learning that *mother* begins with the same sounds as *money* and *Monday;* that *dandelion* and *daffodils* begin like *daddy;* and that *box, bottom, bonfire* and *Bobby* all begin like *bottle.*

NOTE. The breve (˘) over the vowel is to show the teacher that the the beginning of the word is pronounced, not spelled. It is not intended for the pupil's observation or use.

HEARING THE SOUNDS IN FAMILIAR WORDS

The children listen as the teacher pronounces the words in the manner familiar to them. She may pronounce the word *cla-p* and the children respond by clapping. She may say, *ski-p* and the children may skip or show that they recognize the word by answering "skip." She may pronounce the word *stoo-p,* and the children respond verbally or with the act of stooping.

NOTE. The hyphen indicates a pause of a second or two between the beginning and ending in pronouncing the word.

The game may be continued by the teacher's pronouncing the words in the following list as indicated by the hyphen. The pupils may respond to the action word by doing what the word indicates or by pronouncing the word as a whole.

Action Words

ru-n	ho-p	tur-n	stre-tch
smi-le	kno-ck	swee-p	si-t

Things in the Room

The teacher pronounces first the beginning of the word and then the sound at the end of the word as indicated by the hyphen. She may say, "I see something in the room whose name begins with (flă) and ends with (g)." The pupil responds by pronouncing the word "flag." She then continues the "game" by pronouncing first the beginning sounds and then the ending of the word as in the following lists. The pupil responds by pronouncing the whole word, as before.

char-t	boo-k	sea-t	pe-n
ligh-t	hou-se	fi-sh	chair-s

Names of Animals

ca-t	pi-g	fro-g	du-ck	snai-l
do-g	shee-p	mi-ce	gee-se	chi-ck
goa-t	goo-se	sna-ke	bir-d	ba-t

NOTE. These exercises depend for their value upon the degree of accuracy with which the teacher pronounces the speech sounds in the words. It has been found that it is the exceptional teacher who gives the consonants their true value. (See "The Phonetic Study of the Consonents," Chapter 6, for the correct pronunciation of the consonants.)

NOTE. Since the foregoing exercises require the blending of sounds, some beginners in school may not yet be mature enough to blend the sounds into the word whole. In those cases phonic readiness must wait until the pupil is mentally mature enough to blend the sounds in forming the whole word.

HEARING HOW THE WORDS BEGIN

The children listen as the teacher pronounces only the beginning of a familiar word. It may be the name of something in the room. The teacher may say, "I see something and its name begins with (flă)." The pupil answers, "flag." The teacher may say, "I see something whose name begins with (clŏ)." The pupil responds with the word *clock* or *closet*. "I see something in the room whose name begins with (dĕ), and the pupil answers, *"desk."*

NOTE. Since the exercise is an auditory, not a visual, experience, neither the whole word nor its beginning should be written on the chalkboard for the children to pronounce.

The teacher may say, "This time I'm thinking of an animal that gives us wool. Its name begins with (shē)." The pupil answers, *"sheep."* Or the teacher may say, "I'm thinking of a little animal a cat would like to catch. Its name begins with (mou)." The pupil answers *"mouse."*

Continue the game by pronouncing only the beginning of the animal names in the following list, after which the pupil responds with the whole word. The word in parentheses indicates the pupil's response to the teacher's lead.

NOTE. If your pupils are not familiar with the names of the animals in the list, you will, of course, substitute the names of things with which the children are familiar.

lă (lamb)	gōō (goose)	toa (toad)	dŭ (duck)
skŭ (skunk)	bir (bird)	pō (pony)	fĭ (fish)
spī (spider)	rōō (rooster)	snā (snake)	fŏ (fox)

NOTE. Pictures of animals or objects may be used in place of the teacher's pronunciation of the word. In that case the teacher may say, "I see the picture of a big bird whose name starts with (dŭ); and the pupil who is familiar with the bird responds with the word *duck;* or, "I see the picture of an animal whose name starts with (ră)," and the response may be *rabbit* or *raccoon,* according to the picture.

TELLING THE BEGINNING OF THE WORD

This time the teacher pronounces the whole word as indicated by the hyphen. She asks, "What sounds do you hear at the beginning of *mou-se?*" The pupil's response is *mou.* "What sounds do you hear at the beginning of *tree-s?*" The answer, of course, is *tree.*

The teacher pronounces one of the following words and the pupil responds with only the beginning sounds in word, like (mou) in *mouse,* or (lea) in *leaf.*

mou-se	bee-s	bu-s	trai-n	stree-t
tree-s	bir-d	dru-m	tra-ck	schoo-l
lea-f	fi-sh	tru-ck	far-m	clow-n

NOTE. Slow learners may need to hear the word repeated and with a more prolonged pause between the beginnings and endings of the words, for example, like *mou--se, mou--se.* It is important, of course, to pronounce the beginnings clearly but without exaggeration and gear the timing to the pupil's ability to respond.

HEARING LIKE BEGINNINGS IN WORDS

The ability to hear likenesses and differences in words is an essential skill in auditory discrimination. Because the vowel is always blended with the consonant at the beginning of a spoken word or syllable, one hears that words begin alike when both the vowel and consonant sound are the same at the beginning of the word. Hence children can hear that *cat, camel, can, caterpillar,* and *California* begin alike because they all begin with the same vowel and consonant sound. One can hear that *can, cake, comb, cup, cucumbers,* and *cauliflower* do not begin with the same sounds because the vowel sounds differ at the beginning of the words.

Note how easy it is to hear that *bat, band, back,* and *bags* begin alike, and that *bat, big, bears, boys,* and *bugles* do not begin with the same sounds; that *milk, mittens,* and *middle* begin alike, and that *milk, mice, monkey,* and *music* do not begin alike.

The teacher pronounces a familiar word and asks the pupil to name another word that begins with the same sounds as her word. She may name the word *pin* and ask the children to tell the name of something that begins with (pĭ) that they can rest their heads on in bed. The pupil answers "pillow." He may then name other words that begin with the same sounds as *pin* and *pillow.* He may name *pick, pickles, pigeons, picture, pitcher,* and *Pilgrims,* depending upon his auditory knowledge of words.

The word *bus* may suggest *butter, buds, butterfly, bumblebee, buckles, buttons,* even *buck* and *bust.*

The word *sand* may yield *sad, sandals, Saturday, satellite, satisfied,* or even *salamander* and *San Francisco.* In one school a little girl contributed the words *sap* and *sassy.*

The word *flag* will suggest *flat, flash, flashlight, flagpole.*

To the spoken word *stick* the children may respond with *still, stingy, sticky, stiff, stickers, stitches, sting,* and even *stink* and *stinkbug.*

The word *mother* may trigger a whole battery of words with identical beginning sounds like *money, mummy, monkey, much, must, mud, muff, mustard, muffins, multiply, mumps, muscle, muskrat, muss, mutt,* and *mumble.*

HEARING LIKE ENDINGS IN WORDS

We shall now see how children learn to discriminate between the sounds at the *end* of familiar words. The teacher may say, "I am going to pronounce two words while you listen to the sounds at the end of the words. If both words have the same sound at the end, then you must answer *Yes.* If they do not end with the same sound, the answer of course is *No.* Now let's listen closely. Do these two words have the same sound at the end: *si--t, ha--t?*" The pupil should answer, "Yes."

Let's listen again to the same sound at the end of the words. Do you hear the same sound at the end of *si--t, ru--n?*" This time, of course, the answer is "No."

By listening as the teacher pronounces each pair of words from left to right in the following list, children continue their experiences in hearing likenesses and differences at the end of familiar words. The pupil should answer Yes or No depending upon whether both words do, or do not, end with the same sound.

The value as well as the success of the exercise depends upon the clarity and exactness with which the teacher pronounces the consonant at the end of the word. Unless the consonant is pronounced accurately and without exaggeration children cannot be expected to hear the sound at the end of the word.

ba--ck	pi--ck	do--g	be--ll	cu--p	la-p
cla--p	shee--p	do--g	pi--g	ca--tch	hi--ll
shee--p	fi--sh	hou--se	hor--se	hi--ll	sha--ll

NOTE. Slow learners may need repeated experiences in hearing likenesses and differences in sounds at the end of familiar words.

HEARING WHEN WORDS RHYME

The next experience in listening centers around rhyming words. As the teacher pronounces two or three familiar words, the pupils listen to hear whether or not the words rhyme. If they do, the pupil answers, "Yes"; if they do not he answers, "No."

The correct response to the first two words of course is Yes; to the next two words the answer is No.

car, star	trees, bees, sneeze	hat, cat, bat
car, bell	trees, bees, fun	bed, red, green
house, mouse	two, shoe, true	room, broom
house, mice	coat, boat, float	stick, track
chief, leaf	fish, dish, wish	cup, pup, puppy

NOTE. When pictures of animals or objects are used the children match the pictures of the things whose names rhyme.

Visual Discrimination

Visual discrimination is no less important than auditory discrimination in readiness for phonics. Children must be able to distinguish between likenesses and differences in the written forms of words. Exercises like the following are intended to advance the learner on the road to readiness for instruction in phonics.

Children may dictate to the teacher the words they know that begin with the same sounds as *bus, but,* and *buns,* for example. The teacher writes the words on the chalkboard as the children dictate them. Here is a probable list of such words:

bus	buckles	bubbles	bunny
but	buttons	bumblebees	buzz
buns	bumpers	butterfly	buddy

The pupils may encircle the biggest part that is exactly the same at the beginning of all the words in the column, but without pronouncing the words or any part of the word. No attempt should be made to teach children to "read" the words in the list or to recognize them on sight.

Later the teacher may write a word list like the following on the chalkboard. The children may then encircle or underline the biggest part that is the same at the beginning of all the words in each of the columns, but again without pronouncing the words or any part of the words!

You will note that the first three letters are the same in all of the words in the first three columns and that only the first two letters are the same in all of the words in the last two columns.

stick	flag	chickens	rocket	tame
still	flash	children	rods	taste
stiff	flat	chimney	romp	tale
sting	flap	chilly	robbers	take

In the following word list the children are again to show the biggest part that is the same at the beginning of the words in each of the columns. You will see at once that this exercise is more challenging than the previous one, since in the first and fourth columns only the first letter is the same at the beginning of each of the words. In the second column the first two letters are the same and in the third and fifth columns the first three letters are the same in all the words.

NOTE. Word lists like these when written on paper may provide profitable seat work for the children:

apple	ear	stamp	ice	coat
animal	eagle	stand	iron	coast
axe	eat	statue	island	coax

Here is another way for children to indicate like beginnings in words. Lists like the following may be written on the chalkboard or on paper for seat work. The children draw lines to connect the words that begin exactly alike. For example, a line will extend from *dishes* to *dinner* and another from *captain* to *calendar*.

dishes	buckles	bees	turtle
captain	dinner	turkey	places
bunny	calendar	plane	beetles

SEEING LIKE ENDINGS IN WORDS

In the next exercise the children are to match the endings in words. They may encircle or underline the biggest part that is the same at the *end* of all the words in each of the columns. The children will discover that in the first column there is only one letter that is the same at the end of all the words in the column. In the second, third, and fifth columns the last two letters are exactly the same in all the words and in the fourth column the last three letters are the same in all the words in the column.

dog	bell	back	watch	trains
pig	gall	truck	catch	clowns
rug	hill	rock	witch	beans
tag	full	stack	stretch	spoons

NOTE. This exercise too may be performed by the children at their seats.

In exercises like the following the children draw lines to connect the words whose endings look alike, as shown here:

cub	cat	fish	wash
goat	crab	pick	six
toad	man	fox	track
lion	bird	wheel	tail

NOTE. The number and variety of experiences in auditory and visual discrimination depend, of course, upon the pupil's needs in readiness for phonics.

CRITERIA OF READINESS
FOR PHONICS

Under the title "Readiness for Phonics," Josephine Tronsberg offers the following criteria for determining the pupil's readiness for phonics. The child should be ready for phonics:

1. If he can recognize similarities and differences in words he hears.
2. If he can distinguish likenesses and differences in written forms.
3. If he can differentiate between the configuration of written words.
4. If he has acquired the habit of reading for meaning in sentences, phrases or word wholes.
5. If he has mastered a sight vocabulary large enough to give him a basis for generalizing about sounds.
6. If he can use context clues effectively.
7. If he reads rhythmically.
8. If he can read to answer questions.
9. If he has learned to read silently before reading orally.
10. If he has developed a desire to read.[1]

It would seem that when a child has learned to read for meaning and has become interested in reading, is able to follow written directions, to use context clues effectively, to listen to the sounds in spoken words, to hear and see likenesses and differences in the beginnings and endings of words, is able to blend, and can recognize a sufficiently large number of "sight" words to serve as key or cue words for discovering the vowel and consonant sounds, he should be ready for phonics as a means of furthering his pleasure and proficiency in reading.

INSTRUCTION IN PHONICS

We learned in Chapter 2 that in working out an unfamiliar syllable in a new word in reading, both boys, George and John, associated the sounds with the letters in the syllable;

1 *The Reading Teacher,* VIII (October 1954).

then by blending the sounds they identified the word and checked it against the context to see if the word "fit the sense of the sentence," as they said.

In this chapter we shall see how children learn the sounds of the letters in words, vowels, consonants, and consonant blends and to associate the sounds with the letters in identifying the new words in reading situations.

We shall also observe the rules for pronunciation and the most frequently occurring prefixes and suffixes in the children's reading vocabulary, whose ready recognition contributes significantly to proficiency in phonics.

Let us now turn our attention to the sounds of the letters the young learner needs to know for effective functioning of phonics in word perception in reading.

The Vowel and Consonant Sounds[2]

The most frequently occurring vowel and consonant sounds in the children's reading vocabulary as determined by phonetic research are indicated by italic type in the cue word lists on pages 43 and 49. Each of the words in the lists, which presumably was learned as a "sight" word in reading, now becomes the pupil's key or cue word for discovering the vowel or consonant sound in the word. Each sound has its own key or cue word.

Any known word bearing the vowel sound to be learned and which can be pictured may serve as the pupil's key or cue word for discovering the vowel sound, like the words *bag, pig, cake, bees, mouse,* for example. And any known word which can be pictured and in which the consonant comes at the end of the word may serve as the pupil's key for discovering the consonant sound. The known word *boat* is a suitable word for discovering the sound (t) because the sound (t) can clearly be heard in the word *boat*. But the known word *toad,* in which the letter *t* comes at the beginning of the word, would not be so satisfactory for discovering the sound (t) because one hears (toa) in *toad,* rather

---

[2] "An Analysis and Classification of the Sounds in the Children's Reading Vocabulary in Grades 1–3"; unpublished dissertation, University of Iowa, Iowa City, Iowa; and a subsequent "Study of the Reading Vocabulary, Grades 4–6."

than the sound (t). The known word *sheep* is a suitable key word for the consonant sound (p), but not *peas* or *peach* because one hears (pea) in *peach* and *peas* instead of the sound (p).

NOTE. Children who have never seen a *boat* may find the word *cat* or *coat* a more suitable key word for the sound (t); and for some children the word *cop* or *cap* would be preferable to *sheep* as a key word for learning the sound (p).

The picture to illustrate the key word serves a twofold purpose. It enables the pupil to discover the sound to be learned and also provides the means of recalling the sound in case it has been forgotten. The picture of the word *bag,* for example, will serve to recall the "short a" by calling to mind the word *bag,* from which the vowel sound was originally learned. In like manner the picture of the *boat* or the *cat* or *coat,* as the case may be, will recall the key word, which in turn will bring to mind the sound (t) at the end of the word.

THE VOWEL SOUNDS IN THE READING VOCABULARY

Let us now see what vowel sounds children need to know for proficiency in phonics. Each of the vowel sounds is indicated by italic type in the following list of cue words, which presumably are known words in reading. Each known word now becomes the children's key for discovering the vowel sound.

A chart bearing the key or cue words with the vowel sounds indicated by underscoring (or some other means) should be kept on display in the classroom for children's ready reference when needed for independent word perception in reading.

Although all the cue words for the vowel sounds are presented first, it does not mean that all the vowel sounds should be learned before the children are introduced to the consonant sounds. On the contrary, the consonant sounds should not wait until the vowel sounds have been learned. Children need to know the consonant and the vowel sounds in the new word in order to work out the word. If children learned all the vowel sounds before any of the consonants were introduced, their ability to work out a new word in reading would be unnecessarily delayed.

Cue Words for the Vowel Sounds

The "Short" Vowels	*The "Long" Vowels and Diphthongs*				
bag	cake	leaves	ti′ger	mule	mouse
pig	train	ze′bra	bone	mu′sic	cows
bus	clay	kite	boat	news	
tent	ta′ble	pies	crows	coins	
box	bees	fly	mo′tor	toys	

The Various Other Vowels

bird	ferns	horn	book	chairs
church	barn	hawk	goose	

NOTE. For children who are not familiar with the cue words listed here the teacher will substitute words bearing the vowel sounds and with which the children are familiar. The word *pin* or *picture* may be more suitable than *pig* for learning the vowel sound (ĭ), and a saw may be better for learning the vowel sound as in *hawk*, for pupils who have never seen a pig or a hawk.

Now that we have observed the vowel sounds children need to know for proficiency in phonics, let us see how children who have learned to hear the speech sounds in words discover the sounds and then associate them with the letters in working out new words in reading.

The following procedures for learning the "short a," the "long a," and the "long e" are intended as examples to show how children discover all the vowel sounds, and having learned the sounds, to associate them with their letters in working out new words in reading situations.

The "Short a" as in Bag. With the known word *bag* before them on the chalkboard or chart, the children listen to the sounds as they pronounce the word. The teacher asks, "What sounds do you hear at the beginning of *bag?*" Children who have learned to hear the sounds in spoken words will answer, "(bă)" and frame the beginning (ba) in bag. If they have not learned to hear the sounds in spoken words, they may name the letter *b* instead of the sounds at the beginning of the word. (For the benefit of these children, see the exercises in listening at the beginning of this chapter.)

The teacher asks, "What sound do you hear at the end of (bǎ)?" The pupil answers "(ǎ)," as he frames the vowel in *bag.* He has discovered the "short a" and enjoys the rewarding experience of having found out something for himself, instead of having it told to him.

NOTE. The breve (˘) over the vowel shows the teacher that the vowel is to be pronounced, not spelled. It is certainly not intended for the children's observation or as an instructional aid in teaching the sound.

After having learned the "short a" children can associate the sound with its letter as they work out new words or syllables in reading matter like the following lines that have been provided for them. If the pupils know the word *bad,* or if they have learned the sound (d) as in the cue word *bed,* they can identify the syllable *bad* in *badgers* and in *Badlands.* Some children may then be able to guess the word *badgers* in the following line; and those who know the word *lands* or are able to work it out can identify the word *Badlands* and probably read the entire line:

badgers that live in the Badlands.

Unless they are already familiar with the Badlands in South Dakota, the children may even be interested in finding out where the Badlands are.

Having learned the sound (d) the reader can identify the word *Bagdad* in the following line. He already knows the syllable *bag.* He identifies the syllable *dad* by recognizing the vowel sound (ǎ), then (dǎ), and then the syllable *dad.* By blending the two syllables he identifies the word *Bagdad.* He can then read the entire line:

a bag for Mother from Bagdad.

Having learned the sound of the ending *ck,* the reader needs only to blend the beginning and ending sounds to identify the word *back* in the third line and the word *back* may then give the reader the clue to the word *door* in the same line. By blending the known beginning (bǎ) with the ending (tch), the reader identifies the word *batch* in the fourth line.

The known syllables *cat* and *bat* may give the reader the clue to the words *cattle* and *battle* in the fifth line.

The known syllables *sat* and *day* may reveal the identity of the word *Saturday* in the sixth line.

Children should be encouraged to see how many of the "short a" words or syllables they can identify and how many whole lines they can read as they learn how to work out the new words.

badgers that live in the Badlands
a bag for Mother from Bagdad
a rap and a tap at the back door
raccoons and a batch of baboons
cattle and battle to rhyme with rattle

no school on Saturday
camel's tracks in the sand
the band in the band wagon
bats, cats, and dandelions
a tramp to the boys' camp

NOTE. The experience of learning to associate the sounds with the letters in identifying the new words or the unfamiliar components of the words is profitable if the reading matter is provided for the children. It cannot be left to children to choose material appropriate for their needs.

The "Long a" as in Cake.   With the known word *cake* before them on the chalkboard or chart, the children listen to the sounds as they pronounce the word. The teacher asks, "What sounds do you hear at the beginning of *cake?*" Children who have learned to hear the sounds in spoken words will answer, "(kā)," and frame the beginning *ca* in *cake*. Those who have not learned to hear the sounds in spoken words may name the letter *c* instead of the sounds at the beginning of the word. For the benefit of these children, see the exercises in listening at the beginning of this chapter.

When asked, "What sound do you hear at the end of (kā)?" the pupil answers (ā), as he frames the letter *a* in *cake*. He has discovered the "long a" and again enjoys the rewarding experience of having found out something for himself, instead of having it told to him.

NOTE. The macron (‾) over the vowel shows the teacher that the vowel is to be pronounced, not spelled. Indeed it is not intended for the children's observation or as an aid in teaching the sound.

After having learned the "long a," children are ready to associate the sound with its letter in working out new words or syllables in reading matter like the following lines that have been provided for them. If the reader has already learned the sound (n) as in the cue word *clown* he can easily identify the word *cane* by blending the beginning sounds in *cake* with the sound (n). By recognizing the known syllable *can* in *candy,* and with a little help from the context, the reader may be able to identify the entire line:

a big candy cane for Christmas.

Having also learned the sound (m) in the cue word *drum,* children can work out the word *name,* by identifying the sound (ā), then (nā), and then the word *name.* If the reader has learned the sound (g) from the word *dog,* he can work out the word *game* by the same technique. He can identify the word *came* merely by blending the beginning sounds in *cake* with the sound (m). An "educated guess" may reveal the word *rhyme,* in which case the pupil can read the entire line:

a name to rhyme with game and came.

The pupil who has already worked out the word *name,* if he can guess the syllable *nick,* can identify the word *nickname;* and by having worked out the word *game,* he can read *a nickname for a game,* or perhaps even the whole line:

a funny nickname for a game.

Children enjoy the challenge of seeing how many "long a" words they can work out in lines like the following by identifying first the vowel sound, then the beginning of the word, and then the whole word.

They must, of course, know the consonant sounds as well as the "long a" in working out the words. The young learners should be encouraged to read as many of the lines as they can under their own power.

a big candy cane for Christmas	a good place for a bookcase
a name to rhyme with game and came	a blacksnake and a milkshake
a funny nickname for a game	no paste to waste or taste
a cage for a beautiful pet bird	window panes in a jet plane
a cane for a very lame man	a long tale of a whale

NOTE. The so-called "long a," which is usually treated in phonics as a single sound, is actually a diphthong (see "The Phonetic Study of the Vowels," Chapter 8).

The "Long e" as in Bees. With the known word *bees* before them on the chalkboard or chart, the children listen to the sounds as they pronounce the word. The teacher asks, "What sounds do you hear at the beginning of *bees?* Children who have learned to hear the speech sounds in words will answer "(bee)" and frame the beginning *bee* in *bees.* When asked, "What sound do you hear at the end of *bee*," the pupil answers "(ē)," as he frames the two *ee*'s in *bees.* He has discovered the "long e."

After children know the "long e" they can associate the sound with its letters in working out new words or syllables in reading matter in which the sounds occurs as in lines like the following.

If the reader has already learned the sound (f) in the cue word *leaf,* he needs only to blend the beginning (bee) with the ending (f) in order to identify the word *beef.* If then with the help of the context he can guess the words *sandwiches* and *eat,* and he already knows the word *three,* he may show that he can read the line:

three beef sandwiches to eat.

Having learned the sounds (t) and (l) from the cue words, the word *beetle* is readily identified by blending (bee) with the ending (tle). If the reader knows the sounds (j) and (p), he can work out the word *jeep* by identifying the sound (ē), then (jee), and then the word *jeep.* He may then succeed in reading the entire line:

a big beetle in an old jeep.

If the reader has learned the sound (d) he can work out the word *deep* by the same technique by which he worked out the word *jeep.* By recognizing the known syllables *Ten* and *see,* and with a little help from the context, the reader may be able to identify *Tennessee River,* and perhaps the entire line:

the deep water of the Tennessee River.

Not all children, as every teacher knows, are able to use the context with maximum effectiveness as an aid in word perception in reading. But children should be encouraged to let the sense of the sentence help them in working out the new words or the unfamiliar components in the words in their reading.

Some children may be able to identify all the "long e" words in the following lines which have been prepared for them, and even read some of the lines entirely on their own. (See the note on page 45 discussing why the reading matter should be provided for the young learners.)

three beef sandwiches to eat
a big beetle in an old jeep
deep water in the Tennessee River
deep and keep to rhyme with jeep
green cheese for a greedy mouse

a bad bee sting on the knee
a queen bee in a beech tree
shepherds asleep by their sheep
sneezes, wheezes, and breezes
wee little pillows and weeping willows

NOTE. The so-called "long e," like the "long a," is also a diphthong, although it too is usually considered in phonics as a single sound.

THE CONSONANT SOUNDS IN THE READING VOCABULARY

The consonant sounds children need to know for proficiency in phonics are indicated by italic type in the following list of cue words. Each of these words, as in the case of the vowels, is presumably a known word in reading, which now becomes the pupils' key or cue word for discovering the consonant sound.

Note that the consonant is indicated at the end of the word where the sound can clearly be heard when the word is pronounced, except when the sound does not occur at the end of a word or syllable in the reading vocabulary. Since the consonants (h), (j), (w), (wh), and (y) occur only at the beginning and never at the end of a word or syllable in the reading vocabulary, these sounds must be introduced in the initial position of the key or cue words.

Since initial consonants are always blended with the adjacent vowel in a spoken word or syllable, these consonants too are never heard apart from, but always with, the adjacent vowel sound. They must therefore be learned with their vowel sounds as indicated in the cue words.

NOTE 1. Although the consonant (r) occurs at the end as well as at the beginning of a word or syllable, it is presented only in the initial position as in the word *rug,* since the value of the final (r), unlike the initial (r), varies with the geographic origin of the speaker.

NOTE 2. The single letters, *j* as in *jug* and *x* as in *fox,* which actually stand for consonant blends, are included here among the single consonants, since they are usually treated as such in phonics (see "The Phonetic Study of the Consonants," Chapter 6).

Although the cue words for the consonant sounds are presented after the vowel sounds, it does not mean that the consonant sounds should wait until all the vowel sounds have been learned. The pupil needs to know both the consonant and the vowel sounds in working out a new word in reading, the order in learning the sounds of the letters being determined by the pupil's need in word perception in reading.

A chart bearing the cue words (with the sounds of the letters indicated by underscoring) should be displayed in the classroom for children's ready reference as the need for knowing the sounds presents itself.

Cue Words for the Consonant Sounds

boa*t*	picni*c*	wat*ch*	*c*ub	fi*sh*	*j*ug	*y*ard
shee*p*	bu*s*	be*ll*	*cl*own	ca*ve*	*h*unter	*r*ug
tru*ck*	*d*og	be*d*	*dr*um	fo*x*	*w*indow	*king*
boo*k*	pea*ch*	lea*f*	mo*th*	pri*ze*	*wh*ip	

Now that we have observed the consonant sounds children need to know for proficiency in phonics, let us see how they discover the sounds; and having learned the sounds, to associate them with their letters in working out new words or syllables in reading situations.

THE CONSONANTS HEARD AT THE END OF A WORD OR SYLLABLE

The following procedures for learning the consonant sounds (t), (p), and (ch) are intended as examples for all the consonant

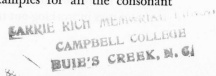

sounds that can clearly be heard at the end of word or syllable as indicated by italic type in the preceding list of cue words.

The Sound (t) *as in* Boat.   With the known word *boat* before them on the chalkboard or chart, the children listen to the sounds as they pronounce the word. The teacher asks, "What sound do you hear at the end of *boat?*" Children who have learned to hear the speech sounds in words will answer "(t)" as they frame the letter *t* in *boat*. They have discovered the sound (t).

Children who have not learned through listening to hear the speech sounds in words are likely to name the letter *t* instead of its sound in response to the question: "What sound do you hear at the end of *boat?*" (For the benefit of these children, see "Experiences in Readiness for Phonics" in this chapter.)

When he knows the sound (t), the child can associate the sound with its letter in working out the new words in reading in which the sound occurs. Having learned the vowel and consonant sounds, the reader can work out the new words in lines like the following, by the simple technique of recognizing first the vowel sound, then the beginning sounds, and then the whole word.

For example, in working out the word *tag* in the first one of the following lines, the reader recognizes the vowel (ă), then (tă), and then the word *tag*. Some children may not need to start with the vowel sound, but go directly from (tă) to *tag*. Still others may not need to work out the word at all. They may, with a little help from the context, be able to identify the word on sight.

In identifying the words *tenpins* and *tennis,* the known syllable *ten* may give the reader the clue to the words' identity. If not, he can work out the unknown syllables in the words by the same simple means by which he worked out the word *tag;* then by blending the syllables in each of the words, the reader identifies the words in the line:

playing tag, tenpins, and tennis.

The words *tick-tack-toe* in the second line of the following list are as easily identified and by the same technique that the youngster uses in working out the word *tag*.

If in working out the word *tiny* in the third line the reader should err by giving the letter *i* its "short" sound (which can be expected), the context will likely come to the rescue, if the pupil is familiar with the spoken word in the line:

> the tinkle of tiny little bells.

By learning how to work out the new words in lines like the following, children are on their way toward independent word perception in reading.

playing tag, tenpins, and tennis	a tadpole and a tomcat
fun playing tick-tack-toe	the tiger and the titmouse
the tinkle of tiny bells	the turtle that lived in a box
tickets to go to the circus	a turkey for a dinner party
two tablets to take to school	a new television set

The Sound (p) *as in* Sheep. With the known word *sheep* before them on the chalkboard or chart, the children listen as they pronounce the word. When asked, "What sound do you hear at the end of *sheep?*" children who have learned to hear the sounds in words will answer "(p)," as they frame the letter *p* in *sheep*. They have discovered the sound (p).

Children who have not learned through listening to hear the sounds in words are almost certain to name the letter *p* instead of the sound in response to the question: "What sound do you hear at the end of *sheep?* (See "Experiences in Readiness for Phonics" in this chapter.)

When he knows the sound (p) the child can associate the sound with its letter in working out the new words in which the sound occurs. Having learned the vowel and consonant sounds, the reader can identify the words in lines like the following, by the familiar technique of recognizing first the vowel sound, then the beginning sounds, and then the whole word.

In working out the word *pocket* in the following line, the technique is the same as it is for one-syllable words. The reader recognizes the vowel (ŏ) then (pŏ), and then *pock*. He then recognizes the second syllable, and by blending the syllables he identifies the word *pocket*.

Some children will no sooner have identified the first syllable in the word than they will have guessed from the context that

the word is *pocket,* and thus they need go no further in working out the word. In the word *pennies* in the same line, the
syllable *pen,* with the help of the context, may give the reader
the clue to the word *pennies.* If not, he can work out the syllables
and by blending them identify the word in the line:

> a pocket full of pennies.

NOTE. One child in working out the word *full* called it (fŭl) instead; whereupon he changed it to *full,* "because," he said, "(fŭl)
didn't make sense and *full* did."

In working out the word *parakeet* in the following line the
technique is the same as for one-syllable words. The reader works
out the syllables, *par* and *keet;* then by blending the syllables
par a keet, he identifies the word in the line:

> a parakeet in the pet shop.

By working out the new words in lines like the following,
children learn to use their "phonetic" ability in word perception
in reading:

a pocket full of pennies	a pitcher of punch for a party
a parakeet in the pet shop	a package from the postman
a pansy with purple petals	the pilot in his plane
pumpkins for a Halloween party	a new pen in a pencil box
a pound of peanuts in a pot	a peck of pickled peppers for Peter

The Sound (ch) *as in* Watch *and* Peach. With the known
words *watch* and *peach* before them on the chalkboard or chart,
the children listen as they pronounce the words. The teacher
asks, "What sound do you hear at the end of *watch?*" Children
who have learned to hear the sounds in words will answer "(ch)"
as they frame the ending (tch) in *watch.* When asked, "What
sound do you hear at the end of *peach?*" the pupils answer "(ch)"
and frame the ending (ch) in the word *peach.* They have discovered the sound (ch) and that it is spelled two ways, *ch* and
tch.

When he knows the sound (ch), the pupil can associate the
sound with its letters in working out the new words in reading
in which the sound occurs. Having learned the vowel and consonant sounds, the reader can work out the one-syllable words in
lines like the following, by the same familiar technique of recog-

nizing first the vowel sound, then the beginning sounds, and then the whole word.

In working out a word of more than one syllable, as in the word *chimpanzee,* in the following line, the technique is the same as for one-syllable words. The reader works out the syllables *chim pan zee;* then by blending the syllables, he identifies the word in the line:

a big chimpanzee on TV.

In working out the words *chipmunk* and *chicken,* the reader works out the syllables in each of the words; then by blending the syllables he identifies the words in the line:

a chipmunk and a chicken snake.

By working out new words in lines like the following, children learn to use their "phonetic" skill and ability in word perception in reading.

baby chicks to hatch out	*cheers* to rhyme with *dears*
a big chimpanzee on TV	lunch time in the kitchen
a chipmunk and a chicken snake	cheese cake and cherry pie
children sitting on a bench	pitching a fast ball
playing checkers with Charley	catching the pitcher's ball

NOTE. Although the sound (ch) is a blend of (t + sh), it is treated here as it is in phonics; namely, as a single sound.

THE CONSONANTS HEARD ONLY AT THE BEGINNING
OF A WORD OR SYLLABLE

The following procedures for learning the consonant sounds (h), (j), and (wh) are intended as examples for all the consonants whose sounds occur only at the beginning, not at the end of a word or syllable, as indicated by italic type in the list of cue words on page 49.

The Sounds (hŭ) *as in* Hunter. With the known word *hunter* before them on the chalkboard or chart, the children listen to the sounds as they pronounce the word. The teacher asks, "What sounds do you hear at the beginning of *hunter?*" Children who have learned to hear the speech sounds in words will answer, "(hŭ)" as they frame (hu) in *hunter*. Children who have not learned through listening to hear the sounds in words are likely to name the letter *h* instead of the sounds at the beginning of the word (see "Experiences in Readiness for Phonics").

When he knows the sounds (hŭ) as in *hunter,* and has learned the vowel sounds, the reader can recognize the beginning sounds in the words like (hă) in *happy* and *hands;* (hĭ) in *history;* (hŏ) in *hollow* and *hobgoblin;* (hou) in *hound;* (hĕ) in *helicopter;* and (ho͞o) in *hoof* in lines like the following reading matter.

NOTE. The diacritical marks over the vowels are intended to show the teacher that the beginnings in the words are pronounced, not spelled. They are certainly not intended for the children's observation, or as an aid in learning the sounds.

Knowing the beginning sounds in a new word and having the context to help him is often all that the reader needs to identify the word. In case he needs to work out the word he can easily do so, when he knows the simple technique for identifying the word in reading. In working out the word *hound,* for example, the reader recognizes the vowel sounds (ou), then (hou), and then *hound* as in the line:

the long ears of a hound.

In working out a word of more than one syllable, as in the word *hobgoblin* in the following line, the technique is the same as for the one-syllable words. The reader works out the syllables *hob gob lin;* then by blending the syllables, he identifies the word in the line:

the tale of a hobgoblin.

Lines like the following can provide a rewarding experience for youngsters who, knowing the vowel and consonant sounds, are learning how to identify new words or the unfamiliar components in the words in reading situations.

the long ears of a hound	a history book to read
the tale of a hobgoblin	a hamburger sandwich
a hummingbird's nest	a happy puppy shaking hands
a helicopter up in the sky	a hornet's sting
a hollow log for a bear	the hoof of a horse

The Sounds (jŭ) *as in* Jug. With the known word *jug* before them on the chalkboard or chart, the children listen as they pronounce the word. When asked, "What sounds do you hear at the beginning of *jug?*" children who have learned to hear the sounds in words will answer "(jŭ)" as they frame (ju) in *jug*. Children who have not learned to hear the speech sounds in words are almost certain to name the letter *j* instead of the sounds at the beginning of the word. (For the benefit of these children, see "Experiences in Readiness for Phonics.")

When he knows the sounds (jŭ) as in *jug* and has learned the vowel sounds, the reader can recognize the beginning sounds in words like (jŏ) in *jolly* and *jockey* and *jogging*, (jĭ) in *jig*, (jă) in *jam* and *January*, (Jü) in *June* and *July*, (jä) in *jars*, and (joi) in the word *joining* in reading matter like the following.

When he knows the beginning sounds in the new word, and has the sense of the sentence in mind, the reader may be able to identify the word on sight. If he needs to work out the word in order to identify it, he can easily do so when he has learned the sounds in the word and how to work out new words.

Should a youngster in working out a new word assign the wrong sound to a letter in the word, he corrects the error, if he comes close enough to the word's identity, and knows the word when he hears it.

For the procedures in identifying new words in reading matter like the following, see the techniques already given for working out the words.

a jolly good time playing "jacks"	the juggler in the TV show
a jigsaw puzzle to work on	new jeans for Jack and Jill
telling jokes just for fun	the jockey on his race horse
boys joining in the fun	jogging along in an old jeep
a baby junco and a blue jay	jars and jars of jam and jelly
January, June, and July	jumping Mexican beans to enjoy

The Sounds (whĭ) *as in* Whip. With the known word *whip* before them on the chalkboard or chart, the children listen to to the sounds as they pronounce the word. When asked, "What sounds do you hear at the beginning of *whip?*" children who have learned to hear the sounds in words will answer "(whĭ)" as they frame (whi) in *whip*.

When he knows the sounds (whĭ) as in *whip* and has learned the vowel sounds, the reader can recognize the beginning sounds in words like (whĕ) in *when* and *whether,* (whā) in *whale,* (whē) in *wheel,* and (whī) in *while* in reading matter like the following.

When he knows the beginning sounds in a new word and has the sense of the sentence in mind, the reader may be able to identify the word on sight. Should he need to work out the word in order to identify it, he can readily do so when he knows the sounds in the word and has learned the simple technique for identifying new words.

the billy goat's whiskers
a whisk broom for the whiskers
a whiff of fresh air
a whale coming up for air
wheels on a wobbly wagon
whether to rhyme with *weather*

the horse's whinny
the puppy's whimper
while the whip-poor-will calls
when boys are whistling
when girls are whispering
asking which ones and why

The Consonant Blends in the Reading Vocabulary[3]

The most frequently occurring initial consonant blends in the children's reading vocabulary are indicated by italic type in the cue word list that follows on page 57. The final consonant blends are indicated in like manner in the subsequent word list.

Each of the words in the lists, which presumably was learned as a "sight word" in reading, now becomes the pupils' cue word for learning the blend. Any known word bearing the consonant blend and which can be pictured may serve as the pupils' cue word for discovering the blend. (For the advantages of having the cue words pictured, see "The Vowel and Consonant Sounds.")

The Initial Consonant Blends

Since initial consonants are always blended with the adjacent vowel in a spoken word or syllable, these consonants are never heard apart from, but always with, their accompanying vowel sounds. The initial consonant blends, then, are learned with the vowel sounds as indicated in the following list of cue words.

---

3 "An Analysis and Classification of the Sounds in the Children's Reading Vocabulary in Grades 1–3"; unpublished dissertation, University of Iowa, Iowa City, Iowa; and a subsequent "Study of the Reading Vocabulary, Grades 4–6."

Cue Words for the Initial Consonant Blends

*st*ick	*sn*ake	*pl*ane	*cr*ab	*tr*ees
*sl*ide	*str*eet	*fl*ag	*dr*ess	*pr*unes
*sp*oon	*bl*ocks	*gl*obe	*fr*og	*qu*een
*sc*out	*cl*ock	*br*idge	*gr*apes	

Now that we have before us the consonant blends that occur at the beginning of a word or syllable in the reading vocabulary, let us see how children discover the blends and then associate them with their letters in working out new words and syllables in reading situations.

The following procedures for learning the consonant blends (st) and (pl) are intended as examples for all the initial consonant blends, indicated by italic type in the cue words above.

The Blend (stĭ) *as in* Stick. With the known word *stick* before them on the chalkboard or chart, the children listen to the sounds as they pronounce the word. The teacher asks, "What sounds do you hear at the beginning of *stick?*" The children who have learned to hear the speech sounds in words will answer "(stĭ)," as they frame (sti) in *stick*.

When he knows the sounds (stĭ) as in *stick,* and has learned the vowel sounds, the reader can identify the beginning sounds in words like (stă) in *stack, statue,* and *stamps;* (stĕ) in *step;* (stŭ) in *stuck* and *stump;* (stē) in *steel;* and (stou) in *stout.*

Since the beginning sounds in a new word may give the clue to the word's identity, the reader may need only to recognize the beginning sounds in order to identify the word. Should he need to work out the word in reading, he can easily do so when he knows the sounds in the word and has learned how to identify new words.

In the word *steamships,* for example, if the beginning *stea,* or the syllable *steam* or *ship,* does not at once reveal the word's identity, the reader can work out each of the syllables by recognizing the vowel sound, the beginning sounds, and then the whole syllable; then by blending the syllables he identifies the word.

In working out the words *stout* and *steel,* the technique is the same as it is in working out the syllables *steam* and *ships* in the line:

steamships made of stout steel.

The most efficient readers in the group may be able to read lines like the following on sight. Others may need to glance only at the beginning of a new word in order to identify the word. Still others may need to work out the new words or syllables by the simple technique for working out the words or syllables.

a stick of sticky candy	steep steps going to the stairs
a stack of stamps to lick	a tree stump stuck in the ground
standing on a stack of stones	stiff and still as a statue
steamships made of stout steel	the Statue of Liberty
the "Stop" and "Go" sign	the United States of America

The Blend (plā) *as in* Plane. With the known word *plane* before them on the chalkboard or chart, the children listen to the sounds as they pronounce the word. When asked, "What sounds do you hear at the beginning of *plane?*" the children who have learned to hear the speech sounds in words will answer "(plā)," as they frame (pla) in *plane.*

When he knows the sounds (plā) as in *plane,* and has learned the vowel sounds, the reader can identify the beginning sounds in words like (plă) in *plants* and *planetarium,* (plĕ) in *plenty,* (plē) in *please,* and (plŭ) in *plump* and *plums* in reading matter like the following.

Since the beginning sounds in a new word may give the clue to the word's identity, the reader may need only to recognize the beginning of the word in order to identify the word. Should he need to work out the word, he can easily do so when he knows the sounds in the word and has learned how to work out new words in reading situations.

One little girl, in working out the word *planetarium* in the following line, came out with (plā′nə·tār·i·əm) and changed it immediately to (plan′ə·tār′·i·əm), having come close enough to the word's identity to recognize the word, since she had the word in her speaking vocabulary.

a visit to the planetarium.

The word *explain* in the next line is easily worked out if the reader knows the syllable *ex* on sight (see the section on prefixes later in this chapter). He then needs only to work out the syllable *plain*, by the same simple technique that has been described in the preceding paragraphs.

something to explain in school.

Children who are able to do so, should be encouraged to read the entire line in reading matter like the following, under their own power.

a visit to the planetarium	a cowboy's plantation on the plains
something to explain in school	a place for plants to grow
plastic bags for sale	a farmer plodding behind the plow
planets in orbit	plenty of plates to wash
plump ripe plums to eat	"Please" and "Thank You"

The Final Consonant Blends

The most frequently occurring final consonant blends in the children's reading vocabulary are indicated by italic type in the following list of words:

Cue Words for the Final Consonant Blends

ta′*ble*	ea′*gle*	poo′*dle*
peo′*ple*	ri′*fle*	bee′*tle*

Now that we have before us the consonant blends that occur only at the end of a word in the reading vocabulary, let us see how children discover the blends and learn to identify them in reading situations.

The following procedures for learning the final consonant blends *ble* and *ple* are intended as examples for all the final consonant blends indicated by italic type in the cue words.

The Consonant Blend as in Ta′ble. With the known word *table* before them on the chalkboard or chart, the children listen to the sounds as they pronounce the word. When asked, "What sounds do you hear at the end of the word *ta′ble?*" the children who have learned to hear the speech sounds in words will answer "(b′l)" or "(bǝl)," both of which are considered correct. The pupil indicates the blend by framing the syllable *ble* in the word *table*.

NOTE. For a description of the pronunciations (b'l) and (bəl), see "The Phonetic Study of the Consonants," Chapter 6.

Having learned to recognize the blend as a unit, children can identify it as a known syllable in the words in which the blend occurs without having to associate the sounds with the letters in the blend. In identifying the word *tumble,* for example, the reader works out the syllable *tum;* then by blending the two syllables he identifies the word *tumble* in the line:

> ready to tumble into bed.

NOTE. For the procedure in working out the syllable *tum,* see the techniques in this chapter for working out the new words.

Simply by blending the "long a" with the syllable *ble,* the reader identifies the word *able* in the line:

> the fun of being able to read.

If the pupil should happen to assign the "short a" to the vowel in the word *able,* he will correct his mistake if he knows the word when he hears it spoken.

Lines like the following provide the opportunity for children who are learning to work out new words in the reading vocabulary to identify the final blend on sight in reading situations.

ready to tumble into bed	the player who fumbles the ball
the fun of being able to read	a scramble for the ball
Mother's new silver thimble	the wind that makes a leaf tremble
the rumble and roar of thunder	fairy tales and fables to read

The Consonant Blend as in Peo'ple. With the known word *people* before them on the chalkboard or chart, the children listen to the sounds as they pronounce the word. When asked, "What sounds do you hear at the end of the word *peo'ple?*" children who have learned to hear the speech sounds in words will answer "(p'l)" or "(pəl)," both of which are accepted in cultivated speech. The pupil indicates the blend by framing the syllable *ple* in the word *people.*

NOTE. For a description of the pronunciations (p'l) and (pəl), see "The Phonetic Study of the Consonants," Chapter 6.

Having learned to recognize the blend as a unit, children can identify it as a syllable in words in which the blend occurs, without having to associate the sounds with the letters in the syllable. In identifying the word *steeple,* for example, the reader works out the syllable *stee;* then by blending it with the syllable *ple,* he identifies the word *steeple* in the line:

a tall steeple on the church.

NOTE. For the procedure in working out the syllable *stee,* see the techniques in this chapter for working out new words.

Upon meeting the word *example,* the skillful reader, unless he identifies the word as a whole, should recognize the familiar syllables, *ex am ple,* which need only to be blended in order to identify the word in the line:

a simple example in arithmetic.

NOTE. See the prefix *ex,* in the list of prefixes on this page.

Lines like the following provide the opportunity for children to identify on sight, and in reading situations, the final consonant blend they have just discovered.

a tall steeple on the church	a sample of good food to eat
a simple example in arithmetic	a purple band in the rainbow
in the shade of the maple tree	the trample of an elephant's foot

Prefixes and Suffixes in Words

It has been found advantageous for children to be able to recognize prefixes and suffixes in words on sight in the reading vocabulary. Children who have learned the consonant and vowel sounds indicated in the cue words in this chapter often find it more fun than work to identify each of the following prefixes and suffixes and to try to discover its meaning in the word in which it occurs.

The most frequently occurring prefixes and suffixes in the children's reading vocabulary are indicated by italic type in the following lists of words.

The Prefixes

*re*turn	*ex*plain	*il*legal	*di*vide	*an*nounce	*pro*duce
*be*fore	*ig*nore	*im*pure	*dis*guise	*un*fair	*con*nect
*de*cide	*se*lect	*in*form	*mis*take	*pre*pare	*com*plete

Having learned to recognize the prefix as a unit, children can identify it as a known syllable in the words in which the prefix occurs without having to associate the sounds with the letters in the prefix.

Children may be expected to assign the "long e" to the prefixes in the words *return, before, decide, select,* and *prepare.* But *Webster's New International Dictionary,* Second Edition, indicates the vowel sound in these prefixes by the symbol (ē); and *Webster's New International Dictionary,* Third Edition, assigns the "short i" to the vowel in the prefix in *return, before, decide,* and *prepare,* and the schwa (ə) to the vowel sound in the prefix in the word *select.* Webster's Third Edition also assigns the schwa to the vowel sound in the prefix in *produce, divide, mistake, announce, unfair, connect,* and *complete;* while Webster's Second Edition indicates the vowel sound in the prefix *produce* with the symbol (ȯ) and with the breve (˘) over the italicized vowel in the prefix in *announce, unfair, connect,* and *complete.*

The Suffixes

farm*er*	want*ed*	kind*est*	care*ful*	glad*ly*	laugh*ing*
sail*or*	watch*es*	fool*ish*	care*less*	kind*ness*	atten*tion*

Having learned to recognize the suffix as a unit, children can identify it as a known syllable in the words in which the suffix occurs without having to associate the sounds with the letters in the suffix.

The suffix *er* in the word *farmer* and *or* in *sailor* have identical pronunciations, indicated as such in Webster's Second Edition, by the symbol (ẽr) and in Webster's Third Edition, by the symbol (ər).

The suffix *ly* as in the word *gladly* is pronounced (lĭ) in Webster's Second Edition and (lē) in Webster's Third Edition. The suffix *ful* in the word *careful* is pronounced (fo͞ol) in Webster's Second Edition and (fəl) in Webster's Third Edition. The suffix *less* in *careless* is pronounced (lĕs) and also (lĭs) in Webster's Second Edition and (ləs) in Webster's Third. The suffix in the word *attention* is respelled by the symbols (shŭn) in Webster's Second Edition and (chən) in Webster's Third Edition.

Rules for Pronunciation and Syllabication

Many teachers find the rules for pronunciation and syllabication useful in word perception in reading. We observed how John applied the rule he had learned for the "long u" in identifying the syllable *sule* in *capsule* and for the "long e" in the syllable *phere* in *atmosphere* (Chapter 2). The following rules are among the best-known and most widely used rules for identifying the vowel and consonant sounds in the children's reading vocabulary.

1. The letter *e* at the end of a syllable usually shows that the first vowel in the syllable has its "long" sound.

   Examples: *gave, hide, refuse, complete, decorate, bone, tune*
   Exceptions: *have, give, come, rule, active, gone*

2. When two vowels come together in a syllable, they usually have the "long" sound of the first vowel.

   Examples: *train, meat, tried, toad, hue*
   Exceptions: *said, plaid, bread, field, cloud, true, steak, break'fast, cou'pon*

3. The vowel in an open syllable is usually "long" when the syllable is accented.

   Examples: *lo'cust, se'cret, hel·lo', con·tri·bu'tion, pu'pils, re·ly', op·por·tu'ni·ty*

4. When there is one vowel in a closed syllable, the vowel is usually "short," unless there is some other factor in the syllable that affects the vowel sound.

   Examples: *swam* and *swarm, con'tent* and *cor'net, pat'ents* and *par'ents, pen'cil* and *per'son, bun'dle* and *burn'ing, cap'tain* and *car'pet*

By pronouncing each pair of words in the preceding list of examples, you will note that the sound of (r) is the factor that affects what otherwise would be a "short" vowel in the closed syllable of the word.

5. When the letter *c* comes before *e, i,* or *y* it has the sound (s).

   Examples: *cent, fence, city, bicycle, cyclone*

6. When the letter *g* comes before *e, i,* or *y,* it usually has the sound (j).

Examples: *germs, bridge, plunge, geography, giant, gypsy*
Exceptions: *get, girl, give, gift, geyser, gears*

The rules for syllabication seem not so well known nor so widely used as the rules for the pronunciation of the consonants and vowels in the reading vocabulary. However, they are being taught. One elementary school student recently reported that the rules he had been taught for dividing words into syllables had started him off in identifying the word *su·per·im·po·si'tion* as readily as if he had been familiar with the word, although he had not seen or heard the word before.

NOTE. For the rules that govern syllabication, see "Syllabication" Chapter 10.

SIGNIFICANCE OF LEARNING
THE SOUNDS IN CONTEXT

It would be difficult to overrate the importance of children's learning the vowel and consonant sounds in context and never in isolation, that is, apart from the words in which the sounds occur in reading. The reasons for learning the sounds within the word whole are well established: (1) It is impossible in the English language to tell the sound of a given letter, except by its pronunciation in the word in which it occurs. How is one to know, for example, whether the letter *a* out of context stands for the sound as in *at, ate, care, are, all, senate,* or *about?* What is true of the vowels pertains equally to the consonants. Take, for example, the letter *s.* Does it say (s) as in *bus,* (z) as in *has,* (sh) as in *sure,* (zh) as in *usual,* or does it have no sound at all as in *island?* The answer is to be had by *hearing the sound of the letter in the word* in which it occurs or by discovering that the letter is "silent." (2) The law of transfer states that a skill, in order to be functional, must be learned in the situation in which the skill is to function. Since the association of the sounds with their letters is intended to function in reading, and since in reading the sounds never occur in isolation, always in word context, the sounds must be taught in the word whole. (3) The emotional factor in learning must not be overlooked. What is more boresome, more deadly to a child's zest for learning than monotonous drill on isolated sounds and their symbols? And how exciting it is to discover the sounds in familiar words, and then find these same sounds again and again in working out new words and phrases in the reading situations!

THE QUESTION OF SEPARATE PERIODS FOR PHONICS

Should time in the school day be devoted specifically to instruction in phonics? This is a question that has often been asked by instructors of reading, particularly on the elementary school level. The answer to the question may be found in the reply to a number of other related questions, namely: Can children be expected to know the sounds of the letters in the reading vocabulary without their having learned the sounds in the words? Should a child's thinking while reading be interrupted with his trying to learn the sounds in a new word in order to identify the word? Is a child likely to know how to attack and work out an unfamiliar word in reading so quickly and easily that he can remain in contact with the author of the sentence while he identifies the new word, if he has not learned how to do it? Can a child be expected to know the techniques best suited in working out a new word without his having had experience in using the techniques?

Suppose we compare instruction in phonics with our educational philosophy in other areas of learning. Is not number computation taught in separate periods in anticipation of problem-solving in arithmetic? Is spelling not being taught to assure its effective functioning in written communication? A child's "phonetic" skill in reading is comparable to his skillful use of numbers in arithmetic, and his ability to spell when his mind is on letter-writing or whatever form of communication the child is engaged in at the time. Like number computation and spelling, phonics too is taught not as an end in itself but as an effective means to a successful end, when a child's reading needs demand it.

It has been found that by effective instruction in phonics children who are educable and able to discriminate between the speech sounds in words, can discover the sounds in known "sight" words; and having learned the sounds, associate them with their letters in working out the new words in reading.

Although the slow learner may never become as adept in using context clues and in judging which of several methods are the most suitable in attacking and identifying an unfamiliar word in reading, by systematic instruction in phonics over a long enough period of time he too may learn to achieve independent word perception in reading. He may be unable to bring critical thinking to the treasures that lie between the covers of the great books, but his ability to cope with the reading vocabulary should be brought on a par with his native capacity to comprehend.

Any child, who because of impaired hearing, or for any other reason is unable to discriminate between the sounds in spoken words, must rely on word-perception techniques other than those recommended for the so-called normal individual. The well-known dictum: "each according to his needs," is as pertinent in phonics as in all other areas of teaching, irrespective of the subject matter to be learned or the skill and abilities to be achieved.

*AN INFORMAL TEST**

COMPLETION

1. The ability to see likenesses and differences in words is essential to a child's success in <u>Visual</u> discrimination.
2. The ability to hear likenesses and differences in words is essential to a child's success in <u>auditory</u> discrimination of sounds.
3. The vowel in a spoken word or syllable is always blended with the consonant that immediately <u>precedes</u> it.
4. One can hear that the words *pig, pins, picture,* and *pillow* all begin alike, because both the consonant and the <u>vowel</u> sounds are the same at the beginning of the words.
5. One can hear that *pig, puppy, pets,* and *parrot* do not begin with the same sounds, because the vowel sounds are <u>not</u> the same at the beginning of the words.

* Answers are listed under the appropriate chapter number in the Appendix.

6. By listening to the speech sounds as he pronounces first the whole word, and then the beginning of the word, the child can discover the vowel _sound_ in the word.

7. Any known one-syllable word that can be pictured may be a suitable key or cue word for children's discovering the vowel _sound_ in the word.

8. Consonant sounds are most clearly heard at the _end_ of a word or syllable.

9. Any known word that can be pictured and in which the consonant sound occurs at the end of the word may serve as the pupil's key or cue word for discovering the consonant _sound_ in the word.

10. By listening as he pronounces first the whole word, and then the consonant sound at the end of the word, the pupil can discover the _consonant_ sound in the word.

11. The ability to blend; to have mastered a sight vocabulary adequate for discovering the vowel and consonant sounds; to have developed the desire to read; to be interested in reading; and to have learned to use context clues effectively are among the criteria of _readiness_ for phonics.

12. A familiar beginning in an unfamiliar word like *sat* in *Saturn* or *satisfied* may give the reader the _clue_ to the word's identity.

13. The meaning or use of the new word in a sentence may give the reader the clue to the word's _identity_

14. If in his trying to work out a new word in reading the child erred in his efforts, but came close to the word's identity, he may with the help of the context be able to _identify_ the word.

15. The consonants (h), (w), (wh), and (y) are heard only at the _beginning_ of a word or syllable in the children's reading vocabulary.

16. Vowel and consonant sounds should be learned in the words in which they occur, not in _isolation_; namely, apart from the word whole.

17. The law of transfer states that a skill, in order to be functional, must be learned in the situation in which the _skill_ is to function.

18. The vowel *e* at the end of a syllable usually shows that the first vowel in the syllable has its _long_ sound.

19. When two vowels come together in a syllable they usually have the "long" sound of the _first_ vowel.

20. It is recommended that phonics like number computation and spelling be taught in a separate period not as an _end_ in itself, but as an effective means to a successful end in children's reading.

4

PHONETICS AND PHONICS

So far we have been devoting our attention to phonics as a means of independent word perception in reading; namely, to the functional aspect of phonics. Let us now see how well informed we are on the subject matter of phonics, and what the science of phonetics has to offer the teacher of reading.

It is generally assumed that the teacher who knows how to teach reading is equally skillful in the field of phonics. While it is true that some of the ablest teachers of reading have also learned to teach phonics effectively, one may be exceedingly successful in creating in his or her pupils the desire to read, in providing a background of experiences for learning to read, in broadening children's interests in reading, and in familiarizing the reader with the "sight" word vocabulary on all levels of learning and be poorly informed or misinformed on the subject matter of phonics and its effective functioning in children's reading.

Mrs. Brown would have recognized in the foregoing statement an accurate description of herself (Chapter 1). She had enjoyed an enviable reputation as a teacher of reading during the period when phonics was banned in her school. But now she was finding that her ability to teach phonics was no match for the success she had formerly enjoyed in teaching beginners to read. She once confessed, "I know so little about phonetics or phonics, I shouldn't be trying to teach it!"

Before proceeding further with our study, let us get together on the meaning of the terms *phonetics* and *phonics*. Although often used interchangeably by educators and laymen alike, the terms are not synonymous, as we shall see.

PHONETICS AND PHONICS DEFINED

The term *phonetics* has long been used to designate the science of speech sounds. This science grew out of the research of many specialists: linguists, anatomists, psychologists, physicians of the throat and nose, teachers of the deaf and dumb, and teachers of voice and has since then been known as the science of speech sounds or the science of sounds used in speaking.

Phonics may be defined as the application of phonetics to the art of reading. It deals with both the speech sounds and the letters that represent the sounds in the reading vocabulary. Phonetics, as we shall see later in the chapter, has its own symbols that stand for the speech sounds in the language. Throughout this book we shall use the term *phonetics* to mean the science of speech sounds and the term *phonics* as a means of independent word perception in reading.

THE NEED FOR A KNOWLEDGE OF PHONETICS

In the so-called "unphonetic" English language, the letters one sees in a word may stand for the sounds one usually associates with the letters in the word, or the spelling of the word may be no indication at all of the sounds one hears when the word is spoken. Because the spelling of a word may give little or no indication of the word's pronunciation, failure to distinguish between letters and sounds in a word accounts for many of the pitfalls in teaching phonics (see Chapter 1).

To Distinguish between Sounds and Letters

In the study of phonetics one learns to *hear* the sounds in a word regardless of the way the word is spelled. Had Mrs. Brown been schooled in the science of phonetics she would have been able at once to distinguish between the so-called "long o" in the words *snow, grown, flow,* and *blow* and the diphthong in *owl, cows, clown, growl,* and *town.* She would indeed have known that the vowels in the two groups of words do not sound alike, even though they are spelled exactly alike.

Had Miss Corwin had a knowledge of phonetics she would not have misled her pupil by directing her to look for the word *hen* in *then* (Chapter 1). She would have known that the letters *th* in the word *then* stand for a single sound, which is neither (t) nor (h), as shown by its phonetic symbol ð. Since there is no sound of *h* in *then,* there is of course no *hen* in *then!*

Miss Corwin, unfortunately, had not learned to distinguish between the letters one *sees* and the sounds one *hears* in a word. According to the letters, one should find the word *hen* in *then,* as well as *hat* in *that, hip* in *whip,* and *hut* in *shut.* But here again the spelling of the words is deceptive. Besides the initial consonant sound, there is an *en* in *then,* an *ip* in *whip,* an *ut* in *shut,* and an *at* in *that.* But that's all!

In another classroom Mrs. Herman, who otherwise was one of the ablest teachers in the school system, was teaching her pupils that the vowel in *put* had the same sound as the vowel in *but.* The words *few, mew, flew, blew,* and *grew* were grouped together as having the "long u" sound. Letters that look alike seem to sound alike, until one has learned to distinguish between the letters one sees in the word and the sounds one hears when the word is spoken.

Mr. Sloan, a conscientious sixth-grade teacher, was troubled because his pupils, as he said, did not have the slightest idea how to attack and "unlock" the unfamiliar words they met in their reading. "And," he added, half humorously, "I haven't the slightest idea how to help them. I don't know the first thing about phonics."

Here was an intelligent teacher directing the attention of his sixth-grade pupils to the word *sure* in *pleasure!* When later the teacher was told that there was no *sure* in *pleasure,* the man was dumbfounded. He finally admitted that he could hear that the sound of *s* in *sure* was not the same as the sound of *s* in *pleasure.* Whereupon he added, "The letter *s* in *pleasure* has the sound of z, like in *seizure!*"

When the young man was told that there is no sound of (z) in *pleasure* or *seizure,* he exclaimed with one sweep of the arm, "I give up! That's too much for me!"

But the man's biggest surprise was still to come—when he learned that the letter *s* in *pleasure* and the *z* in *seizure* have exactly the same sound that one hears at the end of *rouge, garage,* or *sabotage!* "I'll be darned!" he said. "Here I am a college graduate trying to teach children to read and I didn't know until now that there was a sound like that in the English language!"

Perhaps the lesson should have been carried a step further. It might have been interesting to have heard the young man's comment upon learning that the new sound he had just acquired, and which is spelled with the letter *s* in *pleasure* and with the letter *z* in *seizure* and the letters *si* in *division,* is the same sound that occurs twice in the words *judge* and *ginger.* But for a beginner in the study of phonetics, the previous lesson proved to be quite enough.

One is reminded of the German immigrant who was surprised to find that in pronouncing the word *one* he heard the sound (w) at the beginning of the word, but saw no letter there to represent the sound. He was even more surprised when he discovered the spelling of the word *colonel.* He wanted to spell *colonel* "like the kernel of a nut," he said. Having been accustomed to considerable agreement between the spelling and pronunciation of a word in his native tongue, he was astonished to find that the syllable spelled *colo* had exactly the same pronunciation as the syllable *ker* in *kernel.*

It goes without saying that the German had many more surprises as he learned to speak and spell the English language. More than one scholarly foreigner has despaired of ever learning to spell the English language.

The Need To Pronounce Speech Sounds Correctly

Perhaps the most convincing evidence of the teachers' need for a knowledge of phonetics is shown in the faulty pronunciation of the sounds in teaching phonics.

All speech sounds are frequently mispronounced, but the consonants are much more likely to be distorted than the vowels, and some consonants are found to be more difficult than others. The plosives (p) and (b), (t) and (d), and (k) and (g), and the continuants (l) and (r), and the blends formed by these two sounds, present the greatest problem to teachers.

THE PLOSIVES

In pronouncing the plosives, the tendency is to add a vowel sound, resulting in the mispronunciations: (pŭ), (bŭ), (tŭ), (dŭ), (kŭ), (gŭ). The teacher who mispronounces one of the plosives is likely to distort them all and in exactly the same way. Children, of course, imitate their teachers' mistakes as well as their virtues. When a pupil is asked, "What sound do you hear at the end of the word *boat?*" the answer is usually "(tŭ)"; or it may be "(tee)," showing the pupil's confusion between sound and letter. (For the correct pronunciation of the plosives, see Chapter 6.)

THE CONTINUANTS (l) AND (r)

The sound (l) as in *leaf* is usually mispronounced as (ŭl), in this case putting the vowel sound before, rather than after, the consonant as in the plosives. The sound (r) as in *red*, for example, has been mispronounced (ĕr) for generations, as if the word *red* were pronounced *ered; run* were *erun;* or *round* were pronounced *eround*. [See Chapter 6 for the correct pronunciation of the consonants (l) and (r).]

THE (l) AND (r) BLENDS

When (l) is called (ŭl), the blends (pl), (bl), (gl), and (fl) are almost certain to be pronounced as (pul), (bul), (gul), and (ful); as if *please* were correctly pronounced *pulease, black* were *bulack, glass* were *gulass,* and *flag* were *fulag.*

When (r) is called (ĕr), the blends (pr), (br), (gr) , (dr), and (tr) are almost certain to be called (per), (ber), (ger), (der), and (ter). But *proud* is not pronounced *peroud; brown* is not *berown; green* is not *gereen; drum* is not *derum;* and *train* is never pronounced *terain!*

Summary of Points Observed

Many children are learning the sounds of English incorrectly because their teachers have had little, if any, instruction in the science of phonetics.

It is not intended that every teacher of reading should be a phonetician, but everyone who teaches reading should (1) know how the sounds in the reading vocabulary are correctly uttered and how the speech organs function in uttering the sounds; (2) know the relation between the letters that are seen and the sounds that are heard when the word is spoken; and (3) be able to associate the correct sounds with the letters that represent the sounds in the children's reading vocabulary.

In order to achieve these skills and abilities a knowledge of phonetics is essential.

THE PHONETIC ALPHABET

We shall now give attention to an alphabet consisting not of letters like the ABC's, but of symbols, each of which stands for but one sound and that sound only. How different from our conventional alphabet, the ABC's, in which the same letters stand for many different sounds in the reading vocabulary! You have already met three of these interesting symbols; namely ð, ʍ, and ʃ. You will soon meet the rest of the symbols, and unless you already know them you will become familiar with them in this chapter.

How It Came Into Being

The phonetic alphabet dates back to the 1880s when a group of phoneticians from several countries met to form what is known as the International Phonetic Association. This association devised an alphabet known as the International Phonetic Alphabet. It is this alphabet, with slight modifications for the sake of simplicity (the modifications being essentially those used in George P. Krapp's *Pronunciation of Standard English in America*[1]) which is presented in this book.

[1] New York: Oxford University Press, 1919.

Its Value to Teachers

It has already been pointed out that a knowledge of phonetics gives one an understanding of the true relation between sounds and letters in words. The phonetic alphabet is the tool for achieving this understanding, hence its importance to the teacher of phonics.

Since every symbol in the phonetic alphabet stands for one sound and that sound only, there are as many symbols in the alphabet as there are sounds in the language. In contrast to our conventional alphabet of twenty-six letters, the phonetic alphabet provides about forty-one different symbols for the sounds in the English language.

Since every sound has its own symbol, a word that has two sounds has two symbols to represent the sounds. If the word has five sounds, you will see five phonetic symbols in the word. If you see six phonetic symbols in the word, you will hear six sounds when the word is spoken. The number of sounds that you hear always corresponds to the number of symbols that you see in the word. How different when the sounds in a word are represented by the letters of the conventional alphabet! The word *thought,* for example, has seven letters, but only three sounds ðɔːt. The word *box* is spelled with three letters, but it has four sounds bɔks. The word *rocket* with six letters has only five sounds rɔkɛt; and in the word *astronaut,* although it has nine letters, one hears only eight sounds in the word.

Since every sound has its own symbol which stands for that sound and that sound only, it is by means of the phonetic symbols that one learns to hear the sounds in a given word no matter how the word may be spelled.

How many pitfalls in teaching phonics could be avoided if teachers had a knowledge of phonetic symbols to guide them! Familiarity with the phonetic alphabet is the first step in providing a background in phonetics for more intelligent teaching of phonics.

Even though you have never seen the phonetic alphabet, you will have no difficulty in recognizing twenty-one of its symbols, since they look exactly like the letters to which you are accustomed.

COMPARISON OF LETTER AND PHONETIC SYMBOLS[2]

The Consonants

Among the consonants, sixteen of the phonetic symbols look exactly like the letters of the conventional alphabet, as shown by the following comparisons.

Phonetic Symbols   p, b, t, d, k, g, s, z, f, v, m, n, l, r, w, h
Letters   p, b, t, d, k, g, s, z, f, v, m, n, l, r, w, h

You must, of course, think of the phonetic symbols not as letters but as symbols of speech sounds, and as such their value never changes. The symbol **f**, for example, always stands for the sound as in *if*, never for the sound **v** as in *of* (ov). The symbol **g** always stands for the sound as in *get*, never for the sound of the letter *g* as in *gem* (jem), and the phonetic symbol **s** always stands for the sound as in *hats*, never for the sound as in *his* (hiz) or *sure* (shùr).

Unless you are already familiar with the remaining consonant symbols, they may look very strange to you on first sight. But like people you meet for the first time, these characters too will begin to look familiar as you see them again and again in the subsequent chapters of the book.

Here then are the remaining consonant symbols with their corresponding letters of the conventional alphabet.

Phonetic Symbols   ʍ, θ, ð, ʃ, tʃ, ʒ, dʒ, ɪ, ŋ
Letters   wh, th, th, sh, ch, zh, j, r, ng

Note (1) how clearly the phonetic symbol shows that each of the so-called digraphs, *wh, th, sh,* and *ng,* stands for a single sound and not for a blend of two sounds as the letters would seem to indicate; (2) that the single letter *j*, which would seem to stand for one sound, actually stands for a blend of two sounds, the first of which is the sound **d**! and (3) that the letters

[2] Throughout this book phonetic symbols for the speech sounds are indicated in boldface type, the dictionary symbols of the sounds are in roman type in parentheses, and the letters of the alphabet are shown in italic type.

th stand for two different sounds, as shown by the symbols θ and ð.

The Vowels

Among the vowels you will find five familiar symbols: ɑ, e, i, o, and u. To these phonetic symbols the International Phonetic Association assigned their Latin equivalents. These, then, should not prove to be too difficult since you are already familiar with their sounds in words like these:

ɑ as in *a*rm   o as in *o*ld
e as in caf*e*   u as in tr*u*th
i as in pol*i*ce

MATCHING WORDS BY THEIR VOWEL SOUNDS

Here we have two groups of words. The words in Group 1 are phonetically transcribed; those in Group 2 are known as book words. For every word in Group 1 you will find a word in Group 2 to match it. See how readily you can match the phonetic word with its corresponding book word without referring to the preceding words that illustrate the vowel sounds ɑ, e, i, o, and u.

Group 1	Group 2
1. toz	1. two
2. tel	2. tar
3. tu	3. tea
4. tɑɹ	4. tail
5. ti	5. toes
6. bonz	6. bees
7. bek	7. boots
8. buts	8. bones
9. bɑɹn	9. bake
10. biz	10. barn

LEARNING THE REMAINING VOWEL SYMBOLS

Now let us examine the rest of the vowel symbols. Like some of the consonant symbols, these symbols may also look strange to you unless you happen to be familiar with them. If they are new to you, you might like to see how quickly you can become acquainted with these symbols.

æ as in *at*	ɛ as in *end*	ɘ as in t*u*rn
a as in *ask*	ɪ as in *it*	ʌ as in *u*p
ɛː as in c*a*re	ɔ as in *o*dd	ɘ as in *a*go
ɔː as in h*o*rse	ʊ as in f*oo*t	

The phonetic symbol ɘ, known as the schwa, is a very useful symbol as will be seen later in the book. It is the unstressed or lax form of the vowel ʌ as in *up* and is used by phoneticians only in an unaccented, never in the stressed or accented, syllable or word.

ANOTHER EXPERIENCE IN MATCHING

The next exercise in matching presents a real challenge, unless you are already familiar with the symbols. In either case, see how quickly you can match the phonetic word in Group 1 with its corresponding word in Group 2.

Group 1	Group 2
1. læp	1. lost
2. lɛt	2. law
3. lɔst	3. let
4. lɔː	4. lap
5. lʊk	5. look
6. lɘɪn	6. learn
7. past	7. puppy
8. pɛːɪz	8. pig
9. pɪg	9. pears
10. pʌpɪ	10. past
11. ɘlon	11. alone

The Diphthongs

Now that we have observed the symbols for the single vowel sounds, let us turn our attention to the diphthongs, pronounced (dif'thongz), not (dip'thongz), a mispronunciation not infrequently heard.

Since a diphthong is a blend of two vowel sounds, one would expect it to be represented by two phonetic symbols as shown here:

aɪ as in ice	ɑʊ as in out
ju as in use	ɔɪ as in oil

That there should be two vowel sounds in the words *out* and *oil* would seem reasonable enough, since one sees two vowels in these words. But many teachers find it difficult to think of the so-called "long i" and "long u" as being diphthongs. The "long a," "long e," and "long o" are diphthongized too, in the words *day, see,* and *go,* for example. But for the sake of simplicity, these three sounds are classed as single vowels in this book.

TABLE OF THE PHONETIC SYMBOLS

Here you may see all the phonetic symbols with a book word to illustrate each of the consonants, vowels, and diphthongs in the children's reading vocabulary. If you had not seen these symbols before, you might like to have discovered how many of them you could have identified. It will now be interesting to see how many of these once strange-looking characters are beginning to look familiar to you.

Can you read the following quotation without help from the key words in the tables?

"bɔɪ, ʍɒt ə raɪd!"
   Allan B. Shepard, Jr.

Consonants

p, *p*et	ŋ, si*ng*	l, *l*eaf
b, *b*ear	ʍ, *wh*ip	r, *r*ead
t, *t*en	w, *w*ind	ɹ, ca*r*
d, *d*uck	f, *f*ish	h, *h*and
k, *k*ite	v, *v*oice	θ, *th*in
g, *g*oat	s, *s*un	ð, *th*is
m, *m*an	z, *z*ebra	ʃ, *sh*ip
n, *n*est	j, *y*es	ʒ, rou*g*e
	tʃ, cheek	dʒ, jump

Vowels

æ, *a*t	ʌ, *u*p	ɑ, *ar*m	ʊ, f*oo*t
ɛ, *e*nd	i, *ea*t	ɛ:, c*are*	u, f*oo*d
ɪ, *i*t	o, *o*ld	e, *a*te	ə, t*ur*n
ɔ, *o*dd	a, *a*sk	ɔ:, h*orse*	ə, *a*go

Diphthongs

aɪ, *ice*   ɑʊ, *out*
ju, *use*   ɔɪ, *oil*

LETTER SYMBOLS OF SOUNDS

We have just observed the phonetic symbols for the sounds in the words children meet in their reading; and it is by means of these symbols that one learns the true relationship between sounds and their symbols in a given word. But a knowledge of phonetics alone is not enough. The teacher of reading must also know the relation between the sounds and the letters that stand for the sounds in the reading vocabulary.

Since there are only twenty-six letters in the conventional alphabet, and more than forty sounds in the English language, the same letter must stand for many different sounds. The letter *s*, for example, stands for four different sounds; and the letter *a* represents as many as six or seven different vowel sounds in the children's reading vocabulary, as we shall observe in Chapters 7 and 9.

Thus a letter, unlike a phonetic symbol, may represent several different sounds. Some means, therefore, is needed to indicate as accurately as possible the particular sound for which the letter stands in a given word.

THE DICTIONARY'S WAY
OF INDICATING SOUNDS

Although the phonetic symbols provide the exact means of indicating the sounds in words, the authors of dictionaries have devised ways of showing with a fair degree of accuracy the sounds of the letters in any given word.

The vowel sounds are usually indicated by little marks placed over the vowels in the syllables or by respelling the vowels or by both respelling and marking the vowel. The letter *a* as in *all*, for example, is respelled with the letter *o* and marked (ô) in the Thorndike-Barnhart Dictionary and in *Webster's New International Dictionary*, Second Edition, and \ȯ\ in Webster's Third

Edition. The letters *ew* as in *few* are respelled with the letter *u* and marked (ū), except in Webster's Third Edition, in which the letters are respelled and marked \yü\ to show their diphthongal nature.

Consonants are respelled when necessary to show their sounds in words. The letter *s* in *has* is respelled with the letter *z* (haz); and *f* is respelled with the letter *v* in *of* (ov).

It is useful to know the precise meaning of the various marks and symbols used to indicate the sounds in words and to know also that dictionaries vary in their methods of respelling and marking the letters to show how a given word is pronounced.

The following marks and symbols for indicating the vowel and consonant sounds are those found in *Webster's New International Dictionary,* Second Edition, *Webster's New International Dictionary,* Third Edition, and in the Thorndike-Barnhart Dictionary.

For a comparison of the dictionary symbols for the vowel sounds with one another and with their corresponding phonetic symbols, see Table 1. For a similar study of the consonant sounds, see Tables 2 and 3.

Means of Indicating the Vowel Sounds

The marks used by the different dictionaries to indicate the vowel sounds in words are known as diacritical marks. Such marks were originally placed over or under the vowel to indicate the sound of the letter but have long since been placed over the vowels only, with the exception of the hooked "long e," which is used in *Webster's New International Dictionary,* Second Edition, to indicate the "long e" in words when followed by (r), as in the word *here* (hẹr), for example.

Let us begin our study of the dictionary symbols with one that indicates the same vowel sound in each of the three dictionaries.

The two-dot a (ä)

The symbol (ä) is used to indicate the sound of the letter *a* as in the following words in each of the dictionaries:

calm (käm)   farm (färm)   fäth'er (fäth'ər)   al'monds \'ä-məndz\

Let us now take cognizance of the symbols that are used to indicate the vowel sounds in one or two of the three dictionaries under consideration.

The one-dot a (à)

The symbol (à) is used in Webster's Second Edition to indicate the sound of the letter *a* in words or syllables ending in *sk, ss, st, nce, th, nt,* and in some cases in *nd* as well, as in the following examples:

ask (àsk)　　　　　　path (pàth)
pass (pàs)　　　　　　grant (grànt)
last (làst)　　　　　　com·mand′ (kŏ·mànd′)
dance (dàns)

In Webster's Third Edition the symbol (à) is used to indicate the sound of the letter *a* in *father,* as pronounced by speakers who do not rhyme *father* with *bother.*

In the Thorndike-Barnhart Dictionary, in which the symbol (à) is conspicuous by its absence, the speaker is given the choice between the sound (ä) and the "short a" in pronouncing words like those in the foregoing list.

The breve (˘)

This is the diacritical mark which in Webster's Second Edition is used to indicate each of the "short" vowel sounds as in the following examples, and does not occur at all in Webster's Third Edition or in the Thorndike-Barnhart Dictionary.

add (ăd)　　　　end (ĕnd)　　　　inch (ĭnch)　　　　odd (ŏd)　　　　up (ŭp)

The breve is also used in Webster's Second Edition to indicate the "short" vowel sound in unstressed or unaccented syllables as shown by the following examples:

ac·count′ (ă·kount′)　　　　con·nect′ (kŏ·nĕkt′)
si′lent (sī′lĕnt)　　　　cir′cus (sûr′kŭs)
di·vide′ (dĭ·vīd′)

The macron (ˉ)

With the exception of Webster's Third Edition, which uses

the symbol (yü) to indicate the "long u," the macron is used to represent each of the "long" vowels as shown here.

ate (āt)   eat (ēt)   ice (īs)   old (ōld)   use (ūz)

The half-long mark (⁻)

This "semi-macron" is found only in Webster's Second Edition, where it shows the modified "long" (a), (e), (o), and (u) in unaccented syllables as in the following examples:

va·ca′tion (vȧ·kā′shŭn)   o·bey′ (ō·bā′)
e·vent′ (ē·vĕnt′)   u·nite′ (ū·nīt′)

The circumflex (^)

The circumflex, which is often referred to as an upside down *v*, is not found in Webster's Third Edition, but is used in Webster's Second Edition and by Thorndike and Barnhart over the letter *o* to indicate the vowel sound as in *horse* (hôrs) and *saw* (sô), for example. The circumflex is used in Webster's Second Edition over the letter *a* to indicate the vowel sound before (r) as in *care* (kâr) and *bear* (bâr) and over the letter *u* to show the vowel sound before (r) as in *turn* (tûrn), *bird* (bûrd), and *fern* (fûrn), for example.

The short circumflex (˘)

The symbol (ŏ) is found only in Webster's Second Edition, where it is used to indicate the vowel sound that is about half way between the sounds (ô) and (ŏ) as in these words:

soft (sŏft)   lost (lŏst)   dog (dŏg)   cof′fee (kŏf′ĭ)

The tilde (~)

The tilde, which is not found in Webster's Third Edition at all, is used in the Thorndike-Barnhart Dictionary over the letter *a* to indicate the vowel sound before (r) as in *care* (kãr) and *bear* (bãr), for example. It is used in Webster's Second Edition to indicate the unstressed sound (ẽr) as in the following unaccented syllables:

mak′er (māk′ẽr)   mar′tyr (mär′tẽr)
doc′tor (dŏk′tẽr)   mur′mur (mûr′mẽr)
dol′lar (dŏl′ẽr)   cup′board (kŭ′bẽrd)
ta′pir (tā′pẽr)

The long-double o (o͞o)

The symbol (o͞o) is used in Webster's Second Edition to indicate the vowel sound as in the following words:

food (fo͞od)   rule (ro͞ol)   move (mo͞ov)   shoe (sho͞o)

The two-dot u (ü)

The Thorndike-Barnhart Dictionary and Webster's Third Edition both use the symbol (ü) instead of (o͞o) to indicate the vowel sound as in *food, rule, move,* and *shoe,* for example.

The symbol (ü) is also used in Webster's Third Edition to indicate the second element in the diphthong as in the following words:

few \\'fyü\\   tube \\'t(y)üb\\   youth \\'yüth\\

The short-double o (o͝o)

The symbol (o͝o) is used in Webster's Second Edition to indicate the vowel sound as in these words:

foot (fo͝ot)   pull (po͝ol)   would (wo͝od)   bush (bo͝osh)

The one-dot u (u̇)

The Thorndike-Barnhart Dictionary and Webster's Third Edition both use the symbol (u̇) instead of (o͝o) to indicate the vowel sound as in the words *foot, pull, would,* and *bush.*

The symbol (u̇) is also used in Webster's Third Edition to indicate the second element in the diphthong as in these examples:

now \\'nau̇\\   loud \\'lau̇d\\   fu-ry \\'fyu̇ (ə) r-ē\\

The one-dot o (ȯ)

The one-dot *o,* which does not occur in either of the other two dictionaries, is used in Webster's Third Edition to indicate the vowel sound as in *horse* \\'hȯrs\\ and *saw* \\'sȯ\\, for example, and also to indicate the first element of the diphthong as in these words:

coin \\'kȯin\\   boys \\'bȯiz\\

The one-dot e (ėr)

The one-dot (ė) is the Thorndike-Barnhart symbol for indicating the vowel sound before (r) as in the following words:

term (tėrm)   learn (lėrn)   bird (bėrd)   hurt (hėrt)

The hooked long e (ę̄)

The symbol (ę̄) is used in Webster's Second Edition to show the influence of the sound (r) on the "long e" in words like the following:

here (hę̄r)   fear (fę̄r)   deer (dę̄r)   pier (pę̄r)

The italic one-dot a (ȧ)

The symbol (ȧ) is used in Webster's Second Edition to indicate the sound of the letter *a* in unaccented syllables like those in the following words:

a·bout' (ȧ·bout')   a·dult' (ȧ·dŭlt')
com'ma (kŏm'ȧ)   af·fec'tion (ȧ·fĕk'shŭn)

The ligatured t-u (t͡u)

The ligatured t-u, another of the many symbols peculiar to *Webster's New International Dictionary,* Second Edition, shows the pronunciation of the unaccented syllable *ture* in words like the following:

pic'ture (pĭk't͡ur)   na'ture (nā't͡ur)   lit'er·a·ture (lĭt'ẽr·ȧ·t͡ur)

The schwa (ə)

The phonetic symbol known as the schwa, which resembles an upside down *e* and is extensively used in the Thorndike-Barnhart Dictionary and particularly in Webster's Third Edition, does not occur at all in Webster's Second Edition. In the Thorndike-Barnhart Dictionary the symbol (ə) is used only to indicate the sound of the vowels *a, e, i, o,* and *u* in unaccented syllables as in the following examples:

a·bout (ə·bout')   lem'on (lem'ən)
si'lent (sī'lənt)   cir'cus (sėr'kəs)
pen'cil (pen'səl)

In Webster's Third Edition the schwa is used not only to indicate the vowel sound in the unstressed syllables of words like those in the foregoing list but also to represent the "short u" in the accented words or syllables as shown here:

come \'kəm\   but \'bət\   love \'ləv\   hum·drum \'həm-drəm\

Comparison of Vowel Sounds

After having observed the particular letter symbols used to indicate the vowel sounds in English words in *Webster's New International Dictionary,* Second Edition, *Webster's New International Dictionary,* Third Edition, and the Thorndike-Barnhart Dictionary, let us now see how the various dictionary symbols for the vowel sounds compare with one another and with their corresponding phonetic symbols (Table 1).

Observations of the Dictionaries' Symbols for Vowel Sounds

A study of the various symbols used by the dictionaries for indicating the vowel sounds invites some interesting observations.

1. As many as nine different vowel symbols in *Webster's New International Dictionary,* Second Edition, have been replaced by the schwa in Webster's Third Edition.

2. Instead of using the breve to indicate the "short" vowels as in the Webster's Second Edition, the Thorndike-Barnhart Dictionary shows the "short" vowels by leaving the letters unmarked, as does Webster's Third Edition, except for the "short o," which is indicated by the symbol (ä), and the "short u," whose sound is indicated by the schwa.

3. None of the following diacritical marks and symbols, all of which occur in Webster's Second Edition, are found in Webster's Third: the breve, the circumflex, the short circumflex, the italic one-dot a, the ligatured t-u, the half-long symbols (ā̇), (ė), (ȯ), and (û), the italic symbols (ă), (ĕ), (ĭ), (ŏ), and (ŭ), and the symbols (ẽr), (o͞o), and (o͞o).

4. The following symbols for indicating vowel sounds in Webster's Third Edition are not found in Webster's Second Edition: the schwa, the symbols (ər), (ȯ), (u̇), (ü), and the symbols (ȯi), (au̇), (yu̇), and (yü), which indicate the diphthongal nature of the vowels as in *boy, now, fu'ry,* and *few* respectively.

Table 1. Dictionary and Phonetic Symbols

Example	Webster's Second Edition	Webster's Third Edition	Thorndike-Barnhart	Phonetic Symbol
at	ă	a	a	æ
ate	ā	ā	ā	e
ask	à	—	—	a
arm	ä	ä	ä	ɑ
care	â	—	ā	ɛː
va·ca'tion	â	ā	ā	e
a·bout'	à	ə	ə	ə
ac·count	ă	ə	ə	ə
end	ĕ	e	e	ɛ
eat	ē	ē	ē	i
e·vent'	ê	i	i	ɪ
fath'er	ẽ	ə	ə	ə
si'lent	ĕ	ə	ə	ɛ
here	ẹ	—	—	i
it	ĭ	i	i	ɪ
ice	ī	ī	ī	aɪ
pen'cil	ĭ	ə	ə	ɪ
odd	ŏ	ä	o	ɔ
old	ō	ō	ō	o
horse	ô	ȯ	ô	ɔː
soft	ŏ	—	—	ɔ
o·bey'	ō	ō	ō	o
con·nect'	ŏ	ə	ə	ə
foot	o͝o	u̇	u̇	ʊ
food	o͞o	ü	ü	u
out	ou	au̇	ou	ɑʊ
oil	oi	ȯi	oi	ɔɪ
up	ŭ	ə	u	ʌ
use	ū	yü	ū	ju
turn	û	ə	ė	ə
u·nite'	ū	yu̇	ū	ju
cir'cus	ŭ	ə	ə	ə
na'ture	tū̃	chər	chər	tʃəɪ

5. Several of the same symbols in the Thorndike-Barnhart Dictionary and in Webster's Third Edition have taken the place of corresponding symbols in Webster's Second Edition; namely, the symbol (ə) for (ȧ), as well as for all the italized "short" vowels, the symbol (ər) for (ėr), (ā) for (ȧ), (i) for (ė), (ō) for (ȯ), (ú) for (o͝o), (ü) for (o͞o), and (chər) for the symbol (tū̇).

6. Each of the three dictionaries has a very different way of indicating the sound of the letter *u* as in the word *up,* as in the word *turn,* and as in the word *u·nite'.*

7. By its use of the schwa (ə) for the "short u," Webster's Third Edition departs from the traditional representation of the sound (ŭ); namely, by the letter *u* as in *up* and *but,* for example.

8. According to the number of different symbols for the vowel sounds in English words, *Webster's New International Dictionary,* Second Edition, leads the other two by a considerable margin, having thirty-three different symbols to indicate the sounds. The Thorndike-Barnhart Dictionary is next in order with its total of twenty symbols; and finally *Webster's New International Dictionary,* Third Edition, has eighteen different symbols, a little more than half as many as are found in Webster's Second Edition for indicating the vowel sounds.

Means of Indicating the Consonant Sounds

Unlike the vowel sounds, which are indicated in the dictionaries by the use of diacritical marks and/or respelling the vowels, the consonant sounds, with the exception of the barred *th,* are indicated by respelling the letters only.

The letter *c* is respelled (s) as in *cent* (sent) and (k) as in *can* (kan).

The letters *ck* are respelled (k) as in *back* (bak).

The letters *ch* are respelled (k) as in *chord* (kôrd), (sh) as in *ma·chine'* (mə·shēn'), and (kw) as in *choir* (kwīr).

The letter *f* is respelled (v) as in *of* (ov).

The letter *g* is respelled (j) as in *gem* (jem).

The letter *s* is respelled (z) as in *has* (haz), (sh) as in *sure* (shủr), and (zh) as in *pleas'ure* (plezh'ər).

The letters *ph* are respelled (f) as in *tel'e·phone* (tel'ə·fōn).

The letters *qu* are respelled (k) as in *queue* (kū) and (kw) as in *quick* (kwik).

The letters *wh* are respelled (hw) as in *whip* (hwip) and (h) as in *who* (hü).

The letter *x* is respelled (ks) as in *box* (boks), (gz) as in *ex·act'* (eg·zakt'), and (z) as in *xy'lo·phone* (zī'lə·fōn).

The letter *z* is respelled (zh) as in *sei'zure* (sē'zhər) and (s) as in *quartz* (kwôrts).

The letters *ng* are respelled (ŋ) as in *sing* (siŋ) in Webster's Third Edition.

Comparison of Consonant Sounds

In contrast to the wide variance among dictionary symbols for indicating the vowel sounds of English words, the symbols for the consonant sounds as shown in Tables 2 and 3 are conspicuous by their uniformity.

Table 2. Dictionary and Phonetic Symbols
(The Voiceless Consonants)

Example	Webster's Second Edition	Webster's Third Edition	Thorndike-Barnhart	Phonetic Symbol
*p*et	p	p	p	p
*f*ish	f	f	f	f
*h*at	h	h	h	h
*k*ite tru*ck*	k	k	k	k
*s*un	s	s	s	s
*t*en	t	t	t	t
*th*in	th	th	th	θ
*sh*ip	sh	sh	sh	ʃ
*ch*in ca*tch*	ch	ch	ch	tʃ
*wh*ip	hw	hw	hw	ʍ

Table 3. Dictionary and Phonetic Symbols
(The Voiced Consonants)

Example	Webster's Second Edition	Webster's Third Edition	Thorndike-Barnhart	Phonetic Symbol
*b*ear	b	b	b	b
*d*uck	d	d	d	d
*g*old	g	g	g	g
*j*ust	j	j	j	dʒ
*l*eaf	l	l	l	l
*m*an	m	m	m	m
*n*est	n	n	n	n
*r*oar	r	r	r	r, ɪ
*v*oice	v	v	v	v
*w*ind	w	w	w	w
*y*es	y	y	y	j
u′su·al	zh	zh	zh	ʒ
si*ng*	ng	ŋ	ng	ŋ
*th*is	t̶h̶	<u>th</u>	t̶h̶	ð
*z*ebra	z	z	z	z

Observations of the Symbols for the Consonant Sounds

A comparison of the dictionary symbols for the various consonant sounds with one another and with the phonetic symbols shows a striking similarity among the symbols.

Except for the symbol (ŋ) for the consonant sound at the end of *sing,* and the symbol (<u>th</u>) for the sound at the end of *bathe* in Webster's Third Edition, the consonant sounds are indicated by precisely the same symbols in each of the three dictionaries.

Oddly enough, the consonant *ng* is the only one of the five consonant "digraphs" that is respelled with a single symbol in Webster's Third Edition to show its phonemic characteristic. The other four, *sh, wh,* and the voiceless and voiced *th,* continue to retain their digraphic semblance in the dictionaries. One must look to the phonetic symbol for the true nature of each of these consonants.

AN INFORMAL TEST*

1. _Phœnetics_ is the science of speech sounds.
2. The International _Phœnetic_ Alphabet provides a precise means of indicating the pronunciation of a word.
3. Every symbol in the phonetic alphabet stands for one _sound_ and for that sound only.
4. The word *thought* is spelled with seven letters and requires _four_ symbols to transcribe it phonetically.
5. The word *fox* is spelled with three letters and requires _four_ phonetic symbols to transcribe it.
6. The sound _z_ is spelled with the letter *s* in *pleas'ure;* with the letter *z* in *az'ure;* and with the letters *ge* in *sab'o·tage.*
7. The sounds _dz_ occur once in the word *age* and twice in the word *judge.*
8. The consonant sound _ŋ_ is heard once in *sing* and *bank* and twice in *Thanksgiving, banqueting,* and *honking.*
9. The sound _θ_ is the initial sound in the words *thin* and *thank* and the final consonant sound in *bath* and *moth.*
10. The sound _ð_ can be heard at the end of the accented syllable in *both'er, wheth'er,* and *gath'er.*
11. The initial consonant sound in the words *sure, sheep, shine,* and *cha'teau* is correctly represented by the phonetic symbol _ʃ_.
12. The vowel sound in the words *horse, saw, haul, ought,* and *bought* is correctly represented by the phonetic symbol _ɔi_.
13. The phonetic symbol _æ_ corresponds to the letter or dictionary symbol (a) as in *at;* the phonetic symbol _ɪ_ corresponds to the letter symbol (i) as in *it;* and the phonetic symbol _ʌ_ corresponds to the letter symbol (u) as in *up.*

* Answers are listed under the appropriate chapter number in the Appendix.

14. The symbol (ə), known as the <u>schwa</u> is used to indicate the vowel sound in the unaccented syllables in the words *a·cross', o'pen, sel'dom, cir'cus.*

15. A blend of two vowel sounds is a <u>diphthong</u>

16. The phonetic symbol e corresponds to the dictionary or letter symbol <u>ā</u>; the phonetic symbol o corresponds to the letter symbol <u>ō</u>; and the phonetic symbols aɪ to the letter symbol <u>ī</u>.

17. The symbol (ˉ), which is used to indicate the "long" vowel sound is called a <u>macron</u>; the symbol (˘), which indicates the "short" vowel sound, is a <u>breve</u>; the vowel symbol (ʌ) is a <u>circumflex</u> and the vowel symbol (˜) is a <u>tilde</u>.

18. The symbols (ŏ), (o͝o), (o͞o), (à), (â), and (ē) are used to represent vowel sounds in Webster's New International Dictionary, <u>Second</u> Edition.

19. The letter symbols (ȯi), (au̇), (yu̇), and (yü) are used in Webster's <u>third</u> Edition to indicate the diphthongs as in *oil, out, 'fur-i-ous* and *'fu-ture,* respectively.

20. fonɛtɪks ɪz ðə saɪɛns əv spitʃ _____.

5

FUNCTIONING OF THE
ORGANS OF SPEECH

In Chapter 4 we observed the relation between the sounds and the letters that represent the sounds in the children's reading vocabulary. We are now to learn how the speech organs function in uttering the sounds.

THE SPEECH MECHANISM IN ACTION

If only we could see what takes place in the speech mechanism when we talk! We could then see for ourselves how the organs function in producing the sounds.

Let us begin our study by naming the organs of speech and observing the relative position of those indicated in Figure 1. You will, of course, not be guilty of mispronouncing the second syllable in the word *lar'ynx,* the syllable being (ingks), not (niks), as is so often heard even by students of education.

In the pronunciation of a single word, we make marvelously rapid and delicate movements, with complete unawareness of the way it is being done. We learned to do this in babyhood by imitation of the people around us without being aware of the adjustments of the organs of speech in the process.

Let us take, for example, the simple word *cabin* and note what takes place as you pronounce the word. With a mirror you can see what is happening.

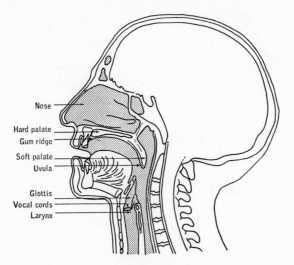

Nose
Hard palate
Gum ridge
Soft palate
Uvula
Glottis
Vocal cords
Larynx

FIG. 1. Organs of Speech

The lips are partly open for *c* (k) (Fig. 2); the front of the tongue is lowered so that the tip touches the lower front teeth, while the back of the tongue strikes sharply against the soft palate. The soft palate is raised, shutting off the nasal passage, thereby letting the air escape through the mouth. At the same time the vocal cords begin to vibrate for (ă) and continue to vibrate to the end of the word. The lower jaw drops, the mouth now opens a trifle wider, and the tongue is slightly arched toward the front (Fig. 3). Now the lips close tightly for (b) (Fig. 4), but suddenly open again for (ĭ).

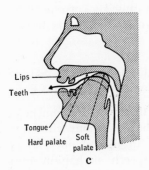

Lips
Teeth
Tongue
Hard palate   Soft palate

c

FIG. 2

To form (ĭ) the open lips are spread as if slightly smiling; the tip of the tongue moves downward, while the front is arched toward the hard palate (Fig. 5). Instantly the tip of the tongue moves upward and presses against the teeth ridge (known also as the *alveoli*), making a complete closure for (n). At the same time the soft palate is lowered, opening the passageway to the nostrils,

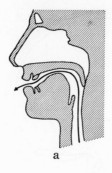

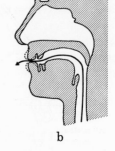

a

b

FIG. 3   FIG. 4

through which the air which has been blocked up in the mouth escapes as we see in Figure 6.

We have completed the pronunciation of the word *cabin*. In the utterance of this simple five-letter word, there are five sounds, each requiring the adjustment of the organs of speech—twenty-five adjustments in all.

To think that all these delicate movements took place in a fraction of a second with incredible accuracy, and without a single voluntary act on our part! Even the

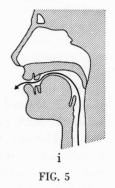

i

FIG. 5

slightest change in any one of these adjustments would have caused a corresponding change in the pronunciation of the entire word.

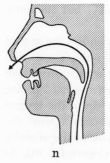

n

FIG. 6

THE SPEECH MECHANISM AS A MUSICAL INSTRUMENT

We know that every instrument in an orchestra must be in harmony with every other instrument. In like manner, every movement of the speech mechanism must be made with perfect precision if the effect is to be pleasing.

We may think of the human speech mechanism as a most complicated musical instrument that operates with the greatest speed and accuracy, and almost wholly without our awareness. In every musical instrument there are three essentials for producing tone:

1. There must be something to vibrate; namely, a *vibrator*.
2. There must be something to cause the vibration; or a *stimulator*.
3. There must be something that amplifies or reinforces the vibration, known as a *resonator*.

In the human speech mechanism the vocal cords act as a vibrator, the breath stream as the stimulator, and the mouth and nasal cavities serve as the resonator.

The Vibrator

We noticed in pronouncing the word *cabin* that the vocal cords started to vibrate with the sound (ă) and continued to vibrate to the end of the word.

If you could look down upon the larynx or voice box, you would notice that the vocal cords are wide apart while breathing. The space between the vocal cords is so wide that in exhalation the air comes out unimpeded, without any noticeable sound. But if you could have looked down upon the larynx during the pronunciation of the word *cabin,* you would have seen that beginning with the sound (ă) the vocal cords were drawn very closely together. When that happened the air in passing through the larynx met with so much resistance that the vocal cords were set into extreme vibration, producing what are known as voiced sounds. Since all the sounds in *cabin,* with the exception of the first consonant, are voiced, the vocal cords which began to vibrate with the utterance of the sound (ă) continued to vibrate to the end of the word.

If you will place your fingertips on the throat just where the Adam's apple is located and utter a voiced sound, you will feel the vibration of the vocal cords. Try it by saying several voiced sounds like (b), (v), (z) and feel the buzzing under your fingertips. Now say the voiceless "twins" of these sounds, (p), (f), (s). This time you did not feel the buzzing sound at all. The buzzing sound, as you may have guessed, was caused by the vibration of the vocal cords in uttering the voiced sounds.

The Stimulator

We have spoken of the breath stream as the stimulator in the human speech instrument. It is the stream of air as it comes from the lungs that sets the vocal cords into vibration and thereby produces the human voice.

The Resonator

It is the resonator that amplifies the tone and gives it its characteristic quality. We know that every musical instrument—the harp, cello, violin, piano—has its own characteristic quality, determined by the resonance chamber, which is also known as the sounding box of the instrument. The resonance chamber of the human musical instrument has an especially wonderful power not given to the man-made musical instruments. It can change its size and shape itself, whereas the sounding box of the other musical instruments remains fixed.

As you stand before the mirror in a bright light and open the mouth for *ah* you will notice that the mouth is like a cavern with the tongue forming a movable floor and the palate as the roof. This oral cavity, together with the nasal cavity, forms the resonance chamber of the human voice. The hard palate forms the front of the roof, and the soft palate the back part. The soft palate, which is also known as the *velum,* is movable, especially its pointed tip, which is called the *uvula.*

Upon leaving the lungs, the air has two possible paths of escape. It may leave through the mouth or the nose. It is the soft palate acting as a door, opening and closing the nasal passage, that determines which path the air will take.

SOFT PALATE ACTION

If you will again stand before the mirror, you can observe the action of the soft palate as it opens and closes the doorway. Say *ah* with the mouth wide open in a good light and notice how the soft palate is raised and pressed against the back wall of the throat. The passage to the nose is closed. Now say *ung* as in *rung,* and notice that the soft palate is lowered against the back of the tongue. The passage to the nose is now open. But the door to the mouth is closed, so that the air can now escape only through the nose.

The soft palate then plays an important part in determining the resonance of the human voice. But it is chiefly by the tongue's action that the resonance chamber in our musical instrument changes in shape.

The quality of one's voice is largely dependent upon the proper action of the soft palate or velum. It is difficult, however, to direct the velum. The following three exercises have proved helpful in gaining control of the velum.

EXERCISE 1

Emphasize the following syllables as you repeat them slowly:

ung-ah; ung-ah; ung-ah; ung-ah-ung;
ump-ma; ump-ma; ump; ma-ump.

Use the mirror in order to see the soft palate lower for (ng) and rise for (ah).

EXERCISE 2

Imitate the ringing of a bell, *ding-dong, ding-dong,* prolonging the nasal (ng) at the end of each of the words.

EXERCISE 3

In the next exercise prolong the syllable *ing,* and make the syllable *ick* short and sharp.

ing-ick; ing-ick; ing-ick;
ing-ick; ing-ick-ing; ick-ing; ick.

Repeat the exercise, but this time whisper the syllables.

TONGUE ACTION

Hold up the mirror so that you can see what a wonderfully flexible mass of muscle the tongue is. Notice how it can be arched and flattened, raised and lowered, and moved in every direction. If you have never tried it, you may wish to see if you can touch your nose with your tongue. Can you dot your chin with the tip of your tongue? Can you narrow your tongue to a point at the tip?

Sluggish and inaccurate tongue action is one of the chief causes of slovenly and indistinct utterance of the speech sounds, and distinct utterance of the sounds is prerequisite to effective teaching of reading and phonics.

Since one should not be made aware of his speech mechanism while talking, exercises for gaining flexibility of the tongue can be profitable as well as amusing.

EXERCISE 1

Thrust the tongue out as far as you can, while someone counts to four. Take care not to let the tongue rest on the lower lip. After the count of four, let the tongue spring back into place quickly. Repeat the exercise five or six times.

EXERCISE 2

Extend the tongue as far as possible. Now point the tongue by making the muscles of the tip as tense as you can. Let the mirror show you how sharp a point you can make. Repeat the exercise.

EXERCISE 3

Point the tongue as before. This time lift the tip slowly and dot the roof of the mouth, first in the front, then in the middle, and then as far in the back as the tongue can reach. Relax and repeat the exercise a few times.

EXERCISE 4

Open the mouth. Say *ah-la-la-la-la* rhythmically, keeping the lower jaw steady. Use the mirror to see that you make this a tongue, and not a jaw, exercise. With every *la* you should feel the tongue tip touching the inner surface, first of the upper teeth and then the lower teeth.

Begin slowly at first, then increase the speed, always keeping the exercise rhythmic. Work for light and quick action of the tongue. You may enjoy singing *la-la* to a familiar melody of your choice.

EXERCISE 5

Say rhythmically, first slowly and then gradually increasing the speed:

tee·dee′; tee·dee′; tee·dee′;
tee·dee·dee′; tee·tee·tee′; tee·tee·tee′;
tee·dee·dee′; tee·tee·tee′; tee·tee·tee′.

LIP ACTION

Lip action plays an important part in clear and distinct speech. This is especially true of the upper lip. Every lip movement usually has a tongue movement that is habitually associated with it. So the movement of the lips serves to indicate the movements of the tongue. If the lips are stiff and inactive in speech, the tongue action is likely to be sluggish. Hence the importance of proper lip action in speaking.

The following exercises are greatly exaggerated, since they are intended to free and strengthen the lips. It is, of course, not recommended that we mouth our words in speaking, as we may seem to be doing in the following exercises.

EXERCISE 1

With your lips parted, that is, with the mouth open, say slowly and with vigorous lip action the following syllables.

ah-you-ee-you; ah-you-ee-you; ah-you-ee-you;
ee-you-ee-you; ee-you-ee-ah-you; ee-you-you-you.

Repeat the exercise and be sure the lips are rounded for the syllable *you* and stretched for *ee*. Let the mirror tell you how well you are succeeding.

Now repeat the exercise with the lips closed, except for the syllable *ah*.

EXERCISE 2

Here is an exercise that should be fun, as well as profitable. Hold the lower lip motionless while extending the upper lip outward and upward to reach the nose. Be sure that the upper lip is free from the teeth. Now close the lips firmly and again extend the upper lip to reach the nose. Repeat the exercise to gain control of the upper lip.

EXERCISE 3

Say the following syllables with vigorous and exaggerated lip action:

wee-woe-wee-woe; wee-woe-wee; wee-wee-wee;
bee-bow-bee-bow; bee-bow-bee; bee-bee-bee.

EXERCISE 4

Repeat the following nursery rhyme with vigorous lip action:

Pat-a-cake; pat-a-cake; baker's man;
Make me a cake as fast as you can.
Pat it, and prick it, and mark it with B;
And bake it in the oven for Baby and me.

EXERCISE 5

Here is another old rhyme to be repeated with vigorous lip action:

Peter Piper picked a peck of pickled peppers;
A peck of pickled peppers Peter Piper picked.
If Peter Piper picked a peck of pickled peppers,
Where are the pickled peppers Peter Piper picked?

AN INFORMAL TEST*

WHICH ONE IS IT?

1. The velum, uvula, alveoli, larynx, and vocal cords, are known as (a) the science of speech sounds; (b) organs of speech.
2. Every speech sound is the result of certain definite adjustments of the organs of speech made (a) voluntarily by the speaker; (b) involuntarily by the speaker.
3. By lowering the soft palate the air is permitted to escape through the (a) nostrils; (b) mouth.

* Answers are listed in the Appendix under the appropriate chapter number.

4. In uttering a voiceless speech sound the vocal cords (a) vibrate; (b) do not vibrate.
5. Whether the air is permitted to escape through the mouth or the nostrils while one is speaking depends upon the raising or lowering of the (a) hard palate; (b) soft palate.
6. The tip of the velum is known as the (a) uvula; (b) alveoli.
7. By placing the fingertips where the Adam's apple is located while uttering a voiced sound one can feel the (a) alveoli vibrate; (b) vocal cords vibrate.
8. In pronouncing a word in which all the sounds are voiced, the vocal cords vibrate (a) during the utterance of the entire word; (b) only during the pronunciation of the beginning of the word.
9. When the soft palate is raised during the utterance of a speech sound, the passage of the breath stream to the nose is (a) closed; (b) open.
10. In uttering the syllable *ah* with the mouth wide open the soft palate is (a) raised and pressed against the back wall of the throat; (b) lowered and pressed against the back wall of the throat.
11. In the human speech mechanism the vocal cords act (a) as a resonator; (b) as a vibrator.
12. The oral cavity, together with the nasal cavity, serves as (a) a stimulator in the speech mechanism; (b) the resonance chamber of the human voice.

6

PHONETIC STUDY
OF THE CONSONANTS

In the foregoing chapters we were concerned with (1) the true relation between sounds and letters in words; (2) the functioning of the speech mechanism in producing the sounds; and (3) the need for teachers to know how the sounds of English are correctly formed. We should now then be ready to devote our attention to a scientific study of a large and varied group of speech sounds, namely, the consonant sounds in the children's reading vocabulary.

DEFINITION AND CLASSIFICATION
OF CONSONANTS

We learned in Chapter 5 that every speech sound is the result of certain definite adjustments of the organs of speech. These adjustments may or may not interfere with the outgoing breath, depending upon the nature of the adjustments. When the adjustments are such that the outgoing breath stream in speaking is obstructed by the organs of speech, the resulting sound is a consonant.

The interference by the speech mechanism may be only partial, as in the case of the sounds f, s, and l, or it may be complete as in the utterance of the sounds b, t, and g. When the obstruction is complete, the resulting sounds are known as *plosives* or *stops*. Those in which the obstruction is only partial, or incomplete are known as *continuants*.

Consonants are also classified as being *voiceless* or *voiced*, depending on whether or not the vocal cords vibrate in producing the sound. We observed in pronouncing the word *cabin* in Chapter 5 that the vocal cords vibrated in uttering the sounds æ, b, ɪ, and n. That was because all the sounds are voiced.

Any sound in a language may be uttered with or without voice. The sound h for example, which in English is a voiceless sound, is voiced in the Czech language; and the Czech has as much difficulty with our voiceless h as we would have in voicing the sound. The Italians and the French lack the sound altogether, and easy as it is for us, they find it a very difficult sound to make. Teachers, of all people, should have no difficulty at all in uttering a sound that is made simply by sighing, h! That is, of course, if they are English-speaking teachers.

DESCRIPTION OF THE CONSONANT SOUNDS

In studying the description of the consonants it should be remembered that in speaking not everyone makes the sounds in precisely the same way. The exact adjustments of the speech organs depend in the case of every speaker on the structure of his organs of speech.

You will find the sounds indicated by their phonetic symbols at the head of each description. Unless you are a student of phonetics, or have mastered the phonetic symbols given in Chapter 4, you might have preferred the letter symbols (th), (th), and (zh) to the symbols θ, ð, and ʒ, for example. But an accurate description of the sounds would be impossible without the phonetic symbols to indicate the sounds. The letters of the alphabet lack the precision that a scientific study of the sounds requires.

In cases in which the consonants can be paired as voiceless and voiced, both sounds are presented at the head of the descriptions.

NOTE. Although the sounds are described individually, it should not be assumed that the sounds should be taught in isolation in phonics or spelling. On the contrary, the sounds should be taught *in the words in which they occur.* (For the reasons for teaching the sounds in context, see Chapter 3.)

The Plosives

Let us now see how the consonant sounds are uttered, beginning with the plosives or stops.

We shall see that there are three pairs of plosives, one of each pair being voiceless and the other voiced: **p, b; t, d; k, g.**[1] There are three essentials for the pronunciation of a plosive.

1. There must be a complete blocking of the outgoing breath stream.
2. The blockage must be released suddenly.
3. The breath must escape with an explosive puff.

Unless the blockage is complete, the air will escape in a continuous stream instead of a sudden puff. Even when the blockage is complete, if the release of the pressure is not sudden, the sound when it occurs at the end of a word will seem to have been left off entirely. An explosive escape of the breath is needed if the final sound is to be clearly heard.

> The sound **p** as in *p*et
> The sound **b** as in *b*ear

The sound **p**. To make the sound press the lips tightly together; then blow them apart suddenly, so that the outgoing breath escapes with an explosive puff.

The sound **p** is a voiceless or whispered bilabial plosive. It is also known as a stop, since the breath stream is completely stopped by the tightly closed lips in producing the sound.

If you closed the lips tightly and blew them apart suddenly, you heard an explosive puff at the end of the sound. You produced the sound **p**, which is frequently mispronounced (pŭ).

---

1 Since these are symbols of sounds and not letters, they must be considered as the sounds (p), (b), and so on, and not as the names of the letters *pea* and *be,* for example.

If you have been mispronouncing the sound p, it will take a little effort to correct the habit. By listening to the sound at the end of the words *cap, cup, hop,* and *leap,* you will hear the difference between p and (pŭ). Hearing the difference between the right and the wrong sound is the first step in correcting the error.

The sound b. This is the voiced "twin" of the sound p. To make the sound press the lips firmly together as you did for p. But this time as you blow the lips apart, let the breath escape with a voiced sound; b is a voiced bilabial plosive or stop. The vocal cords vibrate in producing the sound, as we observed in pronouncing the word *cabin* in Chapter 5.

If you have been calling the sound (bŭ) instead of b, listen closely to the final consonant as you pronounce the words *cub, rob, crab.* Then pronounce the sound b by itself, exactly as you heard it at the end of each of the words.

NOTE. In reading the text the phonetic symbols must be considered as sounds, not as letters of the alphabet.

The sound t as in *ten*
The sound d as in *duck*

The sound t. To make the sound press the tip of the tongue against the teeth ridge (just behind the upper front teeth), known as the *alveoli* (al·vē′ə·li). Then blow the tongue down suddenly so that the breath escapes with an explosive puff.

The sound t is a voiceless or whispered alveolar plosive or stop. If in making the sound the air was completely blocked by the tongue and then released suddenly, the air escaped with an explosive puff.

If you have been accustomed to calling the sound (tŭ) instead of t, you may need experience in hearing the difference between the right and the wrong pronunciation of the sound. As you say aloud the words *bat, sit, cot, cut, meet,* listen to the last sound in each of the words. Then repeat the sound t by itself as you heard it at the end of the word. This is one way of learning to pronounce the sound correctly.

The sound d. This is the voiced "twin" of the sound t. To make the sound press the tip of the tongue against the alveoli as you did for t. But this time as you blow the tongue down suddenly let the breath escape with a voiced sound; d is a voiced, alveolar plosive or stop. You can feel the vibration with your fingertips on the throat where the Adam's apple is located as you utter the sound.

If you are in the habit of pronouncing the sound (dŭ) instead of d, listen to the sound as you hear it at the end of the words *red, mud, bird, head, glad, sled.* Then repeat the sound d by itself until you can make the sound correctly.

> The sound k as in *k*ite
> The sound g as in *g*oat

The sound k. To make the sound press the back of the tongue against the soft palate, known as the *velum;* then blow the tongue down suddenly so that the outgoing breath escapes with an explosive puff.

The sound k is a voiceless or whispered velar plosive or stop. If in making the sound the air was completely blocked by the back of the tongue and then released suddenly, the air escaped with an audible puff.

The sound k is often mispronounced (kŭ) instead of k. By listening to the sound as you hear it at the end of the words *book, cake, walk, truck,* and *stick* you will hear that the sound is k and not (kŭ).

The sound g. This is the voiced "twin" of the sound k. To make the sound press the back of the tongue against the soft palate as you did for k, but this time as you blow the tongue down suddenly, let the breath escape with a voiced sound; g is a voiced velar plosive or stop.

If you have been in the habit of pronouncing the sound (gŭ) instead of g, listen to the sound as you hear it at the end of the words *dog, pig, beg, frog, flag, rug.* Then repeat the sound by itself and hear the difference between g and (gŭ).

Summary

Consonants comprise one of the two classifications of speech sounds. Whether the particular sound in a word is a consonant or a vowel depends on the functioning of the speech mechanism in producing the sound. When the outgoing breath stream is obstructed by the organs of speech, the resulting sound is a consonant. The interference with the outgoing breath may be partial or it may be complete. When the interference is complete, the resulting consonant is a plosive. Plosives are also known as stops, because in producing the sound the outgoing breath is completely stopped before it is released.

Plosives are either voiceless, meaning whispered, or voiced sounds, depending on whether or not the vocal cords vibrate in producing the sound. By placing the fingertips on the throat where the Adam's apple is located one can feel the vibration of the vocal cords when producing a voiced sound. There is no vibration when uttering a voiceless sound.

There are three pairs of plosives or stops: p and b; t and d; k and g. The sound p is a voiceless bilabial plosive and b is a voiced bilabial plosive. The sound t is a voiceless alveolar plosive and d is a voiced alveolar plosive. The sound k is a voiceless velar plosive and g is a voiced velar plosive.

There are three essentials for producing clear and distinct plosives: (1) there must be a complete blocking of the outgoing breath stream; (2) the blockage or interference of the outgoing breath must be released suddenly; and (3) the breath must escape with an explosive puff.

The Continuants

Here, then, is our next classification of consonants. It should be interesting to discover which, if any, of these consonants require relearning and which ones you have been pronouncing correctly.

We observed in pronouncing the plosives that the breath is *completely* blocked before it is released. But in case of the continuants, the breath is only *partially* blocked, thereby causing it to escape in a continuous stream, hence the term *continuants*.

The continuants comprise two classifications, *nasals* and *fricatives*.

THE NASALS

We have three nasal sounds in our language: n, m, and ŋ. All the other sounds in the English language are oral.

Interestingly enough, each of the nasals has a corresponding sound among the plosives. The sound **m**, like **p** and **b**, is also a bilabial sound; **n** is an alveolar like **t** and **d**; and **ŋ** is a velar sound like **k** and **g**. Hence the lips are in exactly the same position for the sounds **m**, **p**, and **b**. The tip of the tongue is in the same position for the sounds **n**, **t**, and **d**, and the back of the tongue is in the same position for **ŋ**, **k**, and **g**.

It makes an interesting game for children to guess whether the teacher is going to pronounce the word *pig, bear,* or *mouse* as she presses her lips together in readiness to say the word and whether she is going to say *nuts, toys,* or *dog* as she presses the tip of the tongue against the alveoli.

The nasals are unlike the plosives in these two respects:

1. Instead of escaping in an explosive puff through the mouth, the air issues in a continuous stream through the nose.

2. All nasals are voiced and thus they have no voiceless counterparts in the English language.

The sound **m** as in *m*an

The sound **m**. This is one of the easiest sounds to make. Simply bring the lips together as you did for **p** and **b**. Keep the lips closed while you make a *voiced* sound through the nose; **m** is a voiced, bilabial nasal, sometimes incorrectly pronounced (mŭ).

If you have been mispronouncing the sound **m**, listen to the sound at the end of the words *drum, ram, him, them,* and *room,* and hear the difference between the sounds **m** and (mŭ).

The sound **n** as in *n*est

The sound **n**. To make the sound press the tip of the tongue against the alveoli as you did for **t** and **d**. Hold the tongue there while you make a *voiced* sound through the nose; **n** is a voiced alveolar nasal, sometimes incorrectly pronounced (nŭ).

You can hear the sound as it is correctly pronounced at the end of *rain, clown, ran, fun, moon,* and *sun.*

The sound **ŋ** as in si*ng*

The sound ŋ. This is the sound, as you can see by the word *sing*, that is spelled with the letters *ng*. The sound ŋ is a difficult sound to make by itself. It is easy enough to say *ing*, *ang* or *ung*, but not ŋ. The sound is correctly made by raising the back of the tongue against the soft palate as for **k** and **g** and holding the tongue there while making a *voiced* sound through the nose. ŋ is a voiced, velar nasal.

It is interesting to note that unlike the other two nasals, **n** and **m**, the sound ŋ occurs only at the end, never at the beginning, of a word or syllable.

Summary

There are three nasal sounds in the English language: **m**, **n**, and ŋ. Unlike the plosives in which the outgoing breath escapes through the mouth in an explosive puff, in uttering the nasals the breath issues in a continuous stream through the nostrils. Moreover, all nasals are voiced with no voiceless counterparts as in the case of the plosives. The nasals, however, have the following characteristics in common with the plosives: (1) in making the sound **m** the lips are in precisely the same position as for **p** and **b**; you can discover this for yourself as you say the words *me, pea,* and *be;* (2) in making the sound **n** the tongue tip is in the same position as for **t** and **d**; say *new, to,* and *do* and you will notice that the tongue is in the same position at the beginning of each of the words; and (3) in making the sound ŋ, the back of the tongue is in the same position as for **k** and **g**; as you say *ing, ick,* and *ig* you can feel that the tongue is in the same position at the end of each of the syllables.

THE FRICATIVES

Our next classification, the fricatives, are perhaps the most challenging of the consonant sounds. Teachers are unlikely to be as familiar with the symbols of some of the fricatives like θ, ð, ʃ, ʒ, ʍ, and j, as with the symbols of the plosives and the nasals. However it is not from choice but necessity that the phonetic symbols are used to indicate the sounds rather than the letters *th, th, sh, zh, wh,* and *y*. The phonetic symbols are needed in order to indicate the sounds precisely.

The sounds f, v, s, z, ʃ, ʒ, θ, ð, ʍ, w, j, h, l, and r are generally known as fricatives. There is, however, a tendency to doubt the accuracy of classifying the last six sounds as fricatives. Some students of phonetics contend that ʍ, w, j, and h function rather as modifiers of vowels than as consonants; and certainly the sounds l and r are frequently vocalic in character.

In studying the fricatives it may be of added interest to observe the shape and position of the channel through which the breath escapes in producing the sound, since it is this channel upon which the characteristic sound of the fricative depends.

Some, but not all, fricatives have voiced or voiceless counterparts. Those fricatives which can be paired as being voiced or voiceless are presented together at the head of the description.

The sound f as in *f*ish
The sound v as in *v*oice

The sounds f and v are excellent examples of fricatives. It is the resulting friction in producing the sounds that gives them their characteristic quality, the friction being caused by the outgoing breath rubbing against the obstructing organs, the upper teeth and the lower lip.

The sound f.   To make the sound place the lower lip lightly against the upper front teeth. Then force the breath out so that it escapes with audible friction. f is a voiceless or whispered labio-dental fricative, sometimes incorrectly pronounced (fŭ).

By listening to the sound at the end of the words *leaf, roof calf, muff, laugh,* and *rough* you will hear that the sound is f and not (fŭ).

The sound v.   This is the voiced "twin" of the sound f. To make the sound place the lower lip against the upper front teeth as for f. But this time force the breath out with a voiced sound. v is a voiced labio-dental fricative, frequently mispronounced (vŭ). The sound can clearly be heard at the end of the words *cave, love, have, move,* and *weave.*

The sound s as in *s*un
The sound z as in *z*ebra

The sound s.   To make the sound bring the sides of the tongue against the upper side teeth; then send a fine stream of air straight out between the front teeth with audible friction. Note the difference between the shape and position of the channel through which the breath escapes in pronouncing f and s.

The sound s is a voiceless alveolar fricative. It can be made by directing the breath stream between either the upper or lower front teeth. Those who form the sound with the tongue tip directed downward need to exert more tongue pressure to avoid a lisped s, as in *thoft thoap and other combuthtible thubthantheth!*

The sound z. This is the voiced "twin" of the sound s. To make the sound bring the sides of the tongue against the upper side teeth the same as for s, but this time send a voiced sound out between the front teeth. z is a voiced alveolar fricative.

The sound ʃ as in *ship*
The sound ʒ as in gara*ge*

The two-letter *sh* as in *ship* may give the impression of a blend of (s) + (h), but these two letters stand for a single sound as shown by the phonetic symbol ʃ.

The sound ʃ. To make the sound place the tongue in contact with the upper side teeth, but not so far forward as for s, so that the groove in the center is broader. Then send the breath straight out between the front teeth. The sound ʃ is a voiceless, alveolar fricative.

Note that the sound ʃ is not nearly so sharp a sound as s.

The sound ʒ. This sound, which was borrowed from the French, is unique in that it has no letter that regularly represents it in the reading vocabulary. It is represented by the letters *ge* in *rouge,* by the letter *s* in *treasure,* by *z* in *seizure,* and by *si* in *division.*

This was the sound you will recall that had Mr. Sloan in Chapter 4 completely fooled in his effort to identify the sound of *s* in *pleasure* and *z* in *seizure.* But Mr. Sloan's confusion is by no means unique. Many teachers have difficulty in identifying the sound ʒ in the children's reading vocabulary.

The sound ʒ is the voiced "twin" of ʃ. To make the sound place the tongue in the same position as for ʃ, but this time send out a *voiced* sound between the front teeth. The sound ʒ is a voiced alveolar fricative.

The sound θ as in *th*in
The sound ð as in *th*is

The consonant *th* is indeed ambiguous! Not only do the two letters stand for but one sound, as shown by the symbols θ and ð but the same letters stand for two different sounds, as in the words *thin* and *this,* for example.

The sound θ. To make the sound place the tip of the tongue against the lower edge of the upper front teeth; then force the breath out with audible friction. The tongue should barely be visible between the teeth. θ is a voiceless interdental fricative. The sound can be heard at the end of *bath, moth, path,* and *myth.*

The sound ð. This is the voiced "twin" of the sound θ. To make the sound place the tongue in the same position as for θ, but this time force the breath out with a *voiced* sound. ð is a voiced interdental fricative. The sound can clearly be heard at the end of the words *bathe, breathe, clothe,* and *scythe.*

The sound ʍ as in *wh*ip
The sound w as in *w*ind

The sound ʍ. Here again we have two letters representing a sound to which the International Phonetic Association assigned the single symbol ʍ. However, since the sound can be correctly formed by uttering **hw** with the lips and tongue in the position for **w**, some writers consider the sound a blend of **hw**. The sound ʍ occurs only at the beginning of a syllable, as in *whip,* and never at the end of a syllable or word.

To make the sound ʍ round the lips as for **u** in *true,* but bring them more closely together than for **u**. Then blow through the small opening between the lips. A piece of tissue paper held in front of the lips should flutter as you blow the sound out. The sound ʍ is a voiceless, bilabial fricative.

The sound **w**. This is the voiced "twin" of the sound ʍ. To make the sound round the lips as for ʍ, but this time blow a voiced sound out through the opening between the lips. **w** is a voiced bilabial fricative. Like its voiceless "twin," the sound w also occurs only at the beginning, never at the end, of a syllable or word.

NOTE. Although the sound w is considered here as a consonant, it is also classed as a semivowel because of the very slight obstruction of the breath in uttering the sound. (For the definition of a vowel, see Chapter 8.)

Teachers are inclined to consider the substitution of w for ʍ as an error in pronunciation. While it is true that American English favors the voiceless ʍ in words that are spelled with the letters *wh* as in *when, where, why,* and *what,* there is a growing tendency in this country to pronounce ʍ and w exactly alike.

The sound j as in *yes*

The phonetic symbol j is almost certain to be confusing. While it looks exactly like the letter *j* as in *jump,* it is not even remotely related to the first sound in *jump.* Moreover, when you meet this symbol again in Chapter 8 you will find it with the diphthongs, of all places!

The symbol y would certainly have been more appropriate than j for the first sound in *yes, yet, your, yard,* and *young.* But the symbol y was reserved by the International Phonetic Association for a sound that occurs in French and German, but not in English.

The sound j. To make the sound raise the middle of the tongue toward the hard palate; then force the tongue down with a *voiced* breath. j is a voiced, palatal fricative.

The sound j has two things in common with the sound w: (1) it is also classed as a semivowel because of the slight obstruction of the breath in producing the sound and (2) it occurs only at the beginning, never at the end, of a syllable or word.

The sound h as in *hand*

The sound h. How wonderful it would be if all the sounds were as easy to make as h. Simply to open the mouth and sigh!

Although this sound is classified as a voiceless, glottal fricative, its true nature is debatable. Some students of phonetics consider the sound merely as the voiceless form of whatever vowel sound comes after it. Others think of it as the characteristic beginning of whatever vowel sound follows h in the word or syllable.

The sound has no voiced counterpart in the English language. Like j, ʍ, and w, this sound also occurs only at the beginning, never at the end, of a word or syllable.

NOTE. The words *humor, humorous,* and *humble* from the French language were originally pronounced with *h* "silent." Today the letter *h* is pronounced in these words.

The sound l as in *l*eaf

The sound l. To make the sound raise the tip of the tongue to the teeth ridge, so that the under part of the tongue touches the upper front teeth; spread the tongue so that its sides touch the side teeth; then force the breath out over the sides of the raised tongue with a *voiced* sound. l is a voiced, alveolar lateral fricative. It has no voiceless counterpart in the English language.

NOTE. The sound l as here described is the sound we hear when *l* comes *before* the vowel as in *leaf, love, lap,* and *lake,* and should never be pronounced (ŭl). When *l* comes *after* the vowel, as in *ball,* its precise quality depends on the vowel sound that precedes it. This variability in the sound l can be heard by pronouncing the words *till, tail, tile, tell, tool, towel,* and *toil.*

CAUTION. The contact of the tongue for l must not be made back of the teeth ridge or a dull, muffled sound will result. The farther back the contact is made the duller the sound becomes. When no contact is made, as is often the case in careless, slovenly speech, the sound takes on the quality of a vowel.

You may wish to see if you can make the contact with the tongue correctly as you pronounce the words that begin with the sound l, and then the words that end with the sound.

The sound r as in *r*ed
The sound ɹ as in bea*r*

Here we have two sounds, r and ɹ, both of which are represented by the letter *r* in the children's reading vocabulary.

The symbol r indicates the sound that is heard when *r* comes *before* the vowel, as in *red*. This sound, usually pronounced (ĕr) in teaching phonics, is undoubtedly the most frequently mispronounced sound in the nation's classrooms.

The sound r. To make the sound, raise the tongue tip toward the teeth ridge, as you did for l. But instead of touching the teeth ridge, curl the tongue tip toward the throat; then force the breath out over the tongue tip with a *voiced* sound. r is a voiced, alveolar fricative.

The symbol ɹ indicates the sound that is heard when it is pronounced *after* the vowel, as in *bear*. Instead of the sound ɹ, some speakers use a more or less neutral sound in words like *bear, war, car, bird, hurt, hear,* and *park*.

There is a tendency in some parts of the country (especially in the Middle West) when pronouncing the sound ɹ to pull the whole tongue back in the mouth as far as possible. This gives a heavy muffled (ĕr) that affects the entire syllable. It is reasonable to assume that when ɹ is made with a vigorously retracted tongue it is not a consonant at all, but a vowel, the tongue tip offering no obstruction to the outgoing breath stream, but merely changing the shape of the resonance chamber. (For the definition of a vowel see Chapter 8.)

Summary

In uttering the sounds f, v; s, z; ʃ, ʒ; and θ, ð the outgoing breath stream escapes with audible friction; hence the term *fricatives*. Each of the voiceless sounds, f, s, ʃ, θ, and ʍ, has a voiced counterpart in the English language. The sounds j, l, and r have no voiceless counterparts.

In uttering the sounds f and v the lower lip is placed against the upper front teeth; hence these sounds are known as labiodental fricatives.

The sounds s and z are known as alveolar fricatives. In making the sounds the sides of the tongue are brought against the upper side teeth, and a fine stream of air issues between the front teeth with audible friction. Some speakers in making the sounds habitually direct the breath stream between the upper front teeth; others make the sounds by directing the air between the lower front teeth.

The sounds ʃ and ʒ resemble s and z. This is understandable, since in making the sounds the tongue is placed in nearly the same position for both pairs of sounds. But because the groove through which the breath stream issues in the center of the tongue is broader for ʃ and ʒ, these sounds are not nearly so "sharp" as s and z.

The sound ʒ is unlike any other sound in the English language in that it has no letter in the alphabet regularly to represent it. This sound is often confused with the sounds ʃ and z. It would be interesting to know how many teachers think that the syllable *sure* in *plea'sure* is pronounced like the syllable *sure* in *sure'ly,* and that the letter z in *a'zure* has the same sound as the letter z in *zoom.*

The interdental fricatives, θ and ð, are also worthy of special mention, in that both sounds are represented by the letters *th,* which are not remotely indicative of the sounds they represent.

Perhaps the difficulty that many teachers have in distinguishing between the voiceless sound of *th* as in *thing, thanks, bath, thumb, three, both,* and *teeth* and the voiced sound of *th* as in *bathe, breathe, smooth, mother, weather, rather, this,* and *these* is because both sounds are represented by the same letters.

Although the bilabial sounds ʍ and w are generally classified as fricatives, their inclusion in this classification is debatable. Some students of phonetics contend that ʍ and w function rather as modifiers of vowels than as consonants. The sound w has the added distinction of being classed as a semivowel as well as a consonant. Note the similarity between the sound w as in *woo* and the vowel sound u as in *truth.*

Although the International Phonetic Association assigned the single symbol ʍ to the initial sound as in *whip,* some students consider the sound a blend of hw. Either way the sound occurs only at the beginning, never at the end, of a word or syllable; and the same can be said of the sound w as in *wind.*

Although the sounds j, h, l, and r are usually considered as fricatives, their status in this classification is controversial. Some phoneticians contend that the sounds j and h, like ʍ and w, function rather as vowels than as consonants; and there is no question but that l and r are often vocalic in character. The precise quality of the final l depends on the vowel sound that precedes it.

The sounds j and h occur only at the beginning, never at the end, of a word or syllable. The sound j, like w, is also classified as a semivowel.

The symbol r indicates the sound that is heard when it occurs before the vowel, as in *red;* and the symbol ɹ indicates the sound after the vowel, as in *bear.*

Consonant Blends

Up to this point we have studied the single-sound consonants, although some of the sounds were represented by two letters, as in the case of *sh, zh, th, th, wh,* and *ng.* Each, however, stands for but one sound, as shown by the phonetic symbols ʃ, ʒ, θ, ð, ʍ, and ŋ, respectively.

We shall now meet some of the consonant blends that also occur in the words children meet in their reading. Oddly enough two of these are one-letter blends! Instead of two letters representing a single sound, we shall see that one letter may stand for a blend of two sounds!

The sounds tʃ as in *ch*eek
The sounds dʒ as in *j*ump

Note that the single letter *j* as in *jump* stands for the two sounds dʒ.

The sounds tʃ. These two sounds constitute such a close blend that they are often considered a single sound. But the International Phonetic Association assigned two symbols to the consonants heard at the beginning of the words *cheek, child,* and *cheer* and at the end of words like *catch, witch,* and *porch.* Hence the general acceptance of the theory that the letters *ch* and *tch* stand for the blend t and ʃ, or tʃ.

To form the blend, raise the tongue tip for the sound t; then go quickly into ʃ. The resulting blend is tʃ. Since the sounds t and ʃ are both voiceless, the blend tʃ is also voiceless. These sounds are frequently mispronounced (chŭ).

Many teachers find it difficult to associate the sounds (t) and (sh) with the letters *ch* as in *cheek*. But (t) + (sh) = (ch).

We have observed that the letters *ch* stand for the blend tʃ at the beginning and at the end of a word. But the spelling *tch* is found only at the end of a syllable or word, as in *catch*.

The sounds dʒ. These sounds constitute the voiced "twins" of tʃ. To form the blend raise the tongue tip as you did for d; then go quickly into ʒ. The resulting blend is dʒ. Since d and ʒ are both voiced, the blend dʒ is also voiced. It should never be pronounced (jŭ).

Teachers usually find it difficult to associate the sounds (d) and (zh) with the letter *j* in *jump*. But the sounds (d) + (zh) = (j) at the beginning of *jump*.

The fact that the sounds of the letter *j* as in *jump* are the voiced counterparts of (ch) as in *cheek* comes to many teachers as a complete surprise, perhaps because it seems a bit difficult to associate (ch) with the sound (j).

When the blend dʒ occurs before the vowel in a word or syllable it may be spelled with the letter *g* as in *gem* or with the letter *j* as in *jump*. But when it comes after the vowel it is spelled *ge* as in *orange* or *dge* as in *badge*.

NOTE. The palatalization of (tụ̄) as in the word *na'ture* (nā'tụ̄r) resembles the blend tʃ and (dụ̄) as in *ver'dure* (vûr'dụ̄r) resembles the blend dʒ.

The sounds ks as in ex·pect'
The sounds gz as in ex·act'

The letter *x* represents another example of a single letter representing a blend of two sounds. When the letter *x* is followed by a voiceless sound, as in the word *ex·pect'*, it stands for the voiceless blend ks; when it is followed by a voiced sound, as in the word *ex·act'*, it stands for the voiced blend gz.

The blend ks. To form the blend raise the back of the tongue against the soft palate as for k; then go quickly into the sound s. The resulting blend is the voiceless ks. Since both k and s are voiceless, one would expect the blend of the two sounds to be voiceless too and it is.

The blend gz. These two sounds constitute the voiced "twins" of ks. To make the blend raise the back of the tongue as for g; then go quickly into the sound z. The resulting blend is the voiced gz. Since both g and z are voiced, the blend of the two sounds is also voiced.

The sounds kw as in *qu*een
The sounds gw as in lan'*gu*age

The blend kw. To make the blend raise the back of the tongue against the soft palate as for the sound k; then go quickly into the sound w. The result is the blend of the two sounds kw.

The blend gw. To form the blend raise the back of the tongue against the soft palate for the sound g; then go quickly into the sound w. The resulting blend is the *voiced* gw.

You will find that the blends kw and gw occur only at the beginning, never at the end, of a word or syllable, as in *queen, quick, lan'guage,* and *pen'guin,* for example.

AN INFORMAL TEST*

WHICH ONE IS IT?

1. A consonant is (a) a speech sound; (b) an organ of speech; (c) a plosive.
2. Every consonant is the result of (a) some interference with the outgoing breath stream; (b) complete interference with the outgoing breath stream.
3. All consonant sounds are either (a) voiced or voiceless; (b) plosives or fricatives.
4. The consonant sound at the end of the word *cup* is (a) a voiced plosive; (b) a voiceless plosive.
5. The consonant sound at the end of the word *man* is (a) a voiceless sound; (b) a voiced sound.
6. The sound t is the voiced counterpart of (a) the sound d; (b) the voiceless counterpart of the sound d.
7. The nasals m, n, and ŋ are (a) voiced sounds; (b) voiceless sounds.
8. The sounds p, b, and m are (a) bilabial sounds; (b) labio-dental sounds; (c) nasals.

* Answers are listed under the appropriate chapter number in the Appendix.

9. The sound **g** is (a) a fricative; (b) a plosive; (c) a nasal.
10. The letter *j* in *jug* stands for (a) a single sound; (b) a blend of two sounds.
11. The letter *x* stands for a blend of two sounds in the word (a) *fox;* (b) *xylophone.*
12. The blend t∫ is the voiceless counterpart of the blend (a) **gz;** (b) **dʒ.**
13. The sound **s** is the voiceless counterpart of the sound (a) ∫; (b) **z.**
14. The words *if* and *of* end with (a) the same consonant sounds; (b) different consonant sounds.
15. The words *fish* and *rouge* end with (a) the same consonant sound; (b) different consonant sounds.
16. The letters *th, sh, wh,* and *ng* stand for (a) single sounds; (b) consonant blends.
17. The sound **ð** is the (a) voiced counterpart of the sound **θ**; (b) voiced counterpart of the sound **f.**
18. The consonant sounds **m, n,** and **ŋ** are classified as (a) plosives; (b) nasals.
19. The word *bathe* ends with (a) a voiced consonant sound; (b) a voiceless sound.
20. The sounds **ʍ, h,** and **w** occur only at the (a) end of an English word or syllable; (b) beginning of a word or syllable.
21. The sound **ʒ** occurs in the words (a) *treasure* and *garage;* (b) *sure* and *sugar.*
22. The sound **z** occurs in (a) *buzz* and *usual;* (b) *buzz* and *has.*
23. The words *thin* and *this* begin with (a) the same consonant sounds; (b) different consonant sounds.
24. The initial consonant sound in the words *rug* and *room* are (a) correctly pronounced (ĕr); (b) incorrectly pronounced (ĕr).

7

THE CONSONANTS
IN RELATION TO PHONICS

We learned from our study in phonetics how each of the consonants in the English language is correctly formed by the organs of speech. We shall now apply what we have learned to a study of the consonants in relation to phonics.

We shall observe (1) the various positions in which consonants occur in syllables, whether at the beginning, at the end, or at both the beginning and the end of the syllable; (2) the letter-to-sound and the sound-to-letter relationships of the consonants; (3) the nature and frequency of occurrence of the consonant blends in the reading vocabulary; (4) the single consonant sounds that are often mistaken for blends; (5) the occurrence of the so-called double consonants; and (6) the so-called silent consonants in the words or syllables.

POSITION OF CONSONANTS
IN SYLLABLES

In studying the position of the consonants in words or syllables, you will find that some consonants occur only in the initial position, that is, before the vowel in the syllable. Others occur after the vowel or in the final position of the syllable, and still others are found in both the initial and the final position of the word or syllable.

Consonants are also said to occur medially in words, as in *accent*. But one may consider a consonant in the middle of the word as being initial or final depending upon whether it comes before or after the vowel sound in the syllable. Accordingly the first *c* in the word *ac'cent* is in the final position and the second *c* is in the initial position of the syllable.

Consonants That Occur Initially and Finally

Let us now see which of the consonants are found both in the initial and the final position in the children's reading vocabulary.

b as in ball and cub	*r* as in rock and star
c as in candy and music	*s* as in sun and bus
d as in dog and bird	*t* as in top and bat
f as in fish and wolf	*th* as in thumb and bathe
g as in goat and pig	*ch* as in chair and peach
k as in king and book	*sh* as in ship and dish
l as in lamb and seal	*v* as in vines and cave
m as in mouse and drum	*x* as in xylophone and fox
n as in nest and sun	*z* as in zebra and prize
p as in pet and sheep	

Consonants That Occur Initially or Finally

The letters *h, j, qu, w, wh,* and *y* stand for sounds that occur only before, never after, the vowel in a word or syllable and the consonant *ng* is found only after the vowel, as illustrated by these examples.

h as in house	*wh* as in whip
j as in jump	*y* as in yard
qu as in queen	*ng* as in sing
w as in wind	

NOTE. The spelling *ck* for the sound (k) and *tch* for the sound (ch) are found only after, never before, the vowel in a word or syllable.

SOUND AND LETTER RELATIONSHIPS

Agreement or the lack of it between sounds and their letter symbols is not the same for all consonants. Some consonant sounds are represented by several different letters and some letters stand for a greater number of different sounds than others.

It should be an interesting observation to note which of the consonant sounds have more than one spelling and which of the consonants stand for more than one sound.

Different Letters for the Same Sound

Each of the following consonant sounds is represented by different letters in the children's reading vocabulary.

The sound **f** is represented by the following six spellings:

f as in i*f*	*gh* as in lau*gh*	*lf* as in ca*lf*
ff as in o*ff*	*ph* as in gra*ph*	*fe* as in sa*fe*

The sound **v** is represented by these different spellings:

v as in *v*ines	*f* as in o*f*	*ve* as in ha*ve*

The sound **k** has eight different spellings:

k as in *k*ite	*ch* as in s*ch*ool	*lk* as in ta*lk*
c as in *c*ome	*qu* as in mos*qu*itoes	*ke* as in ca*ke*
ck as in tru*ck*	*que* as in anti*que*	

NOTE. The sound **k** is consistently spelled *ck* in syllables having the "short" vowel sound as in *truck, back, stick, dock,* and *speck.*

The blend **kw** is represented by two different spellings:

qu as in *qu*een	*cho* as in *cho*ir

The sound **b** has three different spellings:

b as in *b*oy	*bu* as in *bu*oyant	*be* as in tu*be*

The sound **g** is represented by five different spellings:

g as in *g*oat	*gu* as in *gu*ess	*gh* as in *gh*ost
gg as in e*gg*s	*gue* as in catalo*gue*	

The sound **ŋ** has four different spellings:

ng in si*ng*	*n* in thi*n*k
ngue in to*ngue*	*nd* in ha*nd*kerchief

The sound l has these spellings:

l as in *l*amb	*tle* in whis*tle*
ll as in *ll*ama	*le* as in ta*le*

The sound m has five different spellings:

m as in *m*ouse	*lm* as in ca*lm*	*me* as in rhy*me*
mb as in la*mb*	*mn* as in colu*mn*	

The sound n has six different spellings:

n as in *n*ut	*dne* as in We*dne*sday	*pn* as in *pn*eumonia
gn as in *gn*aw	*kn* as in *kn*ow	*ne* as in bo*ne*

The sound t has these different spellings:

t as in *t*op	*bt* as in dou*bt*	*ght* as in ni*ght*
tt as in pu*tt*	*pt* as in *pt*omaine	*te* as in ki*te*
tte as in quarte*tte*	*ed* as in jump*ed*	

The sound d has four different spellings:

d as in *d*og	*ed* as in begg*ed*
ld as in cou*ld*	*de* as in hi*de*

The sounds r and ɹ have five different spellings:

r as in *r*abbit	*wr* as in *wr*ite	*re* as in ca*re*
rr as in pu*rr*	*rh* as in *rh*inoceros	

The sound s has nine different spellings to represent it:

s as in *s*it	*sc* as in *sc*ene	*ps* as in *ps*alm
ss as in mi*ss*	*ce* as in fen*ce*	*st* as in li*st*en
se as in sen*se*	*c* as in *c*ent, *c*ity, bi*c*ycle	*z* as in quart*z*

The sound z has these different spellings:

s as in ha*s*	*z* as in *z*ebra	*x* as in an*x*iety

The sound j has three different spellings:

y as in *y*ou	*j* as in hallelu*j*ah	*i* as in un*i*on

The sound ʃ has twelve different spellings:

sh as in *sh*ip	*ch* as in ma*ch*ine	*ce* as in o*ce*an
s as in *s*ure	*ss* as in ti*ss*ues	*ci* as in suffi*ci*ent

| *si* as in man*si*on | *ssi* as in fi*ssi*on | *scio* as in con*scio*us |
| *ti* as in pa*ti*ent | *cio* as in pre*cio*us | *xio* as in an*xio*us |

The blend **tʃ** has three different spellings:

ch as in *ch*air   *tch* as in wa*tch*   *ti* as in ques*ti*on

NOTE. The blend **tʃ** is consistently spelled *tch* only in the final position in the syllable, as in wa*tch*, wi*tch*, stre*tch*, and cru*tch*.

The sound **ʒ** has four different spellings:

s as in plea*s*ure   *ge* as in gara*ge*
z as in sei*z*ure   *si* as in divi*si*on

The blend **dʒ** has six different spellings:

j as in *j*ump   *di* as in sol*di*er
ge as in pa*ge*   *dg* as in ju*dg*ment
g as in *g*erm, *g*inger, *g*ypsy   *dge* as in ba*dge*

NOTE. When the blend **dʒ** occurs in the initial position in a syllable it is spelled with the letter *j* or *g*; when it occurs before a suffix, as in *judgment,* it is spelled *dg*; and when it occurs in the final position of a syllable it is spelled *ge* or *dge*.

Different Sounds for the Same Letter or Letters

We have just learned which of the consonant sounds have two or more different letters to represent them in the reading vocabulary. We will now see which of the letters or letter combinations stand for two or more sounds.

1. The letter *c* in the initial position of the syllable stands for the sound **k** or **s** depending upon the vowel sound that follows it. It stands for the sound:

k as in *c*ap, *c*ub, *c*oat, and for **s** as in *c*ent, *c*ity, *c*yclone

RULE. When the letter *c* comes before *e, i,* or *y* it has the sound **s**.

NOTE 1. This was the rule, you may recall, that George credited for having known the sound of the letter *c* in the first syllable in *circumnavigate* (Chapter 2).

NOTE 2. The sound s is known in phonics as the "soft" sound of the letter *c* and the sound k as the "hard" sound of *c*.

2.   The letter *g* in the initial position of the syllable stands for g or dʒ, depending upon the vowel that follows it. It stands for the sound:

g as in *gas, gone, gun,* and for the blend dʒ as in *germs, giant, gypsy*

RULE. When the letter *g* comes before *e, i,* or *y* it usually has the sounds dʒ.

NOTE 1. For exceptions to the rule, see Chapter 3.

NOTE 2. The sounds dʒ are known in phonics as the "soft" sounds of the letter *g,* and the sound g as the "hard" sound of *g.*

3.   The letters *gu* stand for a single sound and also for a blend of two sounds:

g as in *gu*ess and gw as in lan*gu*age

4.   The letter *f* stands for the two sounds:

f as in *f*unny and v as in o*f*

5.   The letter *j* stands for a single sound and also for a blend of two sounds:

j as in hallelu*j*ah and dʒ as in *j*ump

6.   The letter *n* stands for two different sounds:

n as in *n*est and ŋ as in thi*n*k and fi*n*ger

RULE. When the letter *n* comes before the sounds g and k it stands for the sound ŋ.

7.   The letters *ng* stand for four different pronunciations. When the word ends in *ng,* or when the suffix *er* is added to the root word to mean "doer," the letters *ng* stand for ŋ as in these words:

si*ng*   si*ng*er   wri*ng*   wri*ng*er

When the letter *n* is a part of the prefix *con* and *g* is a part of the root word, the letters *ng* stand for **n + g** as in:

con*g*lomeration   con*g*ratulation

When the letters *ng* are followed by the letter *e* at the end of a syllable, they stand for **n + dʒ** as in:

plu*nge*   si*nge*   lou*nge*

When the letter *n* before *g* has the sound **ŋ**, the letters *ng* stand for **ŋ + g** as in:

fi*ng*er   co*ng*ress   stro*ng*er

8.   The letter *s* stands for four different sounds:

s as in *s*un   **z** as in ha*s*
ʃ as in *s*ugar   **ʒ** as in mea*s*ure

9.   The letters *ch* stand for three different sounds:

ʃ as in ma*ch*ine   **tʃ** as in *ch*air   **k** as in s*ch*ool

10.   The letters *qu* stand for two different sounds:

k as in mos*qu*itoes and **kw** as in *qu*een

11.   The letters *th* stand for two different sounds:

θ as in *th*ink and **ð** as in *th*is

12.   The letter *x* stands for a single sound and also two different blends:

z as in an*x*iety   **ks** as in bo*x*   **gz** as in e*x*ist

13.   The letter *z* stands for three different sounds:

z as in *z*ebra   **s** as in quart*z*   **ʒ** as in a*z*ure

Summary

The consonants in the English language present an interesting study, because of their variability if for no other reason.

Consonants vary in their position in the syllables in which they occur. Nineteen of the letters (and the combination of letters *ch, sh,* and *th*) are found both in the initial and final position of the syllables. Six of the letters (and combination of letters) *h, j, qu, w, wh,* and *y* occur in the initial position only; and the consonant *ng* is found only at the end, never at the beginning, of a word or syllable.

Consonants also vary in their letter-to-sound and sound-to-letter relationships. We have observed, for example, that the same letter more regularly stands for the same sound, and the same sound is more frequently represented by the same letter, in the case of some consonants than is true of others.

Nine of the consonants, *b, d, k, l, m, r, sh, v,* and *wh,* are relatively more consistent in their letter-to-sound relationships. In contrast to these, the consonant *s* is the most irregular when one considers both its letter-to-sound and sound-to-letter relationships. The letter *s* as we have seen stands for four different sounds, and the sound **s** is represented by as many as nine different spellings. One consonant, however, exceeds the sound **s** in the number of different letters that represent the sound. In its sound-to-letter relationship the sound ʃ wins the prize, having twelve different spellings to its credit!

Among the consonant sounds seven are considered as being consistent in their sound-to-letter relationships: **p, b, h, θ, ð, w,** and **ʍ.** In contrast to these, the blend **dʒ** is spelled six different ways, the sound **s,** as already noted, has nine different spellings, and the sound ʃ has even more.

One needs only to examine the letter-to-sound and the sound-to-letter relationship of the consonants to appreciate a teacher's confusion between letters and sounds in the reading vocabulary and thus the need for a knowledge of the science of phonetics for effective teaching of phonics. The college graduate's confusion between the sound-to-letter relationship of the consonant ʒ is indeed understandable (see Chapter 4).

CONSONANT BLENDS

Description of Blends

We learned in Chapter 5 that every speech sound is the result of a single set of adjustments of the speech mechanism. A blend of sounds requires more than one set of adjustments, depending on the number of sounds in the blend. A blend of two consonants as in *tree,* for example, requires two sets of adjustments of the speech organs in forming the blend; and a blend of three sounds as in *spring* requires three sets of adjustments of the speech mechanism in pronouncing the blend.

In studying the blends it is important to remember that a blend is a combination of sounds, not letters, and that a blend of two sounds may be represented by only one letter, as in the case of *x* and *j.*

The Problem of Correct Utterance

When single consonant sounds are incorrectly uttered, the blends composed of these sounds are certain to be distorted. Ironically, the consonants most frequently mispronounced are the very ones—with the exception of (s)—that form most of the blends in the reading vocabulary. These are the sounds (l) and (r) and the three pairs of plosives: (p), (b); (t), (d); and (k), (g) (see Chapter 4).

It has been found that when a consonant blend at the beginning of a word or syllable is divorced from the vowel with which it is phonetically combined in speech, the blend is usually mispronounced: (gl) as in *glad* is called (gul), (gr) in *green* is called (ger), (tr) in *train* becomes (ter). When the blend is left with its accompanying vowel the blend is correctly uttered: (gla) in *glad,* (gree) in *green,* (trai) in *train.*

You may wish to see for yourself how easy it is to form the consonant blends correctly by pronouncing the blends as indicated by the hyphen in each of these words.

gla-d	grow-l	prou-d	bru-sh
pla-ne	tree-s	clow-n	bla-ck
plea-se	dru-m	tru-ck	cla-p

If now you will pronounce the same blends, but divorced from the vowel sound with which it is combined in speech, as indicated in the following list of words, you will discover the difficulty of avoiding an intervening neutral sound in forming the blends.

gl-ad	gr-owl	pr-oud	br-ush
pl-ane	tr-ees	cl-own	bl-ack
pl-ease	dr-um	tr-uck	cl-ap

Frequency of Occurrence of Blends

The consonant blends, like the single sounds, vary in their frequency of occurrence in the reading vocabulary. The most frequently occurring blends are those formed with (r), (l), and (s).

BLENDS FORMED WITH (r)

There are twelve initial consonant blends in the reading vocabulary in which (r) is one of the sounds: (br), (gr), (fr), (dr), (cr), (pr), (tr), (shr), (thr), (scr), (spr), and (str). Each of these blends is found only at the beginning, never at the end, of a word or syllable.

You might like to see if you can pronounce each of the blends correctly in isolation. Then pronounce the same blends in the following words and observe which is the easier way to form the blends correctly, apart from the adjacent vowel or with the vowel sound.

broo-m	craw-l	tru-ck	scra-tch
fro-g	gree-t	shri-ll	sprou-t
dre-ss	prou-d	thru-sh	stree-t

BLENDS FORMED WITH (l)

There are ten consonant blends formed with (l) in the reading vocabulary. Six of these, (bl), (cl), (fl), (gl), (pl), and (sl), are found both at the beginning and at the end of a syllable. The blend (spl) as in *splash* occurs only at the beginning of a syllable or word. The remaining three, namely, (dl), (kl), and (tl), are found only at the end, never at the beginning, of a word or syllable.

The following list shows the (l) blends that occur both at the beginning and at the end of a word:

*bl*ack	*cl*ap	*fl*ag	*gl*ass	*pl*ease	*sl*ed
ta*bl*e	un*cl*e	ri*fl*e	ea*gl*e	peo*pl*e	mea*sl*es

The next three words show the blends that occur only at the end of a word:

pud*dl*e   an*kl*e   bee*tl*e

BLENDS FORMED WITH (s)

There are thirteen blends in the reading vocabulary of which (s) is the first sound in the blend. Five of these occur both at the beginning and the end as shown in this list:

*sk*ip	*sl*eep	*sm*art	*sp*ot	*st*ick
de*sk*	mea*sl*es	cha*sm*	wa*sp*	gho*st*

Eight of the (s) blends are found only at the beginning of a syllable, as indicated in the following list:

*sc*ooter	*sn*ail	*spr*out	*str*eam
*scr*atch	*spl*ash	*squ*eal	*sw*eep

Single-Letter Blends

We have learned that a consonant blend is a union of two or more consonant sounds. In most blends the number of sounds coincides with the number of letters in the blend, a two-letter blend having two sounds and a three-letter blend having three sounds. But we have already observed two blends, each of which is represented by a single letter. These blends are known as single-, or one-letter, blends.

THE CONSONANT *x*

The letter *x* stands for a blend of two sounds as well as the single sound (z). It stands for the voiceless sounds (ks) and the voiced sounds (gz), as shown by the following examples:

Voiceless (ks)		*Voiced* (gz)	
bo*x*es	te*x*tbook	e*x*hibit	e*x*haust
o*x*en	e*x*cited	e*x*ample	e*x*ert
fo*x*es	e*x*plode	e*x*amine	e*x*actly

RULE. When the letter *x* is followed by a voiceless sound, it usually stands for the voiceless blend (ks); when it is followed by a voiced sound it stands for the voiced blend (gz).

NOTE. The words *boxes, oxen,* and *foxes* illustrate the exceptions to the rule.

THE CONSONANT *j*

The letter *j* oddly enough nearly always stands for a blend of two sounds, the letter *j* in *hallelujah* being an exception to the rule. Teachers who are unaccustomed to thinking of the letter as representing the blend **dʒ** are often amazed at the thought of it. "I don't believe it!" was one teacher's reaction to the novel idea. "How could the word *jump* start with the sound **d** as in *dog?* Impossible!" she said.

Had the teacher observed how the speech mechanism functions in pronouncing the beginning sound in the word *jump,* she would have discovered that the tongue tip is raised for the sound **d,** then goes quickly into the position for **ʒ,** resulting in the blend **dʒ.**

You may be interested in making the same observation as you pronounce each of these words:

jump	joints	judge	journey	Jack
jolly	jokes	junior	jungles	Jupiter

SINGLE SOUNDS MISTAKEN FOR BLENDS

You have learned that the letter combinations *pl, st,* and *dr,* for example, stand for consonant blends. We have also observed that not every combination of consonants stands for a blend of two or more sounds and that there are several letter combinations in the English language, each of which stands not for a blend but for a single sound. Note that each of these two-letter symbols stands for one sound, as indicated by the phonetic symbol for the sound.

th	θ as in ba*th*	*ph* f	as in *ph*onics
th	ð as in ba*the*	*gh* f	as in lau*gh*
wh	ʍ as in *wh*ip	*ng* ŋ	as in si*ng*
sh	ʃ as in *sh*ip		

DOUBLE CONSONANTS

Two identical, adjacent consonants are known as double consonants. Double consonants are found at the beginning of a word or syllable as in *llama*, in the middle of a word as in *balloon*, and at the end of a word as in *ball*. Two identical consonants adjacent to each other stand for a single sound with these exceptions: (1) when the first of the two consonants belongs to the prefix and the second consonant to the root word, as in *dissatisfied* (dis•sat′iz•fīd); and (2) when each of the double consonants stands for a different sound, as in the word *suggest* (səg•jest′) or in the word *accident* (ak′si•dent). In such cases both consonants are pronounced.

The following list shows the double consonant at the end of the syllable representing a single sound.

bell (bel)	miss (mis)	putt (put)
puff (puf)	buzz (buz)	purr (pėr)

In the following columns we also see double consonants of which only one is pronounced when the word is spoken. You will observe that each of the identical consonants represents a single sound and that the sound is not always pronounced with the first syllable in the word. In column one the consonant is pronounced with the vowel in the first syllable; in column two the consonant goes with the vowel in the following syllable.

1.	*2.*
rabbits (rab′its)	commence (kə•mens′)
dinner (din′ər)	sufficient (sə•fish′ent)
carriage (kar′ij)	surrender (sə•ren′dər)
baggage (bag′ij)	suppose (sə•pōz′)
summer (sum′ər)	assignment (ə•sīn′ment)
puppets (pup′ets)	attention (ə•ten′shən)
different (dif′ər•ent)	disappointed (dis•ə•point′ed)
guessing (ges′ing)	addition (ə•dish′shən)

"SILENT" CONSONANTS

Teachers need no introduction to "silent" letters. The term is used in teaching phonics, reading, spelling, and English in the schools. It is used to designate the letters in syllables that are not sounded when the syllable is spoken.

It may be of interest to note that the so-called silent consonants follow a somewhat definite pattern in the case of the letters *b, g, h, gh, k, l, p, t,* and *w*.

The letter *b* is silent when it comes before *t* and after *m*, as shown by these examples:

debt (det)	lamb (lam)	crumb (krum)
doubt (dout)	climb (klīm)	numb (num)
subtle (sut'əl)	comb (kōm)	plumber (plum'ər)

The letter *g* is silent when it is followed by *n* and *m*, as in these examples:

gnat (nat)	gnome (nōm)	phlegm (flem)
gnaw (nô)	gnu (nü)	diaphragm (dī'ə·fram)
gnarl (närl)	gnash (nash)	

The letter *h*, which is never pronounced when it follows the vowel sound in a word or syllable, is frequently silent before the vowel as well. It is also silent when preceded by the letter *r*.

Words in which the letter *h* comes after the vowel:

ah (ä)	hurrah (hu·rô')	hallelujah (hal·ə·lü'yä)
oh (ō)	rajah (rä'jä)	

Words in which the letter *h* comes before the vowel:

hour (our)	honor (on'ər)	exhort (eg·zôrt')
heir (ãr)	honest (on'est)	exhibit (eg·zib'it)
herb (ėrb)	exhaust (eg·zôst')	

Words in which the letter *h* is preceded by *r:*

rhyme (rīm)	rhuematism (rü'mə·tiz·əm)
rhythm (rith'əm)	rhubarb (rü'bärb)
rhinoceros (rī·nos'ər·əs)	rhododendron (rō·dō·den'drən)

NOTE. The word *homage* may be pronounced (om'ij) or (hom'ij), and the word *humble* was formerly, and occasionally still is, pronounced (um'b'l) or (um'bəl) .

The letters *gh* are silent after the vowel sounds (ī), (ā), and (ô), as shown by the following examples, all of which have a high frequency of occurrence in the children's reading vocabulary:

high (hī)	sight (sīt)	eight (āt)	bought (bôt)
sigh (sī)	light (līt)	weigh (wā)	brought (brôt)
night (nīt)	flight (flīt)	weight (wāt)	fought (fôt)
right (rīt)	bright (brīt)	sleigh (slā)	caught (kôt)
fight (fīt)	height (hīt)	straight (strāt)	naughty (nô'ti)

The letter *k* is silent before the sound (n) as shown by these examples:

knee (nē)	known (nōn)	knew (nū)	knot (not)
kneel (nēl)	knock (nok)	knit (nit)	knight (nīt)
know (nō)	knob (nob)	knife (nīf)	knuckles (nuk'əlz)

The letter *l* is silent when it comes before the sounds (k), (d), and (m):

talk (tôk)	chalk (chôk)	yolk (yōk)	balk (bôk)
walk (wôk)	folks (fōks)	stalks (stôks)	

would (wúd)   could (kúd)   should (shúd)

calm (cäm)	psalm (säm)	balm (bäm)
palm (päm)	salmon (sä'mən)	almonds (ä'məndz)

The letter *p* is silent before the sounds (s), (t), and (n), as in these examples:

psalm (säm)   pneumonia (nū·mō'ni·ə)
ptomaine (tō·mān')   pseudonym (sū'dō·nim)

The letter *t* is silent when it is preceded by (s) and (f) as shown by these examples:

listen (lis'n) or (lis'ən)	nestle (nes'l) or (nes'əl)
whistle (hwis'l) or (hwis'əl)	hasten (hās'n) or (hās'ən)
thistle (this'l) or (this'əl)	often (ôf'n) or (ôf'ən)
hustle (hus'l) or (hus'əl)	soften (sôf'n) or (sôf'ən)

The consonant *w* is silent when it is followed by *r* as in these examples:

write (rīt)	wren (ren)	wraps (raps)
wrote (rōt)	wrench (rench)	wriggle (rig'l) or (rig'əl)
wrong (rông)	wrist (rist)	wringer (ring'ər)
wreck (rek)	wring (ring)	wrinkle (ring'k'l) or (ring'kəl)

AN INFORMAL TEST*

1. Is the letter-to-sound relationship the same for all the consonants in the children's reading vocabulary or do the consonants vary in this respect?

2. Does the letter *s* stand for the same sound in *sugar* as in the word *usual?*

3. In which of these words do the letters *th* represent exactly the same sound: *think, this, thistle, bath?*

4. Which of the following letter symbols stand for a blend of two sounds: *gr* as in *green, gh* as in *laugh, x* as in *box, ng* as in *sing, y* as in *yes, j* as in *jump?*

5. The same consonant blend can be heard in two of these words: *queen, antique, mosquitoes, choir.* What is the blend and in which of the words does one hear the blend when the words are spoken?

6. Which of these words do not end with the sound (z): *hats, has, prize, quartz?*

7. Why are both *c*'s pronounced in the word *accent* and not in the word *account?*

8. Which of these blends, (sp), (spl), (tr), (br), (bl), and (tl), occur both at the beginning and at the end of an English word?

9. In which of these words, *chair, school, watch, chorus, choir,* do the letter symbols *ch* represent the sound (k)?

10. What is the first sound in the words *chair* and *chimes?* What is the first sound in the words *gem* and *jet?*

11. In which of these words, *stiff, cough, though, photograph, laugh,* does one hear the same consonant sound as in the little word *if?*

12. What sound is spelled with the letter *s* in *treasure, z* in *seizure, ge* in *camouflage,* and *si* in *division?*

13. Here we have six words in which we see the letter *n: run, nut, think, thin, anchor, stronger.* In which of these words does the letter *n* have the sound (n), and in which does it have the sound (ng)?

14. In which of these words, *singer, finger, congress, wringer, plunge,* do the letters *ng* stand for the sounds ŋ + g?

15. In the blank spaces between the parentheses supply the two blends missing in the following rule: When the letter *x* is followed by a voiceless sound, it usually stands for the voiceless blend (   ); and when it is followed by a voiced sound, it usually stands for

---

* Answers are listed under the appropriate chapter number in the Appendix.

the voiced blend ( ). What is the voiceless blend? the voiced blend?

16. What consonant sound is represented by the letter *s* in the word *sure*, by *cio* in *precious*, by *scio* in *conscious*, by *ce* in *ocean*, by *ti* in *patient*, and by *ssi* in *fission*?

17. Which of these consonants, *h, wh, th, sh, qu, n* and *y*, are sounded only in the initial position in an English word or syllable?

18. Which of these consonants, *m, n, ng, p, v, z, th, wh,* and *sh*, occur both initially and finally in an English word or syllable?

19. What letter is silent in the words *chalk, folks, salmon, calm, would,* and *could*?

20. What letter is silent in the words *pneumonia* and *pseudonym*? in the words *listen* and *soften*? in *debt, lamb,* and *plumber*?

8

PHONETIC STUDY
OF THE VOWELS

After having survived the phonetic study of the consonants in an earlier chapter, the study of the vowels should now be easy by comparison. Teachers usually find the vowels more confusing than the consonants in teaching phonics. It is, however, not the phonetic aspects of the vowels but their sound-to-letter and letter-to-sound relationships that pose the problem in phonics. This is understandable, when a single vowel may represent as many as seven different sounds, and the same sound is spelled in twenty different ways, as will be shown in the next chapter.

First, we shall see what the science of phonetics has to offer the teacher regarding the vowel sounds in the children's reading vocabulary.

DEFINITION OF VOWELS

We know that consonants result when in speaking the outgoing breath stream is either partially or completely obstructed by the organs of speech. Vowels result when the organs of speech merely modify the resonance chamber without impeding the flow of the outgoing breath.

Note the obstruction of the breath in the mouth as you pronounce the sounds b, f, l; then notice the absence of interference by the organs of speech as you say ɑ, e, i, o.

We have learned that the sound w as in *wind* and the sound j as in *yes,* which are classed as consonants, may also be regarded as semivowels because of the slight obstruction of the breath in uttering the sound. We also learned that consonants are either voiced or voiceless, nasal or oral. But all vowels are voiced, and there are no nasal vowels in the English language.

One vowel is distinguished from another by the *quality* of its sound. It is the quality of its sound that differentiates iː in the word *me* from aɪ in *my;* or o in *toe* from u in *true,* for example. The quality of the vowel is determined by the shape of the resonating chamber in forming the sound. Notice the difference in its shape as you pronounce the vowels e, aɪ, o, u, and again as you form the sounds e, o, ɑ.

FACTORS RELATED TO VOWEL QUALITY

We learned that the shape of the resonance chamber determines the quality of the vowel that is uttered; its shape, in turn, is determined by a number of factors of which we are seldom aware when we produce the sounds. These factors are the height of the tongue, the place of its highest point, the shape the lips take in uttering the sound, and the degree of tenseness of the lips and tongue.

Usually when the sound requires a tense tongue, as in the case of the vowels iː and u, the lips are also tense. When the tongue is lax as in uttering the vowel ʌ, the lips are also lax. One can, therefore, get an idea of the tenseness of the tongue by observing the lips.

It is of further significance to note that certain lip positions always tend to be associated with certain tongue positions. For example, when the front of the tongue is raised toward the roof of the mouth, as for the vowel sound i, the lips are spread as in a smile. But when the back of the tongue is raised as for the sound u, the lips are rounded.

CONFLICTING USE OF TERMS

Before proceeding with our study of the vowel sounds, it is important that we understand the use of the terms *long* and *short* in describing vowel sounds. Both terms are used by phoneticians and teachers of phonics, but their meaning depends upon which group is using the terms. In phonics the vowel in the word *cut* is said to be "short" and the vowel in *cute* is called "long." But to the phonetician, the terms *long* and *short* have an entirely different meaning. Whether a sound is long or short as the phonetician uses the term depends on the extent to which the sound is prolonged in the spoken word.

In phonetics then, the vowel in the word *cut* is said to be shorter than the vowel in *cud,* since it does not take so long to say the vowel in *cut* as in *cud.* By the same reasoning, the vowel in *bee* is longer than the same vowel in *beet,* and the vowel in *beetle* is the shortest of the three.

In phonics the terms *short* and *long* are used to indicate two entirely different sounds, namely, (ŭ) in *cut* and (ū) in *cute* or (ĕ) in *bed* and (ē) in *bee.*

It is important as we continue with the study of vowel sounds to keep in mind the meaning of the terms *short* and *long* in phonics, as opposed to their use in the science of phonetics.

DESCRIPTION OF VOWELS
AND DIPHTHONGS

The following section presents the vowel sounds that occur in the reading vocabulary. The sound is indicated by its phonetic symbol and a key word for the sound at the head of each description.

Insofar as possible the vowels are grouped to show their phonetic kinship, like the sounds i and ɪ, for example, and the letter symbols (ē) and (ĭ). Teachers are accustomed in terms of phonics, to think of the sounds (ē) and (ĕ) as belonging together. But actually the sounds (ē) and (ĭ) are related to each other, as shown by the phonetic symbols i and ɪ. The phonetic kinship of i and ɪ is based on the characteristics the sounds have in common in one's speech; namely:

1. the position of the highest point of the tongue;
2. the shape of the lips, whether rounded or spread;
3. the degree of tenseness of the lips and tongue.

The extent to which any two related sounds have these characteristics in common is told in the description of the sounds.

The sound i as in *eat*
The sound ɪ as in *it*

The sound i. This is the sound that in phonics is known as the "long e" sound. Dictionaries indicate the sound by the symbol (ē).

To make the sound, spread the lips as in a smile. Rest the tongue tip against the lower front teeth, with the front of the tongue arched toward the hard palate. You will feel that the tongue and lips are tense as you say i in *eat*.

The sound ɪ. This sound is the lax form of i, and is known in phonics as the "short i" sound. It is indicated in *Webster's New International Dictionary,* Second Edition, by the symbol (ĭ). Thorndike-Barnhart and Webster's Third Edition indicate the sound by leaving the letter *i* unmarked.

To make the sound ɪ, place the tongue in the same position as for i, but do not let the tongue stiffen. The lips are spread, but slightly more open than for i. The tongue and lips are lax, as you say ɪ in *it*. The sound ɪ being the lax form of i leaves no doubt of the kinship between i and ɪ.

You can discover for yourself the relationship between the "long e" and "short i" by comparing the vowel sound in the accented syllable in the word *be'ing* with its sound in the unaccented syllable in the word *be·gin'*. The "long e" in (bē'ing) becomes a "short i" in (bi·gin'). In like manner the "long e" in *re'cess* (rē'ses) becomes a "short i" when the first syllable is unaccented as in (ri·ses').

The sound e as in *ate*
The sound ɛ as in *end*

The sound e. This is the sound that is known in phonics as the "long a" sound. Dictionaries indicate the sound by the symbol (ā).

To make the sound part the lips as in a smile. The tongue is raised toward the hard palate, but not so high or so far forward as for the sound i. The lips and tongue are tense as you say e in *ate*.

It is significant to note that when the sound e is prolonged, as in *say, cafe,* and *weigh,* the sound is diphthongized. The vowels *ei* in *weigh* suggest their diphthongal character eɪ. If the word *weigh* were spelled *wei* it would be spelled phonetically!

NOTE. For the sake of simplicity, the symbol e is used throughout the book to indicate the diphthongal form eɪ as well.

The sound ɛ. This sound is known as the "short e" sound. It is indicated in *Webster's New International Dictionary,* Second Edition, by the symbol (ĕ). It is the lax form of the sound e, as in *ate*.

To make the sound part the lips, but do not spread them as tensely as for e. The lips and tongue are lax, as you say ɛ in *end*.

NOTE. The sounds e and ɛ are related in the same way as i and ɪ are related to each other; and how clearly the phonetic symbols show the relationship!

The sound æ as in *at*
The sound ɛː as in *air*

The sound æ. This sound is known in phonics as the "short a." It is indicated in Webster's Second Edition by the symbol (ă). Webster's Third Edition and Thorndike-Barnhart indicate the sound by leaving the letter *a* unmarked.

To make the sound, part the lips, but more widely than for the sound ɛ as in *end,* as you say æ in *at*. The lips and tongue are lax; care must be taken not to prolong the sound or let it come through the nose. A nasalized æ is not acceptable in English.

The sound ɛː. This sound is indicated in Webster's Second Edition by the symbol (âr) and in Thorndike-Barnhart's Dictionary by the symbol (ãr).

To make the sound place the tongue in the position for ɛ as in *end,* then lower the tongue slightly. The lips and tongue are tense as you say ɛː in *air*.

The sound ɛː occurs only before *r* as in *air, bear,* and *care.* It is an interesting sound, if for no other reason than that there seems to be little uniformity in the phonetic value that speakers assign to this sound. Some Americans use a sound resembling ɛ as in *end,* others use æ as in *at,* and still others use a sound resembling e as in *ate* in pronouncing the words *air, bear, care,* and *there,* for example.

Which of these four sounds do you use? Does your pronunciation of *dairy* rhyme with *merry?* If so, you are probably giving the vowel the same sound as in *end.* Or do you pronounce *dairy* to rhyme with *marry?* In that case you could be assigning to the vowel the same sound as in *at.* Or do you give the vowel in *dairy* the same sound as in *date?* If neither of these fits your case, then you are probably using the sound indicated by the phonetic symbol ɛː.

The sound ɑ as in *a*rm
The sound a as in *a*sk

The sound ɑ. This is the sound your doctor wants you to make when he tells you to say *ah.* To make the sound let your mouth fall open and your tongue lie flat on the floor of the mouth. The lips and tongue are lax as you say ɑ in *arm.* Because your mouth is wide open for ɑ and the tongue is flat on the floor of the mouth, the doctor can look into the throat at will.

The sound ɑ is usually indicated in the dictionaries by the symbol (ä). It may be followed by the letter *r* as in *arm* or not followed by *r* as in *father* (fä′thər).

The sound a. This sound, indicated in Webster's Second Edition by the symbol (à), is an intermediate sound between ɑ as in *arm* and æ as in *at.* It is not recognized as such by Thorndike-Barnhart nor in Webster's Third Edition.

To make the sound open the mouth a little more than for æ and keep the back of the tongue slightly raised so that the sound is farther forward than for ɑ.

It should be said that not all speakers use the sound a. Those who do not have it use a sound that resembles ɑ or æ for the words *ask, path, laugh, aunt, dance,* and *can't,* for example.

Perhaps you pronounce these words with the sound ɑ or æ. Or do you use a vowel sound somewhere between these two extremes?

The sound u as in food
The sound ʊ as in foot

The sound **u**.   This is the sound that has seventeen different spellings in the children's reading vocabulary (see Chapter 9). It is indicated in Webster's Second Edition, by the symbol (o͞o) and by Thorndike-Barnhart and also in Webster's Third Edition by the symbol (ü).

To make the sound round the lips so as to form a small circle. As you round the lips the back of the tongue is raised toward the hard palate. The lips and tongue are tense as you say the sound **u** as in *food*.

The sound **ʊ**.   This sound is the lax form of **u** as in *food;* Webster's Second Edition indicates the sound by the symbol (o͝o) and Thorndike-Barnhart and Webster's Third Edition by the symbol (ü).

To make the sound place the tongue and lips as in the position for **u**. Be sure the lips are rounded as you pronounce the sound **ʊ** as in *foot*. Because the lips are lax, the mouth is slightly more open for **ʊ** than for **u**.

Note how clearly the close relationship between the vowel sounds in *food* and *foot* is shown, not only by the phonetic symbols **u** and **ʊ** but by the letter symbols (ü) and (u̇) and also (o͞o) and (o͝o).

The sound ɔ: as in *or*
The sound ɔ as in *often*

Here again we have two closely related sounds as shown by their phonetic symbols and in this case also by their spelling.

The sound **ɔ:**.   This sound is indicated in Webster's Second Edition and in the Thorndike-Barnhart Dictionary by the symbol (ô) and in Webster's Third Edition by the symbol (ȯ).

To make the sound, round the lips; then draw the lips down to form a long opening. The lips and tongue are tense as you say **ɔ:** in *or*.

When the sound ɔː is spelled with the letter *o* it is followed by *r* as in *horse, corn, north,* and *storm;* but when the sound is spelled with a letter or letters other than *o* it is not followed by the letter *r* as in *all, saw, haul,* and *caught.*

The sound ɔ. This sound is indicated in Webster's Second Edition by the symbol (ŏ) as in the words *soft, lost, cross, tossed,* and *cost.*

To make the sound round the lips as you did for ɔː ; then shift to ɑ as in *arm.* Remember to keep the lips somewhat rounded as you shift from ɔː to ɑ in making the sound.

The so-called "short o" as in *top*

The sound known in phonics as the "short o" has no exact equivalent in phonetics. It is indicated in the Thorndike-Barnhart Dictionary by the symbol (o), in Webster's Second Edition by (ŏ), and in Webster's Third by (ä).

Some speakers use a sound resembling ɑ as in *arm* in pronouncing *top, doll, shop, hot, what, was, wash,* and *watch,* for example. Others use a sound resembling ɔ as in *soft* in their pronunciation of these words.

You might be interested in discovering whether you use the vowel sound as in *arm* or the vowel as in *soft* in pronouncing the following list of words or whether you use a sound resembling ɑ in some of the words and ɔ in others.

top	Tom	golf	foreign	what
doll	on	gods	frogs	watch
clock	box	forest	hogs	was
hop	shop	rockets	was	wasp

The sound o as in *old*

The sound o. This sound, which is known in phonics as the "long o," is indicated in the dictionaries by the symbol (ō).

To make the sound, round the lips, but not so closely as for u in *food.* As you round the lips the back of the tongue is raised toward the soft palate, but not so far back as for u. The lips and tongue are tense as you say o in *old.*

When the sound o is prolonged as in the words *so, toad, cold,* and *snow,* for example, it is diphthongized as shown by the phonetic symbol oᴜ. However, for the sake of simplicity, the symbol o is used throughout this book to indicate the diphthongal form oᴜ as well as the shorter sound o.

The sound ʌ as in *up*
The sound ə as in *a·bout'*

The sound ʌ. This sound, whose phonetic symbol is an upside down v is known in phonics as the "short u" sound. It is indicated in Webster's Second Edition by the symbol (ŭ) and in Webster's Third Edition by the symbol (ə). Thorndike-Barnhart indicates the sound by leaving the vowel unmarked.

The sound ʌ is one of the easiest sounds to make, being little more than a grunt. In making the sound, the lips are slightly open with the corners drawn together. The tip of the tongue rests against the lower front teeth. The tongue and lips are lax as you say ʌ in *up*.

The sound ə. The symbol ə (known as the schwa) is the International Phonetic Symbol used to indicate the unstressed form of the sound ʌ. Thorndike-Barnhart uses the schwa not only to indicate the unstressed "short u" but for several other unstressed vowel sounds in the unaccented syllables of words as well. Webster's Third Edition uses the schwa to indicate both the stressed and the unstressed "short u" as indicated in the words *up* \'əp\ and *up·on* \ə-'pȯn\.

In making the sound ə the tongue and lips are in the same position as for the sound ʌ, but they are more lax for the sound ə than for ʌ.

These two sounds are so nearly alike that you may have difficulty in distinguishing them. If you will listen carefully to the first and second vowels as you pronounce the word *a·dult'* you may be able to experience the difference between ʌ and ə. By pronouncing the accented syllable much more forcibly than the unaccented syllable, you will be sure to detect the difference between the two sounds.

The sound ə as in *turn*
The sound əɪ as in *fath'er*

The sound ə. This sound is heard in words in which the letter *r* is final, as in *fur*, or followed by a consonant, as in *turn*.

It is indicated in Webster's Second Edition by the symbol (ûr) and in Webster's Third Edition by the schwa. Thorndike-Barnhart indicates the sound by the symbol (ėr).

The quality of the sound differs greatly in the speech of different individuals. Speakers who "drop" their final *r*'s form the sound with lips and tongue in somewhat the same position as for the sound ʌ, except that the tongue is higher and the lips are slightly stretched. The resulting sound is indicated by the phonetic symbol ɜ:. The symbol ə is used to show that the *r* is pronounced.

Some speakers in uttering the sound ə curl the tongue tip and pull the whole tongue back in the mouth. This gives the vowel a heavy muffled sound that colors the whole word. This sound is frequently heard in the Middle West in the words *turn, fur, herd, girl,* and *church,* for example.

The sound əɪ. This is the unstressed form of the sound ə and it occurs in the unaccented syllables as in the words *fath'er, doc'tor,* and *col'lar,* for example. Webster's Second Edition indicates the sound by the symbol (ēr). Thorndike-Barnhart and Webster's Third Edition use the symbol ər to indicate the sound.

The diphthong aɪ as in *ice*

The diphthong aɪ. This blend of two sounds is known in phonics as the "long i" sound. The dictionaries indicate the sound by the symbol (ī).

To make the sounds shape the lips and place the tongue in the position for a as in *ask;* then partly close the lips and go quickly into ɪ as in *sit.* See how smoothly you can shift from a into ɪ in forming the blend aɪ.

The vowels *ai* in the word *aisle* suggest their diphthongal character. If the word were spelled *ail,* it would be spelled phonetically!

There are as many as fifteen different ways of spelling the diphthong aɪ in the children's reading vocabulary, as we shall see in Chapter 9.

The diphthong ju as in *use*

The diphthong ju. Here is the symbol that looks like the letter *j* and stands for the first sound in the word *yes!* You first met this sound as a consonant (Chapter 6). You must now think of it as the first sound in the diphthong ju, which is a blend of the two vowel sounds j and u. These are the sounds you are accustomed to think of as the "long u" sound, indicated in the Thorndike-Barnhart Dictionary and in Webster's Second Edition by the symbol (ū). What could possibly be more confusing! Interestingly, however, Webster's Third Edition shows the diphthongal nature of the so-called "long u" by using the symbol (yü) to indicate the sounds.

To make the sounds, shape the lips and bring the tongue in position for ɪ as in *sit;* then go quickly into u as in *food.* The resulting blend is ɪu or ju.

The symbol ɪu would seem to be the more fitting of the two symbols, and some authorities favor ɪu, which certainly would be much less confusing than ju.

NOTE. Many teachers confuse the vowel sound ʊ as in *rude* with the sounds ju as in *use,* perhaps because one hears the sound ʊ in both *rude* and *use.* The only difference between the two sounds is the inclusion of the sound j in the diphthong ju in the word *use.*

Can you hear the difference between the vowels in *few* and *flew?* In *mew* and *moo?*

The diphthong ɑʊ as in *out*

The diphthong ɑʊ. Now here we have two symbols that look as if they stood for the diphthong as in *out,* and they do!

To make the sounds part the lips for ɑ as in *arm;* then quickly round the lips for ʊ as in *foot.* The resulting blend is the diphthong ɑʊ. See how smoothly you can shift from ɑ to ʊ as you try again to form the diphthong ɑʊ. Some persons substitute the sound æ for ɑ as in *arm.* As a result, the word *cow* (kou) is pronounced (kă' o͞o), a form that should be avoided.

NOTE. The diphthong ɑʊ is consistently spelled with the letters *ou* as in *out* or *ow* as in *cow.*

The diphthong ɔɪ as in *oil*

The diphthong ɔɪ. Here we have another diphthong whose symbols look as if they stood for the blend ɔɪ as in *oil*—and sure enough they do. To make the blend round the lips and draw them down slightly for ɔ as in *often;* then quickly spread the lips for ɪ as in *it.* The resulting blend is ɔɪ. See how smoothly you can shift from ɔ to ɪ as you try again to form the diphthong ɔɪ.

NOTE. The diphthong ɔɪ is consistently spelled with the letters *oi* as in *oil* or *oy* as in *boy.*

JUST FOR FUN

ju me nɑu wɪʃ tu si ɪf ju kæn mek ðə rɑrt tʃɔɪs bɪtwin (a) ænd (b) in ðə fɔlowɪŋ stetmɛnts.

*AN INFORMAL TEST**

WHICH ONE IS IT?

1. A vowel is (a) an organ of speech; (b) a speech sound.
2. If in speaking the outgoing breath stream is obstructed by the organs of speech, the resulting sound is (a) a vowel; (b) a consonant.
3. Every vowel sound in the English language is (a) a voiced sound; (b) a voiceless sound.
4. The sounds w and j may be classed as semivowels because (a) the vocal cords vibrate when uttering the sounds; (b) of the slight interference with the outgoing breath in uttering the sounds.
5. The quality of a vowel sound is determined by the shape of the (a) resonance chamber in forming the sound; (b) vocal cords.
6. In uttering the sound o the breath stream is (a) unobstructed by the organs of speech; (b) completely obstructed by the organs of speech.
7. The vowel sound in *said* is the same as the vowel sound in (a) *sail;* (b) *sell;* (c) *seal.*
8. The vowel sound i in *feet* is the tense form of the vowel (a) ɪ in *fit;* (b) ɛ in *fed.*
9. The vowel sound e in *bake* is the tense form of the vowel (a) æ in *bag;* (b) ɛ in *beg.*
10. The sound ʊ in *pull* is the lax form of the vowel u in (a) *pool;* (b) ʌ in *but.*
11. The term *schwa* is (a) just another name for the breve; (b) the name for the symbol (ə).

* Answers are listed under the appropriate chapter number in the Appendix.

12. A diphthong is a blend of (a) two vowel letters; (b) two vowel sounds.

13. The sound ɔ: as in *horse* is (a) always followed by the letter *r;* (b) sometimes followed by the letter *r.*

14. The sound ɛ: as in *care* is (a) always followed by the letter *r;* (b) only sometimes followed by *r.*

15. The sound ə as in *bird* is (a) sometimes followed by the letter *r;* (b) always followed by the letter *r.*

16. The vowel sound u is heard (a) in the spoken words *rude* and *use;* (b) only in the word *rude.*

17. The letter *u* in *mule* stands for (a) a single vowel sound; (b) the diphthong ju.

18. The letter *i* in *kite* stands for (a) a single vowel sound; (b) the diphthong aɪ.

19. The diphthong ɔɪ as in *soil* is (a) consistently spelled *oi* or *oy;* (b) *oi* or *ou.*

20. The diphthong aʊ as in *ouch* is (a) consistently spelled *ou* or *ew;* (b) *ou* or *ow.*

21. The phonetic symbol j indicates the first sound in the word (a) *just;* (b) *you.*

22. The sound ə is the (a) lax form of the sound ʌ as in *cup;* (b) the tense form of the sound ʌ.

23. The vowel sound in *horse* is (a) the same as the vowel sound in *all;* (b) different from the vowel sound in *all.*

24. A diphthong (a) does not always consist of two sounds; (b) always consists of two vowel sounds.

9

THE VOWELS IN THEIR
RELATION TO PHONICS

We found in our study of the consonants that the same letter may stand for a number of different sounds and that the same sound may be represented by a surprising number of different letters. But a study of the speech sounds in the reading vocabulary shows an even greater irregularity among the vowels than we found among the consonants (Chapter 7). Note, for example, the letter-to-sound relationship in the words *busy, bury, burn, but,* and *bulls.* In pronouncing the words one hears five different vowel sounds, and the sounds are all spelled alike, although they are not even related to one another. In the sound-to-letter relationship of the vowels one finds an even greater discrepancy.

Note, for example, the different spellings for the sound (ü) as in the words *truth, blew, blue, rule, fruit, shoes, juice, to, too, two, you, through, whose,* and *route.*

It is understandable that teachers (even those considerably better informed than the young man who said that he didn't know one phonic from another) have difficulty in teaching phonics and that an intelligent teacher like Mrs. Brown in Chapter 1 was confused between the diphthongs in the words *owl, brown, cow, clown,* and *growl* and the so-called digraphs in the words *snow, grown, flow, low,* and *blow.*

SOUND AND LETTER
RELATIONSHIP OF VOWELS

We found in our study of the consonants that agreement or the lack of it between the sounds and their letter symbols was not the same for all consonants. We shall find that what is true of the consonants in this respect is also true of the vowels in the English language. Some vowel sounds are represented by a far greater variety of letters than others and some letters stand for a greater number of different sounds than others. It should be interesting to note the degree of variability among the vowels in the reading vocabulary.

This study will begin with the sound-to-letter relationship and then proceed to the letter-to-sound relationship of the vowels. In studying the vowels in their relation to phonics, one must keep in mind the distinction between letters that are seen in the written word and the sounds one hears when the word is spoken.

NOTE. You will find that the Thorndike-Barnhart symbols are used throughout the chapter for indicating the sounds of the letters, except when it seemed advisable to use the breve to indicate the so-called "short" vowel sound.

Different Letters for the Same Sound

The vowel sound (ā)

The so-called "long a" is represented by ten different letters and combinations of letters in the reading vocabulary, as shown by these examples:

a-e as in cake (kāk)	*ei* as in veins (vānz)
a as in ba'by (bā'bi)	*eigh* as in eight (āt)
ai as in train (trān)	*aigh* as in straight (strāt)
ay as in play (plā)	*ey* as in they (t̶h̶ā)
ea as in break (brāk)	*au* as in gauge (gāj)

Although the sound (ā) is spelled in ten different ways, it is regularly represented by:

1. *a-e* as in *cake, made, safe'ty, mis·take', space*
2. The single vowel *a* in open, accented syllables as in *ba'by, ra'di·o, pa'per, na'vy, sla'ver·y, re·la'tion*
3. *ai* as in *train, hail, trail'er, sail'or, rail'road*
4. *ay* as in *play, cray'ons, gray, birth'day.*

NOTE. The letters *a-e* represent the so-called "long a," except in the words *have* and *bade;* the letters *ai* represent the "long a" except in *said* and *plaid;* and the letters *ay* stand for the "long a" except in unaccented syllables as in *Sun'day.*

The vowel sound (ă)

The so-called "short a" has four different spellings.

a as in hat (hăt)	*ai* as in plaid (plăd)
a-e as in have (hăv)	*au* as in laugh (lăf)[1]

The "short a" is regularly represented by the letter *a* in closed syllables as in *flag, stand, glad, cap'sule, as'tro·naut, sat'el·lite,* and *at'oms.*

The vowel sound (ãr)

The sound (ãr) is represented by eight different letter combinations, as shown here:

air as in chair (chãr)	*ar* as in dar'ing (dãr'ing)
are as in care (kãr)	*eir* as in their (t̶h̶ãr)
ear as in bear (bãr)	*ayer* as in prayer (prãr)
ere as in where (hwãr)	*aire* as in millionaire (mil'yən·ãr')

Although the sound (ãr) has several different spellings, it is regularly represented by only three of them:

1. *air* as in *chair, stairs, fair, re·pair', af·fair'*
2. *are* as in *fare, share, care'ful, scared, com·pare'*
3. *ar* in accented syllables of words as in *dar'ing, shar'ing, star'ing, Po·lar'is, par'ing.*

NOTE. In every case the vowel (ã) is followed by (r), which gives the sound its characteristic quality.

[1] The word *laugh,* which is pronounced (läf) by many Americans, is pronounced with the "short a" in areas too large to be ignored.

The vowel sound (ä)

The sound (ä) is represented by eight different spellings, as shown by these examples:

a(r) as in farm (färm)	*au* as in laugh (läf)
a as in fath'er (fä̵th'ər)	*e*(r) as in sergeant (sär'jənt)
ah as in ah (ä)	*ea*(r) as in heart (härt)
ua(r) as in guard (gärd)	*a*(r)*e* as in large (lärj)

The sound (ä) is regularly represented by only two of its various spellings by:

1. *a*(*r*) as in *farm, arm, barn, gar'den, car'pen·ter, chart, dar'-ling, Kear'sarge, a·larm', dis·arm', Mars*
2. The single letter *a* as in *fath'er, palms, lla'ma, pe·cans', al'monds.*

NOTE. The letters *a*(*r*) represent the sound (ä) much more often than the single letter *a* in the children's reading vocabulary.

The vowel sound (ē)

The so-called "long e" exceeds the "long a" in the number of different letters that represent the sound in the children's reading vocabulary. Note the different spellings for the sound as shown by these examples.

ee as in bees (bēz)	*ei-e* as in seize (sēz)
ea as in meat (mēt)	*ie* as in field (fēld)
e as in e'ven (ē'vən)	*ie-e* as in piece (pēs)
ee-e as in geese (gēs)	*eo* as in peo'ple (pē'pəl)
ea-e as in leave (lēv)	*ey* as in key (kē)
e-e as in com·plete' (kəm·plēt')	*i-e* as in po·lice' (po·lēs')
e(*r*)*e* as in here (hēr)	*ei* as in re·ceive' (ri·sēv')

Although the sound (ē) is represented by so large an assortment of letters, it is most frequently spelled with:

1. The letters *ee* as in *bees, seen, free'dom, sleep, trees, street, beech, bee'tle, be·seech*
2. *ea* as in *meat, bea'ver, tea'pot, steam'ship, ea'gle, sea'sons, wea'sel, feast*

3. The single vowel *e* in the open accented syllables as in *e'ven, se'cret, fe'ver, ze'bra, re'cent·ly, he'ro, im·me'di·ate·ly.*

NOTE. The spelling *e-e* for the sound (ē) has a high frequency of occurrence in words of two or more syllables, but not in words of one syllable, except in proper nouns as in the name *Pete.*

The vowel sound (ĕ)

The so-called "short e" is spelled in ten different ways as shown by these examples:

e as in red (rĕd)	*ue* as in guess (gĕs)
ea as in bread (brĕd)	*a* as in any (ĕn'i)
ie as in friend (frĕnd)	*ai* as in said (sĕd)
eo as in leop'ard (lĕp'ərd)	*ay* as in says (sĕz)
e-e as in fence (fĕns)	*ei-e* as in leis'ure (lĕzh'ər)[2]

The sound (ĕ) is regularly represented by:

1. The single vowel *e* in closed syllables as in *red, get, bell, let'ters, spel'ling, pen'cils, den'tist*
2. The letters *ea* as in *bread, head, in·stead', health, weath'er, feath'ers, meas'ure, pleas'ant.*

The vowel sound (ī)

The so-called "long i," which is actually a diphthong, is treated in phonics as a single sound. It is represented by fifteen different spellings, as shown by the following examples.

I in the word I (ī)	*uy* as in buy (bī)
i-e as in kite (kīt)	*ui-e* as in guide (gīd)
i as in i'ron (ī'ərn)	*eye* as in eyes (īz)
ie as in tried (trīd)	*ye* as in rye (rī)
y as in fly (flī)	*y-e* as in style (stīl)
igh as in high (hī)	*ai-e* as in aisle (īl)
eigh as in height (hīt)	*aye* as in aye (ī)
oi(r) as in choir (kwīr)	

Although the "long i" is spelled in a surprising number of different ways, it is regularly represented by:

[2] The word *leisure* may be pronounced (lĕzh'ər) or (lē'zhər), depending upon the speaker.

1. *i-e* as in *kite, tires, fine, nine'ty, di·vide', de·cide', ex·cite', spine, de·fine'*

2. The single vowel *i* in an open, accented syllable as in *i'ron, ti'ger, ci'pher, u·ni'ted, gi'ant, bi'son, fi'nal·ly, di'a·monds, tri'-an·gle*

3. *ie* as in *tried, cried, re·plied', sup·plied', de·nied', re·lied, mul'ti·plied*

4. The letter *y* in accented syllables as in *fly, mul'ti·ply, re·ply', de·ny', dry, lul'la·by, sup·ply', ty'rant*

5. *igh* as in *high, sigh, night, flight, might'y, fright'ened, de·light'.*

NOTE. The letters *i-e* represent the "long i" except in the words *give* and *live* and in unaccented syllables as in *fer'tile* and *rep'tile.*

The vowel sound (ĭ)

Among the various vowel sounds in the English language, the "short i" is the most irregular in its sound-to-letter relationship. Note the variety of different spellings for the sound, especially in the unaccented syllables in the second column.

i as in sit (sĭt)	*ie* as in po'nies (pō'nĭz)
i-e as in give (gĭv)	*ea* as in guin'ea (gĭn'ĭ)
ie-e as in sieve (sĭv)	*ay* as in Sun'day (sŭn'dĭ)
e as in pret'ty (prĭt'ĭ)	*ia-e* as in car'riage (kăr'ĭj)
ee as in been (bĭn)	*a-e* as in sen'ate (sĕn'ĭt)
u as in bu'sy (bĭ'zĭ)	*e-e* as in priv'i·lege (prĭv·ə·lĭj)
ui as in build (bĭld)	*u-e* as in min'ute (mĭn'ĭt)
o as in wom'en (wĭm'ən)	*y* as in ba'by (bā'bĭ)
y as in cym'bals (sĭm'bəlz)	*ey* as in mon'ey (mŭn'ĭ)
e as in be·gin' (bĭ·gĭn')	*eig* as in for'eign (fŏr'ĭn)

The sound (ĭ) is regularly represented by the single vowel *i* in closed syllables as in *sit, kit'ty, chick, pig, swing, pic'ture, whis'-per, win'ter, ships.*

NOTE. Americans are inclined to assign the "long e" rather than the "short i" to the vowel in the unaccented syllable as in *ba'by, Sun'day,* and *mon'ey,* a tendency that is understandable in view of the phonetic relationship between the vowel sounds (ē) and (ĭ). (See "Phonetic Study of the Vowels," Chapter 8.)

It is of further interest in this connection to note that Webster's Third Edition assigns the "long e" to the vowel in the unstressed syllables as in *ba'by, Sun'day,* and *mon'ey.*

The vowel sound (ō)

The so-called "long o" ties with the "long e" in the variety of letter representations for the sound.

o-e as in bone (bōn)	*ou* as in shoul'der (shōl'dər)
o as in o'pen (ō'pən)	*ou(r)-e* as in course (kōrs)
ow as in snow (snō)	*oa(r)-e* as in coarse (kōrs)
oa as in boat (bōt)	*ou(r)* as in four (fōr)
oe as in toes (tōz)	*oo(r)* as in floor (flōr)
oa-e as in loaves (lōvz)	*ough* as in though (t̶h̶ō)
ew as in sew (sō)	*o(r)* as in porch (pōrch)

Only four of the fourteen different spellings for the sound (ō) may be said regularly to represent the sound:

1. *o-e* as in *bone, a·lone', poles, hole, home, close, rose, tones, sup·pose', joke*

2. The single vowel *o* as in *o'pen, lo'cust, so'lo·ist, sto'ry, o'cean, po'ny, mo'ments*

3. *ow* as in *snow, blow, flown, slow, nar'row, row, grown, spar'rows*

4. *oa* as in *boat, goat, float, toad, foam, coat, loaf, road.*

The vowel sound (ŏ)

The so-called "short o" has two different spellings:

o as in top (tŏp)   *a* as in want (wŏnt)

The "short o" is regularly represented by:

1. The letter *o* in closed syllables as in *top, clock, doc'tor, box'es, rock'ets, mon'ster, dolls, rob'in, for'est, pond*

2. The letter *a* before *w* as in *want, was, wash, wan'der, watch, wasp, wam'pum, wal'let.*

It seems ironic that the vowel sound that has the smallest number of different letters to represent it should have the greatest variety of pronunciations according to popular usage. Some speakers use a sound of "short o" that resembles the vowel sound in *arm,* others use a sound like the vowel in *all,* and still others use a sound that is anywhere between these two extremes.

The vowel sound (ô)

The sound (ô) is represented by eleven different letter combinations as shown by the following examples:

o(r) as in horn (hôrn)	*au* as in fault (fôlt)
aw as in saw (sô)	*o(r)-e* as in horse (hôrs)
a as in call (kôl)	*wo(r)* as in sword (sôrd)
a(r) as in warm (wôrm)	*ough* as in bought (bôt)
oa as in broad (brôd)	*augh* as in caught (kôt)
au-e as in be′cause (bĭ·kôz′)	

The sound (ô) is usually represented by:

1. The letter *o* when it is followed by *r* as in *horn, or, bor′der, or′bit·ing, storm, for, tor′toise, north, morn′ing, dor′mouse*

2. The letter *a* when followed by *w* as in *saw, claws, dawn, fawn, aw′ful, law, crawl, gnaw, draw*

3. The letter *a* when followed by *l* as in *call, wall, ball, al′ways, al·read′y, hall′way, wal′rus, salt*

NOTE. When the sound (ô) is followed by *r* it is spelled with the letter *o;* when it is spelled with the letter *a,* the letter is usually followed by *w* or *l.*

The diphthong (oi)

The diphthong (oi) is represented by three different letter representations as shown by the following examples:

oi as in oil (oil)	*oy* as in boys (boiz)
oi-e as in noise (noiz)	

The diphthong (oi) is represented regularly by:

1. The letters *oi* as in *oil, toil, coils, joints, oint′ment, moist, soil, mois′ture*

2. The letters *oy* as in *boys, toys, des·troy', em·ploy', en·joy', em·ploy'ment, roy'al, oy'sters*
3. The letters *oi-e* as in *noise, voice, re·joice', choice.*

NOTE. When the diphthong occurs at the end of a syllable, it is spelled *oy*, never *oi*. The frequency of occurrence of the diphthong is almost equally divided between the two spellings *oi* and *oy*.

The diphthong (ou)

The diphthong (ou) has twice as many different spellings as the diphthong (oi).

ou as in out (out)	*ou-e* as in house (hous)
ow as in cow (kou)	*ou(r)* as in flour (flour)
ow-e as in browse (brouz)	*ough* as in bough (bou)

The diphthong (ou) is regularly represented by:

1. The letters *ou* as in *out, cloud, mouth, moun'tain, proud, a·loud', ground, found, trou'sers, count'down, thou'sand*
2. The letters *ow* as in *cow, now, how, crown, frown, growl, pow'der, flow'er, tow'els, show'ers, brown, bow-wow.*

NOTE. The frequency of occurrence of the diphthong is almost equally divided between the two spellings *ou* and *ow* in the children's reading vocabulary.

The vowel sound (ū)

The so-called "long u," as we learned earlier, is actually a diphthong, although it is treated in phonics as a single sound. It is represented by eleven different letters and letter combinations, as shown here:

u-e as in mule (mūl)	*eu* as in neu'tral (nū'trəl)
u as in mu'sic (mū'zĭk)	*ewe* as in ewes (ūz)
u(r)e as in pure (pūr)	*eau* as in beau'tiful (bū'tĭ·fŭl)
ew as in few (fū)	*ieu* as in lieu·ten'ant (lū·ten'ənt)
ue as in Tues'day (tūz'dĭ)	*iew* as in view (vū)
ui as in suit (sūt)	

The so-called "long u" is regularly represented by:

1. The letters *u-e* as in *mule, tune, fuse, dis·pute', cap'sule, ex·cuse', in·tro·duce', a·muse'ments, sa·lute'*

2. The single vowel *u* in open, accented syllables as in *mu'sic, pu'pils, cu'cum·bers, op·por·tu'ni·ty, bu'gle, tu'lips, du'ty, su'per·in·ten·dent*

3. The letters *u(r)e* as in *pure, en·dure', cure, se·cure', pro··cure'*

4. The letters *ew* as in *few, new, stew, dew, mew.*

NOTE. It is significant to observe that in each of the examples the sound (ū) is preceded by a consonant other than *j, r, ch, sh,* or an *l* or *r* blend.

The vowel sound (ŭ)

The so-called "short u" is represented by six different letters or letter combinations, as shown here:

u as in cub (kŭb)	*ou* as in dou'ble (dŭ'b'l)
o as in son (sŭn)	*oo* as in flood (flŭd)
o-e as in done (dŭn)	*u-e* as in judge (jŭj)

The "short u" is regularly represented by:

1. The single vowel *u* in closed syllables as in *cub, up, sup'per, but'ter, buds, drum, ducks, lum'ber, stum'ble, plums, brush, hun'dred, pump'kin, hum, sum'mer, fun'ny, jump*

2. The letter *o* as in *son, won, noth'ing, don'key, moth'er, mon'key, won'der·ful, gov'ern·ment, a·mong'.*

The vowel sound (ü)

The sound (ü), the second most irregular of the vowel sounds in the children's reading vocabulary, is represented by seventeen different spellings, as shown by these examples:

oo as in food (füd)	*o-e* as in whose (hüz)
u as in truth (trüth)	*o* as in to (tü)
ew as in blew (blü)	*wo* as in two (tü)
ue as in blue (blü)	*ou* as in you (yü)
u-e as in rule (rül)	*eu* as in rheu·ma'tic (rü·mă'tĭk)

oo-e as in goose (güs) *ough* as in through (thrü)
ui as in fruit (früt) *ooe* as in mooed (müd)
ui-e as in juice (jüs) *ou-e* as in route (rüt)
oe as in shoes (shüz)

The sound (ü) is most frequently represented by:

1. The letters *oo* as in *food, too, tooth, moon, soon, spoon, school, rac·coon', ba·boon', roos'ter, boos'ter*
2. The letter *u* as in *truth, tru'ly, ru'ined, flu'id, ru'ler, Ju·ly', Ju'pi·ter, cru'el*
3. The letters *ew* as in *blew, flew, drew, jew'els, crew, grew, chew*.

NOTE 1. It is significant to observe that in each of the examples in which the letters *u* and *ew* say (ü), the sound is preceded either by *j, r, ch,* or an *l* or *r* blend.

NOTE 2. Students often find it difficult to distinguish between the vowel sound (ü) as in *flew* and the "long u" as in *few;* or the sound (ü) in *rule* and the "long u" in *mule.* Confusion between the sounds (ü) and the diphthong (ū) is understandable, since (ü) is one of the elements in the diphthong (ū); (ĭ + ü = ū).

The vowel sound (u̇)

The sound (u̇), which is sometimes called the short form of (ü), is represented by only six different spellings, as compared with seventeen for the sound (ü):

oo as in foot (fu̇t) *ou(r)* as in your (yu̇r)
u as in put (pu̇t) *u(r)* as in hur·rah' (hu̇·rô')
ou as in could (ku̇d) *o* as in wolf (wu̇lf)

The sound (u̇) is most frequently represented by:

1. The letters *oo* as in *foot, good, book, look, stood, un'der-- stood, shook, text'book*
2. The letter *u* as in *put, pull, push, pud'ding, full, bull'frog, bul'le·tin.*

NOTE 1. The words in which the letters *oo* say (u̇) are greatly outnumbered by the one- and two-syllable words in which *oo* say (ü) in the children's reading vocabulary.

NOTE 2. The sound (ů) as in *put* is often confused with the "short u" in *but,* perhaps because the two sounds are spelled alike.

The vowel sound (ėr)

The sound (ėr) is represented by twelve different letter combinations in the children's reading vocabulary, as shown by these examples:

ur as in burst (bėrst)	*or-e* as in worse (wėrs)
er as in her (hėr)	*our* as in jour′ney (jėr′nĭ)
ir as in bird (bėrd)	*olo* as in colo′nel (kėr′nəl)
or as in work (wėrk)	*eur* as in am′a·teur′ (ăm·ə·tėr′)
ere as in were (wėr)	*ear* as in heard (hėrd)
ur-e as in nurse (nėrs)	*urr* as in purr (pėr)

The sound (ėr) is regularly represented by:

1. *ur* as in *burst, hurt, turn, hur′ry, cur′tain, sur′face, hur′ri-·cane, pur′pose, fur′ni·ture*
2. *er* as in *her, herd, berth, ver′ses, ser′vants, Mer′cu·ry*
3. *ir* as in *bird, third, girl, whirl, cir′cle, squirm, cir·cus, squir′rel, cir·cum′fer·ence.*

NOTE. In every case the vowel (ė) is followed by (r), which gives the sound its characteristic quality. When the sound (ėr) is spelled *or,* it is preceded by (w), as in *work, word, worm, worth, wor′ship, wor′ry, worst.*

The vowel sound (ə)

The sound (ə) is represented by fifteen different letters and letter combinations in the unaccented syllables of words, as shown by these examples.

a as in a·bout′ (ə·bout′)	*io* as in fash′ion (făsh′ən)
o as in at′om (ăt′əm)	*oa* as in cup′board (kŭ′bərd)
u as in cir′cus (sėr′kəs)	*eo* as in sur′geon (sėr′jən)
e(r) as in fath′er (fäthər)	*ro* as in i′ron (ī′ərn)
o(r) as in doc′tor (dŏk′tər)	*y* as in mar′tyr (mär′tər)
a(r) as in dol′lar (dŏl′ər)	*oi-e* as in tor′toise (tôr′təs)
u(r) as in Sat′urn (săt′ərn)	*re* as in a′cres (ā′kərz)
i(r) as in ta′pir (tā′pər)	

Different Sounds for the Same Letter

In your observation of the various letters that stand for the same sound you may have been surprised to find that the so-called "short i" is spelled twenty different ways. But we shall now see that the letter-to-sound relationship of the vowels shows an even greater degree of irregularity than the sound-to-letter relationship.

Tables 4–8 show the various sounds each of the vowels represents singly and in combination with the letters that accompany the vowel in the reading vocabulary.

Table 4.   The Letter A

Letters	Sound	Example	Letters	Sound	Example
a	(ā)	ba′by	aw	(ô)	saw
a	(a)	cap			
a	(o)	want	are	(ãr)	care
a	(ô)	call			
a	(ä)	fath′er	air	(ãr)	chair
a	(ə)	a·bout′			
			a(r)	(ə)	dol′lar
a-e	(ā)	cake	a(r)	(ô)	warm
a-e	(a)	have	a(r)	(ä)	car
a-e	(i)	sen′ate	a(r)	(ãr)	dar′ing
ai	(ā)	train			
ai	(a)	plaid	a(r)e	(ä)	large
ai	(e)	said			
ai	(ə)	moun′tain	ayer	(ãr)	prayer
ai-e	(ī)	aisle	au	(ô)	as′tro·naut
			au	(ä)	laugh
ay	(ā)	play	au	(a)	laugh
ay	(i)	Sun′day			
ay	(e)	says	au-e	(ô)	be·cause′
ay-e	(ī)	aye	augh	(ô)	caught
			aigh	(ā)	straight

NOTE. The various vowel sounds for the letter *a* singly and in combination with the letters associated with it are represented by sixteen different spellings in the reading vocabulary.

Table 5.   The Letter E

Letters	Sound	Example	Letters	Sound	Example
e	(ē)	e'ven	ear	(ėr)	heard
e	(e)	bed	ear	(ãr)	bear
e	(i)	pret'ty			
e	(ə)	si'lent	ea(r)	(ē)	hear
			ea(r)	(ä)	heart
e-e	(ē)	com·plete'			
e-e	(e)	fence	ere	(ãr)	where
			ere	(ėr)	were
ee	(ē)	bees			
ee	(i)	been	eir	(ãr)	their
ee-e	(ē)	geese	ei	(ā)	veins
			ei	(ē)	lei'zure
ea	(ē)	beast			
ea	(e)	bread	ei-e	(ē)	re·ceive
ea	(ā)	break			
ea	(i)	guin'ea	eigh	(ā)	eight
			eigh	(ī)	height
ea-e	(ē)	leave			
			eo	(ē)	peo'ple
er	(ėr)	her	eo	(e)	leop'ard
			eo	(ə)	sur'geon
e(r)	(ä)	ser'geant			
e(r)	(ə)	fath'er	eu	(ū)	neu'tral
ew	(ü)	blew	eau	(ū)	beau'ty
ew	(ū)	few			
ew	(ō)	sew	eur	(ėr)	am·ə·teur'
ewe	(ū)	ewes	eig	(ə)	for'eign·er
			eye	(ī)	eyes
ey	(ā)	they			
ey	(ē)	key			
ey	(ī)	mon'key			

NOTE. The various vowel sounds for the letter *e* singly and in combination with the letters associated with it are represented by twenty-three different spellings in the reading vocabulary.

Table 6. The Letter I

Letters	Sound	Example	Letters	Sound	Example
i	(ī)	ti′ger	ie-e	(ē)	piece
i	(i)	pig	ie-e	(i)	sieve
			ia-e	(i)	car′riage
i-e	(ī)	kite			
i-e	(i)	give	ir	(ėr)	bird
i-e	(ē)	po·lice′	i(r)	(ə)	ta′pir
i-e	(i)	rep′tile			
			igh	(ī)	high
ie	(ī)	tried			
ie	(ē)	field	io	(ə)	fash′ion
ie	(e)	friend			
ie	(i)	ba′bies	iew	(ū)	view
			ieu	(ū)	lieu·ten′ant

NOTE. The various vowel sounds for the letter *i* singly and in combination with the letters that are associated with it have nine different spellings.

Table 7. The Letter U

Letters	Sound	Example	Letters	Sound	Example
u	(ū)	mu′sic	ui	(ü)	fruit
u	(u)	cub	ui	(ū)	suit
u	(ů)	put	ui	(i)	build
u	(ə)	cir′cus			
			ui-e	(ü)	juice
u-e	(ū)	tune	ui-e	(ī)	guide
u-e	(ü)	rule			
u-e	(u)	judge	ur	(ėr)	burn
u-e	(i)	min′ute	u(r)	(ə)	Sat′urn
ue	(ū)	due	ur-e	(ėr)	nurse
ue	(ü)	blue			
ue	(e)	guess	urr	(ėr)	purr
			uy	(ī)	buy
			ua	(ä)	guard

NOTE. The various vowel sounds for the letter *u* singly and in combination with the letters associated with it are represented by ten different spellings.

Table 8. The Letter O

Letters	Sound	Example	Letters	Sound	Example
o	(o)	top	ou-e	(ou)	house
o	(ō)	o'pen	ou-e	(ü)	route
o	(ü)	to			
o	(ù)	wo'man	oe	(ō)	toes
o	(i)	wo'men	oe	(ü)	shoes
o	(u)	son			
o	(ə)	at'om	or	(ėr)	work
o-e	(ō)	bone	o(r)	(ô)	horn
o-e	(u)	done	o(r)	(ō)	porch
o-e	(ü)	whose	o(r)	(o)	or'ange
			o(r)	(ə)	doc'tor
oa	(ō)	boat			
oa	(ô)	broad	or-e	(ėr)	worse
oa(r)	(ō)	oars	o(r)e	(o)	fore'head
oa(r)	(ə)	cup'board	o(r)-e	(ô)	horse
oo	(ü)	food	our	(ėr)	jour'ney
oo	(ù)	foot			
oo	(u)	flood	ou(r)	(ù)	your
			ou(r)	(ou)	flour
oo(r)	(ō)	floor	ou(r)	(ō)	four
oo-e	(ü)	goose	ou(r)e	(ō)	course
			ou(r)e	(ō)	coarse
ow	(ō)	snow			
ow	(ou)	cows	ooe	(ü)	mooed
ow-e	(ou)	browse	Oh	(ō)	Oh
ou	(ou)	loud	olo	(ėr)	ker'nel
ou	(ù)	could			
ou	(u)	dou'ble	ough	(ō)	though
			ough	(ü)	through
oy	(oi)	boys	ough	(ô)	thought
oy	(oi)	oil	ough	(ou)	bough
			ough	(ôf)	cough
oi-e	(oi)	noise	ough	(up)	hiccough
oi-e	(ə)	tor'toise			
			oi(r)	(ī)	choir

NOTE. The table shows the most irregular of the vowels in its letter-to-sound relationship. The various vowel sounds for the letter *o* singly and in combination with the letters associated with it are represented by twenty-six different spellings in the reading vocabulary.

A study of the letter-to-sound relationship of the unique vowel *o* shows that:

1. the letter *o* by itself stands for seven different vowel sounds. It represents the sound (ŏ) in *top,* (ō) in *o'pen,* (ù) in *wom'an,* (ĭ) in *wo'men,* (ü) in *to,* (ŭ) in *son,* and (ə) in *at'om.*

2. the letters o-e stand for the "long o" in *bone,* the "short u" in *done,* and for (ü) in *whose.*

3. in association with *r* the letter *o* is pronounced (ō) in *porch,* (ô) in *horn,* (ŏ) in *or'ange;* and when *or* is preceded by (w) the resulting sound is (ėr) as in *work.*

4. in association with *a,* the letter *o* is pronounced (ō) as in *boat,* (ô) as in *broad,* and (ə) as in *cup'board.*

5. the letters *oo* stand for (ü) in *food,* (ù) in *foot,* and although much less frequently, for (ŭ) in *flood;* and in association with (r) the letters *oo* give us the "long o" in *floor.*

6. the letters *ou(r)* stand for the sound (ù) in *your,* (ō) in *four,* and for the diphthong (ou) in *flour.*

7. the letters *ow* give us the diphthong (ou) as in *cow,* as well as the "long o" in *snow.*

8. the letters *ou* give us the same diphthong as the letters *ow,* as well as (ù) in *could* and the "short u" in *dou'ble.*

9. in association with *i* and *y* the letter *o* stands for the diphthong (oi) as in *oil* and *boys;* and with *i* and *r* the letter *o* stands for the "long i" in *choir.*

10. in association with *lo,* the letters *olo* stand for (ėr) as in *colo'nel!*

11. in association with *ugh,* the letter *o* represents the "long o" in *though,* (ô) in *thought,* (ü) in *through,* (ou) in *bough,* (ôf) in *cough,* and (ŭp) in *hic'cough.*

12. with or without the help of the silent *h,* the letter *O* represents a complete word!

What a letter, remarkable for its versatility if for nothing else!

INCONTROVERTIBLE FACTS[1]

No monk too good to rob, or cog, or plot.
No fool so gross to bolt Scotch collops hot.
From Donjon tops no Oronoko rolls.
Logwood, not Lotos, floods Oporto's bowls.
Troops of old tosspots oft, to sot, consort.
Box tops, not bottoms, school-boys flog for sport.
No cool monsoons blow soft on Oxford dons,

[1] Charles Carroll Bombaugh, *Oddities and Curiosities of Words and Literature* (New York, Dover Publications, Inc.).

Orthodox, jog-trot, book-worm Solomons!
Bold Ostrogoths, of ghosts no horror show.
On London shop-fronts no hop-blossoms grow.
To crocks of gold no dodo looks for food.
On soft cloth footstools no old fox doth brood.
Long storm-tost sloops forlorn, work on to port.
Rooks do not roost on spoons, nor woodcocks snort,
Nor dog on snow-drop or on coltsfoot rolls
Nor common frogs consort long protocols.

GENERALIZATIONS

1.   A single vowel in a closed accented syllable has its "short" sound unless it is influenced by some other sound in the syllable. The consonants that most frequently affect the vowel sounds in the syllable are (r), (l), and (w).

2.   A single vowel in an open, accented syllable is usually "long."

3.   The letter *e* at the end of an accented syllable usually shows that the preceding vowel has its "long" sound.

4.   The "long e" represented by the letters *e-e* rarely occurs in monosyllabic words other than proper nouns.

5.   The letter *o* is the most irregular of all the vowels in its letter-to-sound relationship, in that it has the highest number of different spellings to represent the various vowel sounds for which the letter stands.

6.   The letter *o* singly and in combination with the letters associated with it represents all but seven of the vowel sounds in the children's reading vocabulary.

7.   The letter *e* is the runner-up in its letter-to-sound relationship, having twenty-three different spellings to represent the sounds as compared to the letter *o*'s twenty-six different spellings.

8.   Interestingly enough, the letters *o* and *e* represent the same number of different vowel sounds, and both lack only seven of the different vowel sounds in their letter-to-sound representations in the reading vocabulary.

9.   The letter *a* by itself stands for as many as seven different vowel sounds, including the sound (à) as indicated in *Webster's New International Dictionary*, Second Edition. The letter *a* represents the sound (ā) in *bā'by*, (ă) in *cap*, (ŏ) in *want*, (ô) in *call*, (ä) in *fath'er*, (à) in *ask*, and (ə) in *a·bout'*.

10. The various vowel sounds for the letter *a* singly and in combination with the letters associated with it are represented by sixteen different spellings in the reading vocabulary.

11. The letter *u* singly stands for four different vowel sounds and the letter *i* alone for only two different vowel sounds; the various sounds for the letter *u,* when taken singly and in combination with the letters associated with it are represented by ten different spellings in the reading vocabulary.

12. The vowels *u, ue, u-e, ui,* and *ew* stand for the "long u" except when preceded by *j, r, sh, ch,* or any of the *l* and *r* blends, in which cases they regularly stand for the sound (ü).

13. The sound (ĭ) is the most irregular of all the vowels in its sound-to-letter relationship, in that it is spelled twenty different ways in the children's reading vocabulary.

14. The sound (ü) is the "runner up" in its sound-to-letter relationship, having seventeen different letters and letter combinations to represent it as compared with twenty different spellings for the sound (ĭ).

15. Of all the vowel sounds the so-called "short o" has the fewest number of different letters to represent it in the reading vocabulary.

16. The letters *u-e* stand for the "long u" more frequently than for the sound (ü); and the letters *ue* represent the sound (ü) oftener than the "long u" in the children's reading vocabulary.

17. The sound (ə) is represented by as many as fifteen different letters or combinations of letters in the reading vocabulary.

AN INFORMAL TEST*

WHICH ONE IS IT?

1. A study of the speech sounds in the children's reading vocabulary shows (a) a greater degree of irregularity among the vowels than among the consonants; (b) a lesser degree of irregularity.

2. In its sound-to-letter relationship the sound (ü) has (a) a greater number of different spellings to represent it than the sound (ā); (b) a smaller number of different spellings.

* Answers are listed under the appropriate chapter number in the Appendix.

3. The letter *o* is the (a) most irregular of all the vowels in the reading vocabulary in its letter-to-sound relationship; (b) least irregular.

4. A single vowel in an open, accented syllable usually represents the (a) so-called "long" sound of the vowel; (b) "short" sound of the vowel.

5. The sound (ə) occurs more often in (a) accented syllables of words; (b) unaccented syllables of words.

6. The diphthong (oi) is (a) rarely represented by the letters *oi* or *oy;* (b) regularly represented by the letters *oi* and *oy.*

7. The diphthong (ou) is (a) regularly represented by the letters *ou* or *ow;* (b) almost never represented by *ou* or *ow.*

8. The letters *ow* (a) always represent the sound (ō); (b) sometimes represent the sound (ō).

9. The letters *ea* sometimes represent (a) the vowel sound (ĕ); (b) always represent the vowel sound (ĕ).

10. The vowel sounds in the accented syllables of the words *colo′nel* and *Mer′cu•ry* are (a) entirely different; (b) identical.

11. The sound (ī) is (a) usually represented by the single vowel *i* in an open, accented syllable; (b) seldom so represented.

12. The letter-to-sound relationship of the letter *o* is (a) exactly the same as the sound-to-letter relationship of the letter *o;* (b) not the same.

13. The vowels in the word *few* represent (a) a single vowel sound; (b) two vowel sounds.

14. The letters *u, ue, ui,* and *ew* when preceded by (j), (r), or (ch) represent the (a) vowel sound (ū); (b) vowel sound (ü).

15. The vowel sound (ü) is (a) represented by the letters *a* and *i* in the children's reading vocabulary; (b) never spelled by *a* or *i.*

16. The vowel sound (ä) is (a) spelled by the letters *e(r), ea(r)* and *ua(r)* in the reading vocabulary; (b) never spelled by these letters.

17. The vowel sound (ē) is (a) represented by the letters *ea, ei, eo,* and *ey* in the reading vocabulary; (b) never spelled with these letters.

18. The letter-to-sound relationship of any given vowel is (a) always the same as the sound-to-letter relationship of the vowel; (b) never the same.

19. The sound (ī) having twenty different spellings in the children's reading vocabulary is the (a) most irregular of all the vowels in its sound-to-letter relationship; (b) least irregular.

20. The letter *i* is (a) the most irregular of all the vowels in its letter-to-sound relationship; (b) among the least irregular.

10

THE SYLLABICATION
OF WORDS

We should now be ready for the operation of dividing words into syllables and for the rules that govern syllabication. This chapter will discuss the influence of stress or accent on the vowels in the syllables and on connected discourse as well as on the prefixes and suffixes in words, and the significance of the open and closed syllables in the reading vocabulary.

All this is not nearly so difficult as it may sound. Indeed, if much of what has gone before was new to you, you may now find yourself on more familiar ground.

It has already been shown that when a word has more than one vowel or diphthong the word can be divided into its parts or components; that one or more vowel sounds may be assigned to each of the parts; and that these parts are known as syllables. The word *won'der*, for example, has two syllables; *won'der·ful·ly* has four syllables. We have also seen that every syllable has one vowel sound, unless the vowel is a diphthong, in which case the syllable has two vowel sounds. In the words *cloud'y, boil'ing*, and *flow'er*, for example, one can see the vowels that give the syllables their vowel sounds. But not every syllable in an English word has a vowel that gives the syllable its vowel sound. Take, for example, the unaccented syllables in these two words:

lit'tle (lit″l)   gar'den (gar'd'n)

There is no vowel letter for the sound in the unaccented syllables in these words. The vowel quality is supplied by the consonant (l) in the word (lit″l) and by the consonant (n) in the word (gar′d′n). When the consonants (l) and (n) function as vowels, they are capable of forming a syllable entirely by themselves; hence they are known as syllabic consonants. The consonant (m) as in the words rhythm (rith′m) and chasm (kaz′m) may also be regarded as a syllabic consonant.

The phonetic symbols for the syllabic consonants are indicated in these transcriptions:

little (lɪtḷ)   garden (gɑrdṇ)   rhythm (rɪðṃ)

Let us now see what we can learn about the syllabication of words.

DIVIDING WORDS INTO SYLLABLES

The Dictionary's Way of Showing Syllabication

The dictionary shows the syllables into which a given word may be divided. It indicates where the break comes between the syllables when the word is written and when the word is spoken. The spoken word follows directly after the written word and is always enclosed in parentheses (   ) or within the slant lines \   \, as in Webster's Third Edition.

The syllabication of the spoken word may or may not coincide with the way the word is divided when the word is written. The simple word *selfish* offers an example. When writing the word, it is correctly divided as *self'ish,* but the spoken word is (*sel'fish*).

In a word of three or more syllables the division between the syllables is indicated by a dot (·), except where the dividing point is indicated by the accent mark as in *self'ish·ness, ge·og'ra·phy,* and *a·rith'me·tic.*

NOTE. In Webster's Third Edition the accent mark is placed before the accented syllable, and the division between the syllables is indicated by a hyphen (-).

The accent mark serves a double purpose: (1) it indicates which syllable or syllables in the word are accented or stressed when the word is spoken and (2) it serves the same purpose as the dot or hyphen between the syllables of the word.

In a polysyllabic word with more than one accented syllable, a heavy accent mark (′) is used to show the syllable that has the primary or stronger accent and a light mark (′) is used to indicate the syllable that has the secondary or lighter accent when the word is spoken, as in the words *in′ter·rupt′* and *ge′o·graph′i·cal·ly*, for example. In Webster's Third Edition the secondary accent is indicated by placing the mark in a lower position as in the word *interrupt* \ˌint-ə′rupt\.

Rules for Syllabication

Teachers have reported that they have often found the rules for syllabication helpful in dividing words into syllables. Unfortunately these rules too, like most rules, have their exceptions. Even so, it should be a profitable experience to examine and evaluate the rules for syllabication in terms of the cases to which the rules apply.

WHEN THERE IS ONE CONSONANT BETWEEN THE VOWELS

Upon looking closely at the words in the following list you will find that there is one consonant between two vowels in each of the words and that the consonant occurs either with the vowel that follows the consonant or the vowel that precedes it in the syllabified word.

Unless you already know the answer, it might be interesting before reading the rule to discover what determined the placement of the consonant with reference to the vowels in syllabifying the words in the list.

he′ro	her′o·ine	ra′dar	rad′i·cal	rock′ets
fa′mous	fam′i·ly	sta′tion	stat′ues	grav′i·ty
na′tion	nat′ur·al	pe′ri·od	per′il	cour′age
pi′lot	pic′a·dor	po′lar	pop′u·lar	mon′ey
Ve′nus	vet′er·an	de′cent	dec′i·mals	cov′er
me′di·um	med′i·care	ro′bot	rob′in	fath′er

The rule. When there is one consonant between two vowel sounds, the consonant usually goes with the next syllable, if the preceding vowel is "long," and with the preceding syllable if the vowel is "short" or has a sound other than "long."

NOTE. Words like *sail'or, jok'ing, div'er,* and *lat'est* are not subject to the rule and may not be regarded as exceptions, since the root word retains its identity when the suffix is added.

WHEN THERE ARE TWO OR MORE CONSONANTS
BETWEEN THE VOWELS

In the next list of syllabified words you will find that there are two or more consonants between the vowels in each of the words. It might be an interesting experience, before reading the rule, to see what determined the placement of the consonants with reference to the vowels in the syllabified words in the list.

se'cret	sec're·tar·y	tel'star	as'tro·naut
pro'gram	prog'ress	cap'sule	ther·mom'e·ter
o·blige'	ob'li·gate	his'to·ry	cir·cum'fer·ence
ta'ble	tab'let	stron'ti·um	at'mos·phere
fre'quent	frac'tions	per'fect	ob·struc'tion
fra'grant	frag'ments	mi'cro·phone	bac·te'ri·a

The rule. When there are two or more consonants between the vowels in a word all the consonants go with the next vowel, if the preceding vowel is "long"; if the vowel is not "long," the first consonant stays with the preceding syllable and the others go with the following syllable.

WHEN THE CONSONANTS BETWEEN THE VOWELS ARE IDENTICAL

The next list shows the syllabication of words having two identical consonants between the vowel sounds:

bal·lis'tic	ap·proach'	ac·count'	sug·gest'
mis'siles	flut'ter	sum'mer	run'ning
strug'gle	hud'dle	whin'ny	shuf'fle
ac'ci·dent	con·nect'	rub'bers	puz'zling

The rule. When there are two identical consonants between the vowel sounds the word is divided between the consonants.

NOTE. Words like *guess'ing, putt'er, fuss'i·ness,* and *stuff'y* are not subject to the rule and may not be regarded as exceptions, since the root word remains unchanged when the suffix is added.

WHEN EACH OF TWO ADJACENT VOWELS FORMS A SYLLABLE

The following list of words presents what might be called another interesting example of syllabication. In each case the division comes between two adjacent vowels in the word:

ru′in	nu′cle·ar	gi′ant	fi′er·y
du′el	her′o·ine	nu′cle·us	pi·a′no
cre·ate′	fu′el	Su·ez′	po′et·ry
flu′id	qui′et	ge·og′ra·phy	re′al·ly
li′ons	co·in·cide′	co·op′er·ate	

The rule. When each of two vowels in a word forms a separate syllable, the word is divided between the vowels.

WHEN THE WORD IS A COMPOUND WORD

We have now come to another group of words, a relatively large group in the children's reading vocabulary and one which should be relatively easy to syllabify:

count′down	or′bit	rat′tle·snake	hon′ey·bee
Red′stone	flag′pole	cop′per·head	tooth′brush
Sky′bolt	sun′set	flash′light	bath′robe
fall′out	rain′bow	thun′der·storm	down′stairs

The rule. When a word is composed of two complete words, the word is divided between the words in the compound word.

NOTE. It is not intended that children should be taught the textbook rules for syllabication until after they have stated the rules in their own words, based on their observation of a sufficiently large number of syllabified words in each of the following categories: (1) words having one consonant between two vowels; (2) words having two or more consonants between the vowels; (3) when the consonants between the vowels are identical; (4) when there are two adjacent vowels between the consonants; and (5) when the words are compound words.

CLASSIFICATION OF SYLLABLES

Syllables may be classified (1) as open or closed and (2) as accented or unaccented. Whether a syllable is open or closed depends upon the sound with which the syllable ends, whether with a vowel or a consonant sound. You have already had considerable experience with open and closed, accented and unaccented, syllables on the preceding pages of the chapter. We shall now see if we can broaden our experience on these topics, beginning with open syllables of words.

Open Syllables

A syllable that ends with a vowel sound is known as an open syllable. There is at least one open syllable in each of the words in the following list, and in some words there are as many as three open syllables. You will observe, too, that a single vowel may constitute a syllable and that the vowel in the open syllable is "long" when the syllable is accented.

se′cret	to·ma′to	po′nies	fre′quent
sta′tion	po·ta′to	ti′ger	o·bey′
sea′sons	vol·ca′no	ea′gles	o·be′di·ent
free′dom	tor·na′do	sto′ries	ra·di·a′tion

The rule. When an open syllable is accented, the vowel in the syllable is usually "long."

NOTE. There are fifteen unaccented, open syllables in the following list of words and the vowels in these syllables do not have the "long" vowel sound:

di·vis′i·ble	ca′pa·bil′i·ty	mul′ti·pli·ca′tion
o′be′di·ent·ly	jus′ti·fi·ca′tion	re·spon′si·bil′i·ty

Closed Syllables

A syllable that ends with a consonant sound is known as a closed syllable. In the following list there is at least one closed syllable in each of the words, and in some words every syllable is closed.

At·lan′tic	grav′i·ty	shop′ping
Pa·cif′ic	mech·an·ism	mon′sters
In′di·an	mer′chants	moc′ca·sin
Ant·arc′tic	ship′yard′	form′less
Cas′pi·an	land′mark′	func′tion·al
A′dri·at′ic	lol′li·pop	hob·gob′lins
Med′i·ter·ra′ne·an	watch′man	meg′a·tons

The rule. The vowel in a closed, accented syllable is usually "short" unless the vowel is influenced by some other sound in the same syllable.

NOTE. In the preceding list there is one vowel in each of six closed, accented syllables whose sound is influenced by an adjacent sound in the syllable. Can you name each of the six syllables?

Stressed or Accented Syllables

In pronouncing a word of two or more syllables one notices that at least one of the syllables sounds more forceful than the others. It is pronounced with stronger breath impulse and is often, although not always, higher in pitch. Such a syllable, we say, is stressed or accented. In the word *candy,* for example, the syllable *can* has the strong beat and is the accented syllable in the word, and *dy* has the light beat. In *can·teen'* the last syllable is accented. In *can·ta'ta* the accent is shifted to the second syllable in the word.

You may be interested in discovering whether you use a higher pitch as well as greater force in pronouncing the accented syllable than in pronouncing the unaccented syllable in each of these words, or whether the degree of pitch and force vary with different words:

res'cue	a·mong'	de·gree'	o'ver
a·do'	al'ways	nev'er	stu'pid
fun'ny	pu'trid	love'ly	bril'li·ant
hor'rid	se·cure'ly	beau'ty	glo'ri·ous

THE PROBLEM OF STRESS
OR ACCENT

It must be said that the matter of accent in the English language is a bit confusing. On first sight it would seem that there is no general custom. Take, for example, the words *im'age, im·ag'ine,* and *imag·i·na'tion.* Here the stress falls on a different syllable in each of the words. The lack of uniformity can, of course, be explained by the varied composition of the English language. The basis of English is Anglo-Saxon, a branch of the Germanic language. Beginning with the Norman Conquest in 1066 many French words found their way into English. As a consequence, we have two opposing tendencies in placing the accent on words. While the German tendency is to stress the chief syllable of the word, which is usually the first syllable, the French tend to throw the stress toward the end of the word. Because the first tendency is the stronger, we have words of French origin like *barrier, bureau,* and *danger,* which over the years have conformed to the English custom of accent. The tendency of shifting the stress forward in the word is discernible in the manner in which the words *adult, recess, resource,* and *research* are currently pronounced by some speakers, namely *ad'ult, re'cess, re'source, re'search.*

The following guides in placing the accent in a word may prove helpful, although like most rules they too have exceptions.

1.   Words that are used as both nouns and verbs have the accent on the first syllable when used as nouns and on the second syllable when they serve as verbs. The noun is *per'fume,* the verb, *per·fume'.* The noun is pronounced *con'duct,* the verb is *con·duct'.*

2.   Words having three or more syllables are apt to have both a primary accent and a secondary accent as well, as *des'ti·na'tion, con'sti·tu'tion,* and *per'me·a·bil'i·ty,* and some polysyllabic words like *hydrotherapeutics* have two secondary accents: *hy'dro·ther'-a·peu'tics.*

3.   In counting we accent the first syllable of the word as *thir'teen, four'teen, fif'teen, thir'ty-one, thir'ty-two, thir'ty-three.* But when naming these numbers both syllables are accented equally. We say *thir'teen', four'teen', fif'teen', thir'ty-one', thir'ty-two', thir'ty-three'.*

THE INFLUENCE OF STRESS
OR ACCENT

Now that you have had experience with both accented and unaccented syllables in words, you should be ready to learn how stress or the lack of it affects the vowel sound in the syllable.

We shall study its influence both on the *quantity* and the *quality* of the vowel sound.

The Quantity of the Vowel Sound

It is understandable that the stronger the accent on a syllable, the more its vowel sound is prolonged, and the tenser are the tongue and lips in uttering the sound. The lighter the accent, the shorter is the vowel sound. Accent, then, or the lack of it, affects the amount or quantity of the sound in the spoken syllable. That is, one hears less of the vowel sound in an unaccented syllable because it is shorter than the sound in the accented syllable of the word. To illustrate:

The sound of the vowel *a* is shorter in the unaccented syllable in *a·tom'ic* than in the accented syllable in *at'om.*

The sound of the letter *e* is shorter in *chil'dren* than in the accented syllable in *pen'cil.*

The "short *i*" is shorter in the unaccented syllables in *I·tal'·i·an* than in the accented syllable in *It'a·ly.*

The "short *o*" is shorter in *cor·ral'* than in the word *cor'al.*

The "short *u*" is shorter in *up·on'* than in the word *up'per.*

The "long *o*" is shorter in the word *o·bey'* than in the accented syllable *old.*

The "long *u*" is shorter in *u·nite'* than in the accented syllable in *un'ion.*

By pronouncing first the unaccented and then the accented syllable in each of the words you will note the difference in the amount of the vowel sounds in the syllables. The quantity of the vowel sound, then, depends upon whether the syllable in which the sound occurs is accented or not.

The Quality of the Vowel Sound[1]

We have just observed how stress or the lack of it affects the amount of the vowel sound that is heard when the syllable is spoken. We shall now see that some vowels differ in *quality* as

---

[1] The vowel sounds indicated in the unstressed syllables in the respelled words are those found in the Thorndike-Barnhart Dictionary and in Webster's Second Edition, but do not in every case conform to the effect of the lack of stress on the vowel sounds in Webster's Third Edition.

well as *quantity* when the accented syllable becomes unaccented. To illustrate:

The "short *a*" in *at'om* becomes the sound (ə) when the vowel is unaccented, as in *a·tom'ic* (ə·tom'ik).

The "short *o*" in *cor'al* becomes the sound (ə) when the vowel is unaccented, as in *cor·ral'* (kə·ral').

The "short *u*" in the word *up'per* becomes the sound (ə) when the vowel is unaccented, as in *up·on'* (əp·on').

The "long *a*" in the words *age, ace, ate,* and *day* becomes the "short i" when these syllables are unaccented, as in *bond'age* (bond'ij), *pal'ace* (pal'is), *sen'ate* (sen'it), and *Sun'day* (sun'di).

The "long *e*" in the word *be* becomes the "short i" when the syllable is unaccented, as in *be·long'* (bi·lông').

The "long *i*" in *pi'ous* becomes the "short i" when the vowel is unaccented, as in *im'pi·ous* (im'pi·əs).

The "long *i*" in the word *by* becomes the "short *i*" when the syllable is unaccented as in *ba'by* (bā'bi).

The vowel sound (ãr) in *par'ent* becomes the sound (ər) when the vowel is unaccented, as in *pa·ren'tal* (pə·ren'təl).

The sound (ä) in *par'ti·cle* becomes the sound (ə) when the vowel is unaccented, as in (pər·tik'yə·lər).

Accent, then, or the lack of it, affects all vowels in the amount or quantity of the sound that is heard when the syllable is spoken, and some vowels are affected in the quality of the sound as well.

DEGREES OF STRESS IN CONNECTED DISCOURSE

In our study of syllables we found that not every syllable in a word is equally stressed or accented when the word is spoken. Words also vary in the degree of stress with which they are spoken in connected discourse.

In speaking or in reading aloud, we stress some words more than others. Take, for example, the simple sentence *The girl ate the apple and a piece of cake.*

The words *girl, ate, apple, piece,* and *cake* are stressed or accented, since they carry the message. The words *the, and, a,* and *of* are not nearly so significant. They serve mainly as the connecting links in the sentence, so we make them less noticeable by not accenting them.

In order to give cadence to the sentence one should weaken the connecting words. The word *the* has two weak forms in connected speech. It is pronounced (thə) before the consonant sound, as in the word *girl,* and (thi) before a vowel sound, as in *apple.* The word *and* is weakened into (ənd) or (nd). The word *a* is weakened into (ə), and the word *of* becomes (əv).

PREFIXES AND SUFFIXES OF WORDS

Prefixes and suffixes constitute a distinctive form of unstressed syllables in many words the children encounter in their reading and spelling. The able reader usually recognizes these unaccented syllables on sight as meaningful components of the word (see Chapter 3).

You may be interested in observing the pronunciation of each of the unstressed syllables, particularly its vowel sound, in the respelled word. You will, of course, keep in mind that the "short" sound of the vowel is indicated by the unmarked letter in the syllable.

Prefixes of Words

an·nounce′ (ə·nouns′)	im·per′fect (im·pėr′fekt)
be·long′ (bi·long′)	in·crease′ (in·krēs′)
con·spire′ (kən·spīr′)	ir·reg′u·lar′ (ir·eg′yə·lər)
de·fend′ (di·fend′)	mis·take′ (mis·tāk′)
dis·miss′ (dis·mis′)	pre·pare′ (pri·pâr′)
em·plane′ (em·plān′)	pro·claim′ (prō·klām′)
en·train′ (en·trān′)	re·turn′ (ri·tėrn′)
ex·plain′ (eks·plān′)	se·cure′ (si·kūr′)
il·legal′ (il·ē′gəl)	un·real′ (ən·rēl′)
ig·nore′ (ig·nōr′)	

Suffixes of Words

THE SYLLABLE *ed*

The letters *ed* form a separate syllable when preceded by *t* or *d,* as shown by these examples:

or'bit·ed	seat'ed	weed'ed	load'ed
last'ed	want'ed	land'ed	seed'ed
skat'ed	act'ed	wad'ed	brand'ed
count'ed	light'ed	fold'ed	need'ed

NOTE. The word *crook'ed* and the poetic pronunciation *bless'ed,* in neither of which the ending *ed* is preceded by *t* or *d,* are exceptions to the rule.

THE SYLLABLES *er, est, or,* AND *en*

Of these, the syllables *er* and *est* have a much higher frequency of occurrence in the children's reading vocabulary than *or* and *en.*

farm'er	hunt'er	short'est
bank'er	high'est	lov'li·est
bak'er	low'est	sail'or
plumb'er	hard'est	act'or
speak'er	soft'est	jan'i·tor
teach'er	neat'est	gov'er·nor
paint'er	old'est	wood'en
preach'er	new'est	fall'en
wait'er	long'est	wool'en

THE SYLLABLE *ing*

This is an interesting ending in that it is often preceded (1) by *ing,* as shown by the examples in the first column; (2) by a double consonant, as indicated by the examples in the second column; and (3) by neither of these, as shown by the third column of words.

ring'ing	run'ning	laugh'ing
sing'ing	hum'ming	jok'ing
bring'ing	hop'ping	sleep'ing
swing'ing	ship'ping	dream'ing
wing'ing	clap'ping	roar'ing
sting'ing	step'ping	pleas'ing

THE SYLLABLES *ful, ness, less,* AND *ish*

Of these endings, the first three occur much more often in the children's reading vocabulary than the syllable *ish.*

List 1

joy'ful	glad'ness	joy'less	fool'ish
wish'ful	sad'ness	thank'less	boy'ish
truth'ful	good'ness	thought'less	girl'ish
thank'ful	swift'ness	point'less	child'ish
grate'ful	sure'ness	use'less	sheep'ish
bash'ful	light'ness	speech'less	sel'fish
fruit'ful	bus'y·ness	fear'less	tick'lish

List 2

truth'ful·ness	fool'ish·ness	self'less·ness
thank'ful·ness	boy'ish·ness	fear'less·ness
grate'ful·ness	sel'fish·ness	use'less·ness
fright'ful·ness	child'ish·ness	thought'less·ness
thought'ful·ness	sheep'ish·ness	taste'less·ness

THE SYLLABLE *tion*

This unstressed ending ranks among the highest in frequency of occurrence in the children's reading vocabulary. It is regularly pronounced (shən). Its pronunciation (chən) in the word *question* (kwes'chən) is an exception to the rule.

ra·di·a'tion	rev·o·lu'tion	re·ac'tion	*Sh-en*
grav·i·ta'tion	cir·cu·la'tion	frac'tions	
el·e·va'tion	fric'tion	lo·co·mo'tion	
at·ten'tion	hab·i·ta'tion	mul'ti·pli·ca'tion	

THE SYLLABLE *ture*

This syllable is notable for the controversy it invites among speakers. The purist is likely to prefer the pronunciation *ture* to rhyme with *pure*. Webster's Second Edition indicates the pronunciation as (tür) and Thorndike-Barnhart respells the syllable (chər). The word *lec'ture,* then, may be pronounced (lek'tür), (lek'tür), or lek'chər), depending upon the speaker who is using the word.

If you have not already done so, you might like to ascertain how you would pronounce the last syllable in these words:

lit′er·a·ture   fea′ture   ges′ture
ad·ven′ture   pic′ture   fix′ture

SYLLABLES FORMED WITH (l)

The Syllabic *l*

We are now returning to the syllable already discussed that had
no vowel to give the syllable its vowel sound. It was in the word
lit′tle, you may recall, that you were introduced to the syllabic *l,*
in the unstressed syllable *tle.*

The term "syllabic *l*" is indeed appropriate for a consonant
that can function to give the syllable its vowel sound. You will
see by the respelling of each of the words in the following list
that the letter *l* stands alone as the unstressed or unaccented
syllable of the word.

The symbol (′l) is used in Webster's Second Edition for indicating the syllabic (l), and the symbol ḷ as shown by the transcriptions in the second column of words, is the phonetic symbol for
the syllabic *l.*

bot′tle (bot″l)	botḷ
ap′ple (ap″l)	æpḷ
wig′gle (wig″l)	wɪgḷ
puz′zle (puz″l)	pʌzḷ
fid′dle (fid″l)	fɪdḷ
whis′tle (hwis″l)	ʍɪsḷ
peb′ble (peb″l)	pɛbḷ
pad′dle (pad″l)	pædḷ

The Syllable (əl)

Thorndike-Barnhart and Webster's Third Edition indicate the
unstressed syllables formed with (l) by the symbol (əl). Note the
use of the schwa in the respelled words in these columns.

bot′tle (bot′əl)	fid′dle (fid′əl)
ap′ple (ap′əl)	whis′tle (hwis′əl)
wig′gle (wig′əl)	peb′ble (peb′əl)
puz′zle (puz′əl)	pad′dle (pad′əl)

NOTE. Cultivated speakers tend to show a preference for the pronunciation indicated by the symbol ('l), which is identical to the sound that is indicated by the phonetic symbol l.

Syllables Consisting of *l* Blends

The syllabic *l* is not always alone in the unstressed syllable of the word. It is frequently accompanied by another consonant with which it forms a blend of the two sounds, as shown by the following examples.

The respellings of the unstressed syllables show the two opposing pronunciations of the *l* blends. Those in the first column of words show the pronunciation of the *l* blends in Webster's Second Edition, which, as has already been pointed out, is identical to the syllabic *l*. The respellings in the third column show Thorndike-Barnhart includes the schwa in the pronunciation of the *l* blends:

ta'ble	(tā'b'l)	(tā'bəl)
un'cle	(ung'k'l)	(ung'kəl)
poo'dle	(poō'd'l)	(pü'dəl)
ri'fle	(rī'f'l)	(rī'fəl)
ea'gle	(ē'g'l)	(ē'gəl)
an'kle	(ang'k'l)	(ang'kəl)
mea'sles	(mē'z'lz)	(mē'zəlz)
peo'ple	(pē'p'l)	(pē'pəl)
bee'tle	(bē't'l)	(bē'təl)

SYLLABLES FORMED WITH *y*

The letter *y* is also deserving of special mention in connection with the unstressed syllables of words, for several reasons. (1) The letter *y* represents an entire syllable as in the word *read'y;* (2) it forms unstressed syllables with nearly every consonant in the alphabet; and (3) the syllable *ly,* when preceded by the suffix *ful,* gives us a number of colorful adverbs, as shown by the examples in List 2 which follows.

NOTE. The syllable *ly* outnumbers all the other unstressed syllables formed with the letter *y* in the children's reading vocabulary.

List 1

read′y	ris′ky	gyp′sy	sim′ply
ba′by	glad′ly	emp′ty	coun′try
i′cy	en′e·my	i′vy	laun′dry
can′dy	po′ny	co′zy	sym′pa·thy
en′er·gy	sto′ry	an′gry	ge·og′ra·phy

List 2

joy′ful·ly	thought′ful·ly	re·gret′ful·ly
glee′ful·ly	thank′ful·ly	bash′ful·ly
truth′ful·ly	de·light′ful·ly	sor′row·ful·ly
grate′ful·ly	hope′ful·ly	mourn′ful·ly

NOTE. The letter *y*, which is consistently pronounced with the "short i" in the unaccented syllables of words in both the Thorndike-Barnhart Dictionary and in Webster's Second Edition, is pronounced with the "long *e*" in Webster's Third Edition.

*AN INFORMAL TEST**

WHICH ONE IS IT?

1. Dictionaries indicate (a) how words are divided into syllables when written and spoken; (b) the syllabication of the spoken words only.
2. The syllabication of the spoken word (a) always coincides with the way the written word is syllabified; (b) sometimes coincides with the syllabication of the written word.
3. In a polysyllabic word the dividing points between the syllables are indicated by means of a dot (·) and the accent mark (′) or marks in (a) Webster's Second Edition; (b) Webster's Third Edition.
4. A syllable that ends in a consonant sound is known as (a) an open syllable; (b) a closed syllable.
5. The quantity of the vowel sound in a syllable depends upon (a) whether or not the syllable is accented; (b) the nature of the vowel.

* Answers are listed under the appropriate chapter number in the Appendix.

6. The sound of the letter *a* is (a) shorter in the word *a·bout'* than in the word *ask;* (b) longer than in the word *ask.*

7. The so-called "long *e*" in the word *see* becomes the (a) "short *i*" in the word *se·cure';* (b) "short *e*" in the word *se·cure'.*

8. The "short *o*" in *cor'al* becomes the (a) "long *o*" in the unaccented syllable as in *cor·ral';* (b) vowel sound (ə) in *cor·ral'.*

9. The pronunciation of the unaccented syllable in *bot'tle* (bot"l) is (a) the same as in the respelled word (bot'əl); (b) not the same.

10. The unstressed syllables (p'l) and **pl** are pronounced (a) alike; (b) differently.

11. The "short *u*" in an accented syllable becomes the (a) "long *u*" when the syllable is unaccented; (b) sound (ə) when the syllable is unaccented.

12. The letters *ed* form a separate syllable in a word (a) when they are preceded by *t* or *d;* (b) only when they are preceded by a voiceless consonant.

AN EXERCISE IN SYLLABICATION

You might now like to put to the test the rules for syllabication presented in this chapter by syllabifying the following lists of words.

The accent mark (') should, of course, be placed after the accented syllable or syllables in the word, and the dot (·) should be used to show the dividing point between the syllables not indicated by the accent mark, unless you are being guided by Webster's Third Edition, in which case the accent mark is placed before the accented syllable and the hyphen is used to show the dividing point between the syllables.

After you have syllabified the words in each of the lists you may want to check your work by the dictionary.

List 1

Each of the words in this list has at least one open, accented syllable in which the vowel has its "long" sound:

vitamins	constitution
carbohydrates	confederation
sulphathiazole	multiplication
automation	universe
vernalization	examination
unusual	pursue
herbaceous	representation

List 2

In each of the following words there are two or three closed syllables, at least one of which is accented.

prefabricate	polysyllabic	visibility
preferential	prophylaxis	spectacular
nicotinic	exquisite	subtraction
barbiturate	escalator	prognostication
polliniferous	recognizable	rhododendrons

List 3

The following assortment of words should prove both interesting and challenging to syllabify. In the list are (1) compound words; (2) words with double consonants, some of which are root words; and (3) words with two adjacent vowels between the consonants.

coercible	wigwagging	society
poetry	buzzards	progressive
noseband	missing	countdown
fiery	immediately	accidentally
quietly	agrobiology	sugar-coated
dresses	pettifogging	colloquialism
shrewmouse	huggermugger	hieroglyphics
	radiometeorography	

nɑu hɑu wɔz ɪt? dɪd ju tʃɛk juɪ wəɪk wɪð ðə dɪkʃənɛːɪɪ tʊ dɪskʌvəɪ hɑu wɛl ju ɪəlɪ dɪd?

11

THE PROBLEM
OF PRONUNCIATION

Most cultivated individuals are interested in the proper pronunciation of words. The teacher of reading and phonics, however, has a professional as well as a personal interest in the matter. The teacher must know how the words in the pupils' reading vocabulary are pronounced in accordance with pronunciations that are acceptable in cultivated English speech.

The teachers' problem in regard to the pronunciation of words in the United States is aggravated by the absence of a standard of pronunciation. There is no mode of pronunciation that is recognized as standard by speakers in the various areas throughout the country. One uses the term *correct pronunciation,* but what is correct pronunciation? One would find it difficult indeed to give a precise definition of the term. Perhaps the best one can do is to say that the pronunciation of a particular word is correct when it is used by a sufficiently large number of cultivated speakers throughout the nation. But such a definition depends for its accuracy upon knowledge that is hardly obtainable; namely, what constitutes a sufficiently large number of users, and who are the cultivated speakers who are to make the judgment for the country as a whole?

Authorities, so-called, may also disagree, and since the pronunciation of words varies among people in areas too large to be ignored, it is obvious that conformity of pronunciation is not to be found throughout the length and breadth of our land.

One can, of course, heed the pronunciation of cultivated speakers and consult the dictionary on the pronunciation of any word about which there is doubt, or which one has met only in reading. But it must also be remembered that the chief function of the dictionary is not to dictate how a word should be pronounced but rather to record the pronunciations prevailing in the best current usage.

While it is not the purpose of this chapter to deal with the problem of pronunciation on the whole, it is the intention to call to the mind of the teacher (1) some of the commonest errors in the pronunciation of English words, recognized as such by people of education and culture and (2) pronunciations about which there seems to be no general agreement among discriminating speakers and which vary with the individual's habits and tastes.

ERRORS IN PRONUNCIATION

If phonics is to serve well the purpose for which it is being taught, the teacher must be sensitive to the manner in which the words in our language are habitually mispronounced. He must be able to identify the nature of the error responsible for the faulty utterance of the word. A single sound, inaccurately spoken in a word causes the entire word to be improperly pronounced.

Consonants may be slurred, weakened, transposed, added, replaced by another consonant, or omitted altogether.

In some words it may be the vowel rather than the manner in which the consonant is formed that is responsible for the error in pronunciation. In others, both the consonants and the vowels may be incorrectly uttered when the word is spoken. These and many other inaccuracies, all of which have been heard by listening to children's speech in their classrooms, and which are subsequently described in the chapter, result in the slovenly pronunciation of some of the commonest words in the English language.

In each of the following word lists, the particular nature of the irregularity or error in pronunciation is indicated.

NOTE. It is important to keep in mind that the word lists are representative rather than complete. Teachers will no doubt be able to add many other examples from their own experiences in listening to children's conversation in school and on the playground as well.

The Thorndike-Barnhart symbols are used to indicate the pronunciations throughout the chapter, except when it seemed advisable to use the breve, the short-circumflex *o,* or any of the other symbols from *Webster's New International Dictionary,* Second Edition, to indicate the vowel sound in a given word.

When the Sound t Is Slurred

The sound (t) is likely to be slurred when it comes between two vowels, as in the following list of words. Because the vowels are voiced, the consonant too is likely to be voiced. The slightly voiced (t) causes the word *water* to sound like *wader* and *little* to sound like *liddle,* for example.

Proper usage requires a distinct, clear cut, though not exaggerated (t) in the pronunciation of these words:

wa′ter	bet′ter	pret′ty	Ju′pi·ter
lit′tle	but′ter	ket′tle	ex·ci′ted
scoot′er	let′ter	hot′ter	Sat′ur·day
la′ter	af′ter	u·ni′ted	bat′tle

When Final Plosives Are Weakened

Americans habitually use more force in beginning a syllable than in ending it. Consequently, the final consonant in the syllable often becomes so weak that it vanishes altogether. This is particularly noticeable with the final stops or plosives: (p), (b); (t), (d); (k), (g). We observed in Chapter 6 that there are three requirements in uttering a distinct plosive. If any of these is omitted or slighted the result is an indistinct or weakened sound. An inaudible plosive at the end of a syllable is evidence of a slovenly habit of speech.

It requires some effort to produce a clear, distinct plosive at the end of a syllable as in *keep,* for example; and when the sound is followed by another plosive, as in *kept,* even greater effort is needed to pronounce the two plosives distinctly. Consequently, about the best one usually does is to explode the (p) and neglect the (t). The result is *kep'* instead of *kept.*

The secret, of course, is to linger long enough on the sound (p) to allow time for the tongue to get into position for (t); the sound (p) can then explode nicely into (t), resulting in the distinct pronunciation *kept.*

Before instructing your pupils on the secret of pronouncing two final plosives in a syllable, you may wish to see how clearly you habitually pronounce the following words:

jum*ped*	dire*ct*	rub*bed*	beg*ged*
cre*pt*	subtra*ct*	bob*bed*	wag*ged*
clap*ped*	ki*cked*	grab*bed*	buz*zed*

After having tested your skill in pronouncing the syllables ending in two plosives, you may wish to see if you can do as well with words ending in three consonants, at least one of which is a plosive, as in the next list of words. In pronouncing such syllables, even greater effort is required for distinctness. It is little wonder, then, that the word *asked* (having three final consonants, two of which are plosives) is so often pronounced with only one final plosive as in *ast* or *ask.*

When children take time enough for a distinct (s) in the word *asked,* they will be ready for the sounds (kt) that follow. Thinking of the sound (s) as a springboard for "getting set" for the final plosives may also prove helpful in pronouncing the word correctly.

You may be interested in noting the effort that is required for distinct pronunciation of each of these words, in which *one* of the *three* final consonants is a plosive:

a*sks*	ta*sks*	arti*sts*	ba*nks*
ne*sts*	tu*sks*	fore*sts*	tru*sts*
co*sts*	wri*sts*	cla*sps*	mou*nds*
ta*stes*	locu*sts*	wa*sps*	thousa*nds*
de*sks*	gue*sts*	ri*sks*	hundre*dths*

In the next list the final plosive is followed by the syllable *ly.* In pronouncing the final syllable in words like these, one should not stop at all between the plosive and the following syllable, but explode the sound (t), (d), or (k) at once into the syllable (lĭ).

exact*ly*	fond*ly*	quiet*ly*	awkward*ly*
quick*ly*	glad*ly*	distinct*ly*	swift*ly*

NOTE. Although phoneticians usually transcribe the unstressed *ly* as lɪ, giving the vowel the sound that is known as the "short *i*" in phonics, Webster's Third Edition respells the syllable as (lē).

When Final Nasals Are Faulty

Because Americans are accustomed to use less force in ending a syllable than in beginning it, the final nasals too are often weakened, or omitted. In pronouncing the nasals **m**, **n**, and **ŋ**, the outgoing breath stream should be completely blocked in the mouth, and with the lowering of the soft palate, the air should escape only through the nose. But when the blocking of the air is imperfect in forming the final sound, as in *train, swim,* and *ring,* some of the air issues through the mouth. The result is a weakened or omitted consonant and a nasalized vowel, both of which are objectionable.

You may find it interesting at this point to observe how well you pronounce the final nasals in words like those in the following list. It was noted in Chapter 6 that for the sound **n** as in *train* the air is blocked with the tip of the tongue against the upper teeth ridge; for the sound **m** as in *swim* the air is blocked with the lips; and for the sound **ŋ** as in *ring* by the back of the tongue against the soft palate. If the air is completely blocked as you pronounce the final consonant in the following words, you will hear a pleasing vowel sound and a distinct nasal at the end of the words:

trai*n*	cla*m*	spi*n*	cli*mb*
swi*m*	clow*n*	ru*n*	stru*ng*
ri*ng*	swi*ng*	clea*n*	stro*ng*
pla*ne*	broo*m*	dru*m*	spri*ng*

When Final Fricatives Are Weakened

Correctness of speech requires that the fricatives, like the plosives and nasals, be clearly heard at the end of a spoken word.

We learned in Chapter 6 that in forming the consonants **s, z, f, v,** and **l,** although the blockage of the breath stream in the mouth is incomplete, there is enough obstruction to produce audible friction as the air issues from the mouth. When too little time is allowed for the necessary adjustments by the organs of speech, these sounds may be so weakened that they become inaudible. When a word ends in three consonants, for example, *months,* it is necessary to linger slightly on the first of the trio of sounds before uttering the fricatives that follow. When there is a succession of four fricatives, as in the word *twelfths,* one needs to linger on the first two before uttering the next two fricatives in the word.

By giving each of the final consonants in the following words their full value, one appreciates the difficulty of achieving distinctness without exaggeration in forming the final fricatives in the pronunciation of the words:

fi*fth*	ba*ths*	wo*lves*	mou*ths*	eleve*nth*
fi*fths*	ba*thes*	va*lves*	mo*nths*	twe*lfth*
si*xth*	she*lves*	de*pth*	four*ths*	twe*lfths*

When Middle Sounds Are Slovenly Treated

The lack of accuracy in pronunciation is evident in the manner in which the middle consonants and vowels are treated in words of two or more syllables. In some words the consonant is habitually slurred or omitted—when, for example, *gov′ern·ment* is pronounced *gov′er·ment.* In other words, the vowel sound may be missing, as in *op′ra* for *op′er·a.*

In the first word list that follows, the consonant that is prone to be slurred is indicated by italic type. In the second list the vowel that is likely to be mistreated is similarly indicated.

Can you guess the mispronunciation that is likely to be substituted for the correct utterance of each of the words in the following lists?

List 1

arc*t*ic	so*l*dier	a*ll* right	di*ph*thong
su*r*prise	lib*r*ary	woul*d*n't	di*d*n't
Feb*r*uary	recog*n*ize	di*ph*theria	gover*n*ment

List 2

opera	fina*l*ly	di*a*mond	comfor*t*able
re*a*lize	re*a*lly	cons*o*nant	partic*u*lar
usu*a*lly	sim*i*lar	f*o*r instance	

NOTE. In the words *finally* and *really,* not only the vowel sound in the second syllable but the entire syllable is likely to be omitted. In slovenly speech the third syllable in the word *comfortable* is often omitted.

When Sounds Are Transposed

The reversal of sounds in spoken syllables accounts for some of the commonest errors in pronunciation. The words in the following list are among the chief offenders.

In each of the words the syllable in which transposition of sounds occurs is indicated by italic type. You will observe that it is usually the first, or the last, syllable of the word in which the sounds are transposed. For example, when *pre·scrip'tion* is called *per·scrip'tion,* the reversal of sounds is in the first syllable. When *chil'dren* is pronounced *chil'dern* the error is in the last syllable of the word.

Can you tell how each word in the list is mispronounced when the order of the sounds in the syllable is reversed? You may also find it profitable to see how many words you can add to the list from your own experience as a teacher.

chil'*dren*	in'*tro*·duce'	lar'*ynx*
hun'*dred*	i'*ron*	phar'*ynx*
pre·served'	*per*·spire'	*pre*·scrip'tion
pro·nounce'	*pret*'ty	*pro*·nun'ci·a·tion

When (ü) Is Substituted for the "Long u"

Words like *due, new,* and *suit* are frequently mispronounced (dü), (nü), and (süt). Teachers are often uncertain whether *due* should be pronounced (dü) or (dū) or whether the name of the color is (blü) or (blū). You know, of course, that the difference between (ü) and (ū) is the difference between the single vowel sound and the diphthong. The phonetic symbols ʊ and **ju,** as you have already observed in Chapter 8, show the relationship between the single sound (ü) and the diphthong (ū).

In determining whether the vowel in a given word stands for the single sound (ü) or the diphthong (ū), the following rule may serve as a guide.

The rule. When the vowels *u, ue, u-e, ew, iew, ui, eu, ieu, eau,* or *ue* are preceded by the consonants (j), (r), (ch), or (sh) or by a blend formed by (r) or (l) they stand for the sound (ü); when preceded by any other consonant or consonant blend these vowels represent the diphthong (ū).

By applying the rule to the following words, you will find that the words in the first list are correctly pronounced with the vowel sound (ü), and those in the second list with the diphthong (ū).

List 1

blue	chew	true	flew	grew
blew	juice	drew	rule	prunes
glue	jewels	grew	June	shrew

List 2

due	suit	duty	stupid	costume
dew	stew	pupil	avenue	neutral
new	view	fuel	duet	nuisance
tune	cute	music	Tuesday	beautiful

NOTE. When the sound (ü) is substituted for the sounds (ū) in pronouncing the words in the second list, the error lies in omitting the first element, **j** in the diphthong **ju**.

When an Unstressed Syllable Is Mispronounced

Errors in pronunciation vary in degree. Some are slightly irregular, while others are unacceptable to the point of being offensive, and like uncouth manners, put their possessor at a disadvantage. The substitution of the syllable (un) for (ing) or (in) in words like *do'un, look'un,* and *go'un* belongs to the second of the two categories.

The chief offender in the use of (un) for (ing) is not the consonant but the vowel sound in the syllable. If your pupils say *do'in* for *do'ing,* *look'in* for *look'ing,* and *go'in* for *go'ing,* you might leave well enough alone; for although American usage prefers the syllable (ing) to (in) in words like these, many cultivated speakers use the syllable (in) instead of (ing)—but hardly (un) for (in)!

Of the three pronunciations indicated here, only the first one may be considered unacceptable.

look'un, look'in, look'ing	laugh'un, laugh'in, laugh'ing
walk'un, walk'in, walk'ing	wash'un, wash'in, wash'ing
noth'un, noth'in, noth'ing	sing'un, sing'in, sing'ing
sleep'un, sleep'in, sleep'ing	slid'un, slid'in, slid'ing

When Sounds Are Added to Words

Here is a type of mispronunciation as familiar as it is objectionable. Who has not heard the word *you* pronounced *youz,* and *your* as *yourn?* And where is the teacher who cannot add many more words to this particular list of inaccuracies?

you(z)	his(n)	twice(t)	drown(ded)	attack(ted)
your(n)	her(n)	across(t)	height(th)	
our(n)	once(t)	stole(d)	nowhere(z)	

When Vowels and Consonants Offend

Many teachers have heard the words in the following list incorrectly spoken by children and adults. If you too have heard them you will know at once the precise manner in which these words are mispronounced. In some words it is the vowel that is at fault, *milk* being called *meelk* and *fish, feesh.* In others the consonant is mispronounced, *chim'ney* being called *chim'ley* and *tre·men'-dous, tre·men'jous.* When *rinse* is called *rensh* and a *pump'kin* is a *pung'kun,* both consonants and vowels are at fault. When *ac·cept'* is called *a·cept'* and a *pic'ture* is a *pi'ture* a consonant is omitted in each of the words; and when *e·lev'en* becomes *lev'en* an entire syllable is missing!

The letters whose sounds are often mispronounced are indicated in the following list of words by italic type. Can you guess the mispronunciation that is likely to be substituted for the correct utterance in each of these words?

m*i*lk	c*a*n	err	le*ng*th	someth*ing*
f*i*sh	catch	d*ea*f	stre*ng*th	noth*ing*
chim*n*ey	o*i*l	e*s*cape	*p*retty	inst*ead*
ri*n*se	ag*ai*n	*a*ny	pu*mp*kin	favor*i*te
acce*p*t	c*ow*	m*a*ny	eleve*n*	valent*i*ne
pi*c*ture	s*u*ch	d*i*shes	m*ea*sure	tremen*d*ous
g*e*t	si*n*ce	gather	hero*i*ne	ha*n*dkerchief
j*u*st	s*ays*	colu*m*n	*I*talian	pron*u*nciation

When the Accent Is Misplaced

People who do not habitually add, omit, slur, transpose sounds in words, or mispronounce the vowels and consonants, sometimes err in misplacing the accent in words. The following lists are representative of many words in this category.

In the first list the accent is often misplaced on the second syllable of the word. In the second list the accent may be considered as being incorrectly placed on the third syllable of the word.

List 1

the′a·tre	ped′es·tal	in′fa·mous
per′go·la	mis′chie·vous	prof′i·ta·ble
ad′mir·a·ble	com′par·a·ble	trib′une

List 2

in·ex′o·ra·ble	mu·nic′i·pal	su·per′flu·ous
in′ter·est·ing	dec′or·a·tive	in·com′pa·ra·ble

VARIABILITY IN ACCEPTABLE PRONUNCIATIONS

American usage allows one considerable latitude of speech, and the pronunciation of words is no exception. While some pronunciations, as has been pointed out, are unquestionably incorrect, others are debatable. There are many words whose pronunciation is baffling to educators and laymen alike; and the teacher's problem of distinguishing between pronunciations that are considered acceptable and those that are incorrect according to the so-called best usage is not an easy one.

We hear one person say *ad·ver·tise′ment;* an equally authoritative speaker says *ad·ver′tise·ment.* One speaker rhymes *creek* with *seek,* another, with *trick.* There are three current pronunciations for the word *data.* It would seem that one of these must be less desirable than the other two. If so, which one, and according to whose judgment?

Variable Vowel Sounds

1. The letter *a* represents one of the controversial vowel sounds, having three distinct values in a certain classification of words. In pronouncing these words, some speakers give the vowel the quality of Webster's Second Edition, (à); others, the sound (ä) as in *father;* and still others habitually assign to these words the sound (ă) as in *add.*

You may be interested in noting which of the three vowel sounds (à), (ä), or (ă), you are accustomed to using in the pronunciation of these words. It might be even more interesting to discover how consistent you are in the use of the sound. Do you assign the same vowel sound to all the words in the list? If not, what variations are you accustomed to?

ask	grasp	pass	laugh
task	grant	bath	France
half	plant	fast	demand
dance	path	can't	example
aunt	grass	chance	command

2. The value of the vowel sound in the next list of words seems to depend upon the dictionary and upon the speaker who is using the word. In a college class a student using the word *soot* pronounced it (sŭt). When the instructor looked puzzled the student changed her pronunciation to (süt). At this the instructor still seemed baffled. Suddenly his face lighted up as he said, "Oh, yes, yes, indeed, (sŭt)!"

Webster's Second Edition assigns the sound (o͞o) to the words *soon, spoon, root, roof,* and *room;* the sound (o͝o) to the word *poor;* the sound (o͝o) or (o͞o) to the word *soot;* and (o͞o) or (ou) to the word *route*. The Thorndike-Barnhart Dictionary assigns the sound (ù) or (ü) to the words *soot, root, roof,* and *room;* the sound (ù) to the word *poor;* and (ü) or (ou) to the word *route*.

What vowel sound are you accustomed to in the pronunciation of each of these words?

| soon | root | room | poor |
| spoon | roof | soot | route |

3. The pronunciation of *or* in a word or syllable is unpredictable. Are the letters pronounced (ôr), (ōr), or (ŏr)? How can one tell? In Webster's Second Edition the word *for* is pronounced (fôr); the word *force* is (fōrs); and in the word *for'est,* the syllable *for* is pronounced (fŏr).

The respelled words in the following list indicate the pronunciation of *or* in Webster's Second Edition. It is, however, exceedingly doubtful that many speakers make the distinctions among the sounds (ōr) in *store,* (ŏr) in *for'est,* and (ôr) in *for'ty.*

store (stōr)	porch (pōrch)	port (pōrt)
forest (fŏr'ĕst)	por'ridge (pŏr'ĭj)	north (nôrth)
for'ty (fôr'tĭ)	or'ange (ŏr'ĕnj)	stork (stôrk)
horse (hôrs)	morn'ing (môrn'ing)	sto'ry (stō'rĭ)
tor'rent (tŏr'ĕnt)	torch (tôrch)	tor'toise (tôr'tŭs)

4. The so-called "short o," which is spelled with the letter *o* as in *top* and with the letter *a* as in *what,* is also noteworthy for its variability in pronunciation.

Although Webster's Second Edition assigns the so-called "short o" to each of the words in the following list, popular usage does not comply with the dictionaries' degree of uniformity. While some speakers habitually use a sound resembling Webster's (ŏ) as in *soft* for all the words in the list, many persons use the sound (ä) for some of the words, (ŏ) for other words, and still other people use a sound somewhere between (ä) and (ô).

Unless you have already done so, you might like to determine what vowel sound you are accustomed to using in the pronunciation of each of the words in the list. Do you make any distinction between the vowel sound in *top, doll,* and *hop,* and *on, of, frog,* and *golf,* for example?

top	from	hot	what
doll	fond	shop	want
hop	not	got	was
on	hog	stop	watch
of	pond	rocket	wash
frog	odd	shot	wasp
golf	spot	pocket	wander

5. In the pronunciation of the next list of words Thorndike-Barnhart indicates a choice between the "short *o*" and the sound (ô) and Webster's Second Edition indicates the sound by the symbol (ŏ). Popular usage, however, shows as little agreement in the value of the letter *o* in these words as in the preceding list.

While some speakers habitually use the sound (ŏ) in all the words, others assign this sound only to some of the words. Still others use the "short *o*" in pronouncing the words *dog, log, office, coffee, often,* and even *off,* and either (ô) or (ŏ) for the rest of the words in the list:

dog	off	cross	long
log	soft	lost	songs
office	cost	tossed	strong
coffee	loss	frost	belong
often	cloth	across	gong

6. The vowel sound in the monosyllabic words and in the accented syllables in the next list is indicated by the symbol (ô) in Webster's Second Edition and the Thorndike-Barnhart Dictionary. But the same degree of variability exists in pronouncing these words as in the foregoing lists. While usage generally favors the vowel sound (ô) or (ŏ) in the pronunciation of these words, it is not unusual to hear the words *water, caught,* and *taught* pronounced (wŏ'tər), (tŏt), and (kŏt) respectively. Indeed, both dictionaries indicate the "short *o*" as well as the sound (ô) in the pronunciation of *wa'ter.*

wa'ter	ought	cause
caught	bought	be·cause'
taught	brought	a·broad'
fought	thought	daugh'ter

Other Choices in Pronunciation

The words in the lists that follow offer a choice between two different pronunciations in current usage. Although the first pronunciation is considered correct, the other pronunciation is also used by reputable speakers.

You may be interested in observing the lack of agreement in the pronunciation of these words by men and women of education and culture.

1. Note that the two pronunciations in the first list of words differ in the placement of the accent on the spoken syllables and that shifting the accent from one syllable to another in the word almost invariably changes the value of the vowels in the affected syllables.

> inquiry (in·kwīr′ĭ) or (in′kwi·ri)
> exquisite (eks′kwi·zit) or (eks·kwiz′it)
> harass (har′əs) or (hə·ras′)
> bouquet (bü·kā′) or (bō′kā)
> acclimate (ə·klī′mit) or (ak′li·māt)
> abdomen (ab·dō′mən) or (ab′də·mən)
> concentrate (kon′sen·trāt) or (kən·sen′trāt)
> horizon (ho·rī′zən) or (hor′i·zən)
> direct (di·rekt′) or (dī′rekt)
> hospitable (hos′pi·tə·bəl) or (hos·pit′ə.bəl)
> lamentable (lam′ən·tə·bəl) or (lə·men′tə·bəl)
> advertisement (ad·vėr′tis·mənt) or (ad·vər·tīz′mənt)
> illustrate (il′əs·trāt) or (il·lus′trāt)
> controversial (kon·trō·vėr′shəl) or (kon′trō·vėr′si·əl)

2. In the next list of words the two pronunciations differ in the values attached to the vowels and consonants in the words. The difference between the two pronunciations of *forehead* depends upon whether or not the letter *h* is pronounced in the second syllable of the word. Whether the word *creek* is pronounced (krik) or (krēk) is determined by the speaker's preference for the vowel sound (ĭ) or (ē) in pronouncing the word.

forehead (for′ed) or (for′hed)
creek (krēk) or (krik)

*absorb (ab·sôrb′) or (ab·zôrb′)
*absurd (ab·sėrd′) or (ab·zėrd′)
inherent (in·her′ənt) or (in·hēr′ənt)
apricots (ā′pri·kots) or (ap′ri·kots)
isolate (ī′sō·lāt) or (is′ō·lāt)
Polaris (pō·lâr′is) or (pō·lar′is)
Russians (rush′ənz) or (rush′i·ənz)
biography (bi·og′rə·fi) or (bī·og′rə·fi)
radio (rā′di·ō) or (rad′i·ō)
radiator (rā′di·ā·tər) or (rad′i·ā·tər)
direct (di·rekt′) or (dī·rekt′)
**civilization (siv·i·li·zā′shən) or (siv·i·lī·zā′shən)
**Americanization (ə·mer·i·kən·i·zā′shən) or (əmer·i·kən·ī·zā′shən)

3.   The two pronunciations in the following words differ in the placement of the accent on the syllables in words of French origin. Each of these words was originally accented on the final syllable, but there has long been a growing tendency to shift the accent to the first syllable of the word. This tendency is reflected in some of the new dictionaries, which show two pronunciations, one with the accent on the last syllable, which still seems to be the preferred pronunciation, and the other with the accent on the first syllable of the word.

You may be interested in ascertaining which of these choices you are accustomed to:

recess (ri·ses′) or (rē′ses)
address (ə·dres′) or (ad′res)
research (ri·sėrch′) or (rē′sėrch)
detail (di·tāl′) or (dē′tāl)
defect (di·fekt′) or (dē′fekt)
adult (ə·dult′) or (ad′ult)
detour (di·tūr′) or (dē′tūr)
allies (ə·līz′) or (al′īz)
resources (ri·sôrs′əz) or (rē′sôrs·əz)

* Because the vocal cords vibrate in pronouncing the syllable *ab* in the words *ab·sorb′* and *ab·surd′*, the tendency is to continue the vibration into the next syllable. This accounts for the almost universal pronunciation of *ab·zorb′* for *ab·sorb′* and *ab·zurd′* for *ab·surd′*.

** The weak vowel (ĭ) is preferred to the diphthong (ī) in the unstressed syllables in the words *civilization* and *Americanization* because it fits more smoothly with the rhythm of the words.

4. The following words, also from the French, are often Anglicized. When the French pronunciation was attempted, care was exercised not to change the final sound (zh) into (dzh), namely, (j). The blend (dzh) was considered correct only in the Anglicized pronunciation of the word, as shown in the second respellings, but this seems no longer to be the case.

> garage (gǝ·räzh′) or (gar′ij)
> prestige (pres·tēzh′) or (pres′tij)
> mirage (mǝ·räzh′) or (mir′ij)
> sabotage (sab′ǝ·täzh′) or (sab′ǝ·tij)
> camouflage (käm′ǝ·fläzh′) or (kam′ǝ·fläj)

5. These two words from the French were originally pronounced with the letter *h* "silent," a pronunciation that can still be heard, although most speakers seem to prefer the pronunciation of (h) in these words:

> humble (hum′bǝl) or (um′bǝl)
> humor (hū′mǝr) or (ū′mǝr)

6. The following list of words presents another choice in the pronunciation of English words. One often hears Americans give the words *been* and *again* their British pronunciation. But American usage still favors the pronunciation of these and the following words as indicated by their first respellings.

> again (ǝ·gen′) or (ǝ·gān′)
> been (bin) or (bēn)
> either (ē′t̶h̶ǝr) or (ī′t̶h̶ǝr)
> neither (nē′t̶h̶ǝr) or (nī′t̶h̶ǝr)
> often (ôf′ǝn) or (ôf′ten)
> process (pros′es) or (prō′ses)
> issue (ish′ü) or (is′ū)
> schedule (sked′ūl) or (shed′ūl)

7. Our next and last list of words is almost certain to invite controversy. Teachers usually consider it incorrect to pronounce *when* as *wen* and *which* as *witch,* but many proper British speakers make no distinction between the sounds (hw) and (w) in these words. Although the prevailing usage in America is indi-

cated in the first respelling of the words, the second pronunciation is followed by some Americans as well as foreigners:

when (hwen) or (wen)
which (hwich) or (wich)
where (hwãr) or (wãr)
why (hwī) or (wī)
white (hwīt) or (wīt)
while (hwīl) or (wīl)
what (hwot) or (wot)
whether (hweth′ər) or (weth′ər)

NOTE. The choice between (hw) and (w) does not apply to the pronunciation of the words *who, whom,* or *whose,* since these words begin with the sound (h) and not (hw) or (w).

WHICH DO YOU PREFER?

1

Weather it rain, or weather it snow;
We shall have weather, weather or no.

2

Whether it rain, or whether it snow;
We shall have weather, whether or no.

*AN INFORMAL TEST**

TRUE OR NOT TRUE

1. The pronunciation of any English word is never debatable. It is either right or wrong.
2. If someone's pronunciation of a word is not indicated in Webster's *New World Dictionary,* or in Webster's *New International Dictionary,* Third Edition, one may be sure that the pronunciation is wrong.
3. There is a difference between the pronunciation of a word that is acceptable and one that is considered incorrect by American standards of good speech.
4. The pronunciations (droun′dəd) for *drowned,* (ə·tak′təd) for *at-*

* Answers are listed under the appropriate chapter number in the Appendix.

tacked, and (strenth) for *strength,* while not preferred, are nevertheless acceptable by American standards of speech.

5. The substitution of (gō′un) for *go′ing* is much more objectionable than that of (gō′in) for *go′ing.*

6. The person who says (gō′in) for *go′ing* is leaving off the sound of (g).

7. When the word *new* is pronounced (nü), the error lies in the omission of the first vowel in the diphthong (ū).

8. There is a growing tendency in America to shift the accent from the last to the first syllable in many words of French origin.

9. In the words *who, whose,* and *whom* the letters *wh* are pronounced (hw).

10. The word *advertisement* is correctly pronounced either (ad·vėr′-tis·ment) or (ad·vər·tīz′ment).

11. The word *garage* is correctly pronounced either (gar′ij) or (gə··räzh′).

12. The words *diphtheria* and *diphthong* are incorrectly pronounced (dip′thēr·i·ə) and (dip′thong).

13. The word *water* is properly pronounced (wô′tər) or (wô′dər).

14. When *pretend* is pronounced (pər·tend′) the error lies in the reversal of sounds in the first syllable of the word.

15. When *pronunciation* is called (prō·noun·si·ā′shən) the error lies in having substituted a diphthong for the single vowel sound in the second syllable of the word.

16. The word *tremendous* is correctly pronounced (tri·men′jəs).

17. The word *mischievous* is incorrectly pronounced (mis·chē′vəs) or (mis·chē′vi·əs).

18. The vowels *ue* are correctly pronounced (ü) in the words *cue, avenue,* and *Tuesday.*

19. The word *prescription* is correctly pronounced either (pri·skrip′-shən) or (pər′skrip·shən).

20. The pronunciations (yüz) and (yürn) for the word *you* are acceptable by American standards of speech.

21. It is the function of the dictionary to record the pronunciations prevailing in the best present usage, rather than to dictate what that usage should be.

22. There is complete agreement among educated people in America on the pronunciation of any English word.

12

"PHONETIC" INSTRUCTION, THEN AND NOW

There is probably no form of instruction in the elementary schools of America with a more remarkable history than the teaching of phonics, which goes as far back as the 1780s when Noah Webster introduced the idea of teaching the "powers" as well as the names of the letters of the alphabet in beginning reading. By virtue of the alphabet method, the prevailing approach to reading, the little "abc-darians" spelled out their words in reading: *c-a-t, cat; m-o-u-s-e, mouse.* With the advent of "phonetic" instruction in the schools, the little "scholars" were now learning to sound out: (k-ă-t) *cat;* (m-ou-s) *mouse,* as well as to spell the words. This method was a forerunner of the phonetic approach to reading, which competed with the alphabet method over a period of nearly fifty years as the "more sensible" approach to reading instruction in the schools.

THE NEW NATION'S NEED FOR "PHONETIC" INSTRUCTION

America was still in its infancy when the nation was making unprecedented demands on its schools. While these demands did not interfere with the customary instruction in the ABC's, they pointed up the need for systematic teaching of the sounds of the letters in the English language. "Phonetic" instruction was specifically prompted (1) by the desire to unify the English language by ridding it of its numerous dialects and (2) by the prevailing emphasis on elocution, designed to impress the youth with what were heralded as the "noble sentiments of liberty and patriotism to be transmitted into the breasts of the rising generation." Since oratory and purification of the language demanded exactness in pronunciation and enunciation, which were to be achieved by a thorough knowledge of the sounds of the letters, the need for "phonetic" instruction in the schools was too obvious to be questioned.

One of the chief proponents of "phonetic" instruction, as might be expected, was Noah Webster himself, author of *The American Speller,* generally known as the "Blue Back Speller," which was really not a speller but a reader.

THE ALPHABET-PHONETIC METHOD

It must not be assumed that the advent of "phonetic" instruction in the schools sounded the death knell of the ABC approach to reading. Far from it! Beginners in reading now had to learn both the sounds and the names of the letters of the alphabet.

As the instructor pointed to a letter displayed before the class, the pupils were to tell first the name of the letter and then its sound: *a,* (ă); *b,* (b); *c,* (k); *d,* (d); *e,* (ĕ), and so on, to the end of the alphabet. Woe unto the little unfortunate ones who could not respond promptly and correctly! Donned in dunce caps in the corner of the room, they remained the objects of ridicule until they could satisfy the unrelenting demands of the schoolmaster.

When all the letters and their sounds had been learned, whole sentences could be sounded out and read: (k-ă-t) *cat;* (k-ă-n) *can;* (k-ă-tch) *catch;* (m-ou-s) *mouse:*

A cat can catch a mouse.

Reading was like a game of word calling, in which competition among the scholars was encouraged. The speediest in calling out the words was considered the ablest in the class. How different from the concept of reading today!

It is interesting to note that although the students were now being taught to sound out the words in their readers, learning the names of the letters continued to be the most important first step on the road to reading.

THE ALPHABET METHOD CONDEMNED

From Noah Webster we proceed to a contemporary of his, although a much younger man, the distinguished educator Horace Mann.

Among the Americans who went to Europe, particularly to Germany, during the middle of the 1800s to study Prussian instructional principles and practices, none was more respected than Horace Mann.

Mann's glowing reports on the teaching he had observed in Germany were to influence instructional methods on this side of the Atlantic and led eventually to the disrepute of the alphabet method of teaching reading. In his Seventh Annual Report to the Board of Education of Massachusetts, Mann had this to say:

> I am satisfied that our greatest error in teaching children to read lies in beginning with the alphabet; in giving them what are called the "Names of the Letters," *a, b, c,* etc. How can a child to whom nature offers such a profusion of beautiful objects,—sights, sounds and colors—and in whose breast so many social feelings spring up;— how can such a child be expected to turn with delight from all these to the stiff and lifeless column of the alphabet?

In the paragraph that follows Mann continues:

> Although in former reports I dealt at length on what seems to me the absurdity of teaching reading by *beginning with the alphabet,* yet I feel constrained to recur to the subject again,—being persuaded that no thorough reform will ever be effective in our schools until this practice is abolished.

THE "PHONETIC" METHOD EXTOLLED

In Mann's report on the methods of instruction he had observed in Germany, he leaves no doubt of his unqualified preference for the phonetic method to the ABC approach to reading.

Mann pointed out:

> Here [in the Prussian school] the names of the letters were not given as with us, but only their *powers,* or the sounds which those letters have in combination. The letter *h* was first selected and set up in the reading frame, and the children, instead of articulating our phonetical *h,* merely gave a hard breathing,—such a sound as the letter has in the word *house.* Then the diphthong (au), [the German word for *house* is spelled *Haus*] was taken and sounded by itself in the same way. Then the blocks containing *h* and *au* were brought together and the two sounds were combined. Lastly, the letter *s* was first sounded by itself, then added to the others, and then the whole word was spoken.
>
> Compare the above with that of calling up a class of "abc-dari-ans"—or what is more common a single child,—and while the teacher holds a book or card before him, with a pointer in his hand, says *a* and he echoes *a;* then *b* and he echoes *b;* and so on until the vertical row of lifeless and ill-favored characters is completed; and then remanding him to his seat and to sit still and look at vacancy. If the child is bright, the time which passes during the lesson is the only part of the day in which he does not think. Not a single faculty of the mind is exercised excepting that of imitating sounds; and even the number of these imitations is limited to twenty-six. A parrot or an idiot could do the same thing.

One wonders how any method of instruction could have withstood so devastating a blast!

In 1844 Horace Mann wrote his caustic criticism of the ABC method of teaching reading in the American schools. By 1850 the protest against the alphabet method had gained considerable momentum, but Horace Mann did not live to see it outmoded in the schools. However, by the time of his death in 1859 the alphabet-phonetic method, which required instruction in the sounds of the letters as well as their names, was replacing the ABC method of beginning reading.

A NEW APPROACH TO READING

The first primer based on the word method of teaching reading was published in 1840. The word method exemplified an entirely new philosophy of beginning reading that was the exact opposite of the ABC or the alphabet-phonetic approach. The new method of teaching reading with instruction in phonics was favorably received by educators throughout the country. However, in spite of the fervor for what was being heralded as the "more sensible word method with phonics," and the mounting criticism of the ABC method and the phonetic approach to reading, the majority of instructors clung to the method to which they and their teachers had been accustomed. Tradition was too strong to overcome easily. It was not until 1880, more than a generation after the publication of the readers by Bumstead and Webb, based on the word method of instruction, that the alphabet-phonetic method was generally condemned and the word method with instruction in phonics was taking its place in the public schools of America. And who will say that in a little school somewhere, some little beginners are not still being taught to read as were the "abc-darians" more than a century ago?

It was in the middle of the 1800s, when the alphabet-phonetic approach was being superseded by the word method of teaching reading, that the famous McGuffey Readers were published—the readers that were recommended for adoption in the public schools of Twin Lakes, Wisconsin, in 1960, "chiefly because of their phonetic approach to reading."

THE ADVENT OF ORGANIZED
SYSTEMS OF PHONICS

The 1880s marked the beginning of two new educational practices. One was the sentence and story method of teaching reading, the subsequent development of the word method. The other practice was the elaborately organized systems of phonics. Although the systems varied somewhat in methodology, carefully organized programs of phonics were an inseparable part of each succeeding basic reading system for the next forty years.

This new development in phonics is not to be confused with the alphabet-phonetic approach to reading, which was not in any sense a part of a basic reading system.

The Need for Phonics

The demand for instruction in phonics resulted from the growing dissatisfaction with the word method of teaching reading. Even before the introduction of the sentence and story methods, the word method was under severe attack by its opponents. It was pointed out that children were not learning to read as well as they should. The falling off in reading ability, it was said, was particularly conspicuous in the middle and grammar grades, where the inability to call the words readily interfered with efficiency in reading.

The following quotation from an educational journal published over sixty years ago has overtones of the criticism directed against the so-called look-say method of teaching reading today. Let us see what the critics at the close of the nineteenth century had to say about the whole-word method of reading instruction in the schools:

> There is quite a general complaint that the pupils in the upper grades are not able to read with ease and expression. They have so little mastery over the words that an exercise in reading becomes a laborious effort in word calling. Pupils usually read very well through the first three readers, according to our present standard of reading in these grades. But the trouble begins in the fourth reader, and by the time the class is in the fifth, the reading recitation is torture to the teacher and a hateful task to the pupil.
>
> There can be no good reading without the ability to call words readily, and it may be well to consider whether the methods of teaching primary reading are not at fault in preparing the pupil for the advanced reading.
>
> While he (the pupil) should be learning independence in making out his words, he learns dependence, and his dependence increases with the increases in difficulties.

Synthetic Methods of Phonics

Since the "New-fashioned Word Method" of teaching reading was generally believed to be responsible for the poor reading in the schools, the pendulum began to swing away from the *whole* word to the *sounds* that compose the word. Instead of teaching word wholes, the trend was now in the opposite direction; namely, toward the synthetic approach to reading.

THE POLLARD METHOD OF PHONICS

The children's inability to call words readily captured the imagination of poet Kate Harrington, later known as Rebecca S. Pollard, who, in her manual on the synthetic method of teaching reading published in 1889, posed this question: "Instead of teaching the word as a whole, and afterward subjecting it to phonic analysis, is it not infinitely better to take the letters for the starting point, and with these sounds lay a foundation firm and broad, upon which we can build whole families of words for instant recognition?"

From Sounds to Sentences. The first step in "laying the firm foundation" was to teach the sounds of the letters, vowels, and consonants. The sounds were then combined into "families": *at, ate, et, eet, it, ite, ot, ote, ut, ute, oot, out, igh,* and *old,* for example. Then came the task of blending the sounds into words: *c-at, cat; f-at, fat; s-at, sat; m-at, mat;* and lo the pupils could read:

> The fat cat sat on the mat!

Here, then, we have an example of the synthetic approach to reading—beginning with a single sound and proceeding to a combination of sounds, then to the whole word, and from the word to the sentence, and finally from the sentences to the story. The synthetic method thus begins with the smallest unit in reading and proceeds to the largest.

It is understandable that a procedure so clearly logical could have gained general approval in the schools nearly three quarters of a century ago. It is also seen why such a seemingly sensible approach to reading is making a strong appeal to the layman today, who is clamoring for its return to the nation's schools.

Classroom Procedure. How teachers and pupils alike must have groaned under the load imposed upon them by the Pollard method of learning to read! How much pupils had to learn before they could experience the fun of reading. No wonder the author of the method embellished her teaching with every known form of entertainment: storytelling, dramatization, singing, drawing, coloring, even ladder climbing and window framing! The devices at least were interesting, although they must often have stolen the show from the lesson. Even so, the author seems never to have lost faith in their efficacy. Mnemonics were her stock in trade.

To attract the little learners to the sounds of the letters, Rebecca Pollard invented the Johnny stories. She then put the sounds into jingles, which were sung to familiar tunes. Through singing the songs the sounds were to be impressed on the children's minds. Thus learning, drilling, and reviewing were uplifted on the wings of song!

The first sound to be learned was the little lamb's cry: (ă), (ă), (ă), which was introduced by the first of the Johnny stories. A ladder was drawn in colored chalk on the blackboard and the drilling was underway. At the precise instant that the teacher's pointer touched each letter on the ladder's rung, the pupils sang its sound to the scale—up and down, and down and up. The next morning the children found the lamb's sound represented by (ă) in a window frame on the blackboard, from which the day's drilling proceeded. A picture of a lamb was then put on display. For busy work the children drew pictures of a lamb with the letter *a* beside it and marked the letter with a breve to show its sound (ă).

Each day a new Johnny story introduced another sound, until all the vowel and consonant sounds had been learned—the sound (m-m) of the bee's humming, the (p!p!) of the puffing steamboat, (ch! ch!) of the steam locomotive or the sneeze, the pigeon's (d! d! d!), the frog's (g! g!), the bee's (z-z-z), the angry cat's (f! f!), and the dog's (er-er).

As each new sound was introduced it was added to the *Songs of the Sounds*. By the time the last sound had been learned, the song had grown to twenty-four stanzas in length!

As the number of sounds increased, Miss Pollard found vehicles for the verses in the old familiar tunes of "Yankee Doodle," "Comin' Through the Rye," "Here We Go 'Round the Mulberry Bush," and "John Brown's Body"; even "My Country 'Tis of Thee" was not too sacred to serve the little learners' needs.

The "Crooked Letter S," sung to the air of "Tramp, Tramp,

Tramp the Boys Are Marching," is representative of the *Songs of the Sounds.*

> When we find this crooked mark
> After voice or vowel sounds;
> We must try once more to think
> That the bees are buzzing 'round;
> And s,s,s,s,s,s,s,s,s say.
>
> S,s,s, the bees are buzzing;
> Busy fingers, faces bright;
> And remember every day
> That what e'er we do or say,
> We must always try to do and say aright!

The Pollard system did not suffer for want of enthusiastic support. Not only educators, who believed that the phonetic approach to reading would succeed where the word method had failed, but distinguished intellectuals, among them Edward Everett Hale, spoke out boldly in its favor. Sarah Winter Kellogg, one of Boston's distinguished pedagogs, took particular delight in sponsoring the Pollard system. On one occasion, while introducing the author of the new system at a teachers' meeting, Miss Kellogg confessed that the audience would perceive, even before she had spoken ten words, that her pronunciation and enunciation were incorrect. It was so, she explained, because she had not learned to speak and read by the Pollard synthetic system.

"I stand befor' you," Miss Kellogg said, "as the livin' example of how a smaht child can be spoiled foh' want of the Pahlud!"—after which the educators were admonished to put the "Pahlud" system in their schools.

Before the turn of the century, beginners in school in all parts of the country were "climbing" the ladder rungs, hillsides, and plum trees pictured on the blackboard, as step by step they sounded their way to the top imitating the teakettle's (s-s), the tick-tock's (t! t!), the angry cat's (f! f!), and the dog's (er-er). And has not the sound of *r* been known as (er) ever since in "phonetic" and reading instruction in the schools?

Today we frown upon artificial stimuli in teaching, and rightly so. But who will say that letter sounds are not still being plucked from trees on the chalkboard or whirled into place on a merry-go-round and on phonic wheels in classrooms today?

The author of the family phonograms, or the final-blend method, as it is called, built more firmly than she knew. The Pollard synthetic method, the first of the elaborately organized systems of phonics, set the pattern for all the final blend systems that followed; and the Pollard synthetic method of generations ago can be observed as the "family method" of phonics in more than one primary classroom even to this day.

THE RATIONAL METHOD

The Rational Method, published in 1894, was the work of Edward G. Ward, Superintendent of Public Instruction in Brooklyn, New York. In his series, consisting of a primer and six readers, the author combined his "phonetic" method with the word method of teaching reading. Instead of beginning with the sounds of the letters in the alphabet and building whole "families" of words as by the Pollard system, Ward began with a stock of words to be learned *on sight,* after which the pupils were given intensive training in phonics. Part I of the primer was intended for sight reading only, Part II, for sight and "phonetic" reading.

Sight reading was defined as the reading of sentences in which the words were recognized as word wholes, and on sight. *"Phonetic" reading* was the reading of sentences composed largely of "phonetic" words to be identified as such. Ward's Rational method required the mastery of eighty-four sight words like *a, the, is, are, do, does, have,* and *said,* for example, before any reading from the primer was permitted.

Ward's manual of instructions for teachers left little or nothing to the teacher's imagination or ingenuity and was entirely devoid of the devices that glamorized Miss Pollard's teaching. It was intended, it seemed, that the little Wardians were to take their lessons straight.

While the beginners in school were preparing for their first sight-word reading, they were also learning their first stock of phonograms, as they were called. The list comprised nine "simple phonograms" like *ing, ings, ight,* and *ights,* each of which was taught in isolation and drilled until mastery was achieved.

After having mastered the first thirteen phonograms, there was one more river to cross before the pupils were permitted to begin Part II in their primer. The "phonetic" words that occurred in the first lesson had to be mastered.

In his manual of instructions to teachers, Ward proclaimed: "By way of preparation for each lesson in Part II have the phonetic words that occur therein written on the blackboard with proper marks and read by the scholars several times if necessary, as a blend drill."

After his mastery of both the sight words and the "phonetic" words in a given lesson in Part II of the primer, the pupil was permitted to test his power by reading the lesson from the book.

In lessons like the following taken from the primer, the words that were marked diacritically were to be "sounded out"; those that were left unmarked were to be recognized on sight, as word wholes, with the exception of the phonograms, which were underscored.

> Oh, fīe! What a slȳ boy you are! It is not rigẖt to tell līes. You may well sīgẖ. It is mēạn to be so slȳ. Never tell līes, my boy!
>
> Here is a boy that never tells līes. He āịms to do rīgẖt. If he fāịls, he tells me so.

While pupils were sounding their way through the diacritically marked sentences, another system of phonics was competing for recognition. The Gordon Readers, published in 1902, showed both the Pollard influence of "phonetic" instruction and Ward's efforts at reconciling the word method with phonics in beginning reading.

THE GORDON SYNTHETIC METHOD

In Emma K. Gordon's system of phonics the "families" became truly prolific. Two of the Gordon charts bore a total of 140 "family" names: *at, ake, ine, ilk, oke, otch, un, une, eel, oop, ack,* and *ouch* to name but a dozen! On a third chart intended for teaching, one found drills and reviews of such "phonograms" as *ble, bble, tion, sion, igh, ight,* and *ights.*

Additional drill was provided through the use of phonic cards, of which there were sixty-five, bearing the vowels, single consonants, and consonant blends!

While emphasizing the need for teaching sight words as word wholes, Miss Gordon left no doubt of her faith in the efficacy of phonics in beginning reading. In the *Teachers' Manual for the Gordon Readers* the author pointed out:

> The method of teaching reading presented in this manual recognizes (1) that the child must master certain phonic facts before he can have power to solve word problems for himself; and (2) that it is not possible to reduce every word in the language to a phonic basis, and exceptions to phonic rules should be taught as sight words or word-wholes.

One must bear in mind that the *ability to read* in Miss Gordon's day was judged by the pupil's skill in recognizing the words in the sentences. *Reading* was still believed to be as it had been for more than a hundred years, an exercise mainly in word recognition and pronunciation. Reading skill and ability were appraised in terms of speed in word recognition and accuracy in pronunciation. It is not difficult, then, to appreciate the emphasis that was placed on drills aimed at complete mastery of the "family" names and the blending of the sounds into words for instant recognition.

Blending the consonant with the "family phonogram" as in *s-at, sat; w-ill, will,* and *l-ike, like,* for example, is known as the *final blend method of phonics.* The Pollard, Ward, and Gordon systems were based on this method of blending.

THE BEACON METHOD OF PHONICS

For nearly a quarter of a century, the final-blend method was accepted without question as the means of blending sounds into words. In 1912, it met its first opposition by what is known as the *initial method of blending* the sounds. This method of blending originated with James H. Fassett, Superintendent of Schools in Nashua, New Hampshire, and was incorporated in the Beacon reading system. By the Beacon method of phonics children were taught the vowel and consonant sounds in isolation the same as before from the blackboard, phonic charts, and cards: *f, s, t, a, b,* and so on. After having learned to respond to each of the letter sounds separately, the next step was that of blending the consonant and vowel into *fa, sa, ba, ta.* The final step was the blending of the sounds into words like *fa-t, fat; sa-t, sat; ba-t, bat; ta-t, tat.*

The Beacon method, like its predecessors, was based on the synthetic approach to phonics, beginning with the smallest unit, the letter sound, then blending the sounds into larger units, and finally into whole words. Like its predecessors, too, it was a "sounding" method of phonics. Children were taught to identify an unfamiliar word by "sounding it out." It differed from the earlier systems of phonics in its method of blending. While children in some schools were still blending *c-at* into *cat, p-ig* into *pig, sh-eep* into *sheep, f-ish* into *fish,* and *r-un* into *run,* in other schools primary pupils were blending *ca-t* into *cat, pi-g* into *pig, shee-p* into *sheep, fi-sh* into *fish,* and *ru-n* into *run.*

Ten years after the publication of the Beacon method the teachers' manual by Fasset and Norton was published. In explaining the method, the authors pointed up these distinguishing features: (1) careful attention to the blending of the consonant with the vowel that follows the consonant in a word or syllable; (2) ample practice of the short vowel sounds in ideal syllables; (3) clear differentiation between words that are "phonetic," and words that are "unphonetic," adequate preparation for "natural syllabification and spelling," the use of the dictionary; and (4) the inclusion of the best standard of pronunciation.

Fasset, like Ward, made a clear distinction between sight words, which were to be taught as word wholes, and "phonetic" words, which were to be identified by the sounds of the letters in the word. Provision for drill on the sight words was prominent in the Beacon primer as it had been in Ward's readers. But the Beacon primer, unlike Ward's, used no diacritical marks intended to assist the reader in sounding out the "phonetic" words.

In the Beacon method of learning to read, the emphasis was on the reader's skill in word recognition. The children who could most readily unlock the unfamiliar words in reading were considered to be the ablest readers in the class. The bigger the words, the better! But the shift in emphasis from the mechanics of word recognition to comprehension in reading, to the meaning of the symbols rather than their form, was soon to come.

From the time of the Pollard synthetic method of reading until 1928, all of the various systems of phonics had three characteristics in common: (1) they were based on the synthetic approach to phonics, which began with the smallest units, namely, the individual sounds, which were then blended into larger units and finally into the word-whole; (2) the sounds of the letters, vowels, and consonants were taught in isolation, that is, apart from the words in which the sounds occurred; and (3) their objective in teaching phonics was to enable the children to sound out the unfamiliar words in reading.

The Analytic Approach to Phonics

The word method of teaching phonics by Anna D. Cordts provided the first analytic approach, as opposed to the synthetic methods of teaching phonics. Starting with the whole word the pupil proceeded to the parts or components of which the word or syllable is composed. "Phonetic" units, vowel and consonant sounds, were learned not apart from but always in the words in which they occurred. The children discovered each "phonetic" unit themselves from a word they already knew and which had become the key word for the unit. The word *candy*, for example, was the key word for the beginning (ca) as in *cattle, calendar, camera, cavities, castle, California*. The vowel (ir) was discovered from the key word *bird*, the diphthong (ou) from the key word *mouse*, and the consonant sound (p) from the key word *sheep*, for example.

The "phonetic" units, then, were learned not in isolation as before, but in the words in which they occurred. Instead of sounding out an unfamiliar word in reading, children identified the word by its known parts or components.

The program provided for individual differences among children. It supplied experiences in listening, in hearing the "phonetic" units in spoken words, in auditory and visual discrimination, and in blending the sounds to form the whole word.

A readiness program in phonics accompanied readiness in reading, and like the instructional program in phonics, it was the result of phonetic research[1] and educational experiment in phonics.

OPPOSITION TO TRADITIONAL METHODS OF PHONICS

It had now been nearly a century and a half since Noah Webster advanced the idea of teaching the "powers" of the letters as well as their names, and forty years since the publication of the first elaborate system of phonics for promoting efficiency in reading.

Before the end of the 1930s phonics had fallen into ill repute, and the erstwhile indisputable aid to reading was under attack by supervisors of elementary education and by reading instructors in the teachers' colleges of America.

Among the reasons for the educators' objection to phonics were the overemphasis on the mechanics of reading and the practice of instructing children to sound out the new words they encountered in reading, a procedure that had become traditional in the schools.

The Progressive Movement in education was playing no small part in lowering the esteem in which phonics had so long been held. The traditional methods of "phonetic" instruction, with the emphasis on drill, were anathema to the proponents of progressive education.

While the progressive movement in education was making itself felt, several other developments in educational thought were taking place, all of which were having an unfavorable effect on the traditional methods of "phonetic" instruction.

THE INFLUENCE OF EXPERIMENTAL RESEARCH

Among the factors that had a decisive bearing on "phonetic" instruction in the schools were the results of experimental research in the field of education.

[1] "An Analysis and Classification of the Sounds in the Children's Reading Vocabulary in Grades 1–3"; unpublished dissertation, University of Iowa, Iowa City, Iowa.

The Effect of "Phonetic" Instruction on Reading

Not least among the investigations of classroom practice and procedures were the studies that were conducted to determine the influence of phonics on children's reading in the schools. When it was found that pupils who rated highest in their ability to sound out the unfamiliar words in reading consistently made the lowest scores in speed and comprehension, phonics was declared to be a handicap in reading. With the rapidly mounting interest in reading speed and comprehension, the continuing decline in the status of "phonetic" instruction in the schools was inevitable.

As early as 1916 the handwriting on the wall was clearly discernible. The following conclusions by Mary A. Gruppe in her study "Phonics in Relation to Reading" substantiated the reports of other studies on the effect of phonics on children's reading in the elementary schools.

1.   The ability to pronounce new words is certainly not the most important factor in learning to read.

2.   Reading is not word pronunciation or word recognition. It is gathering thought from the printed page.

3.   The association which is important to make is between the idea and the symbol. The thought symbol would suggest its thought without interference of the association of sound and letter.

4.   Our slow, mechanical word calling readers have generally become so through training of phonetic analysis; and our quick thought gathering readers have been trained by associating the symbol with the thought.[2]

From her study, "Phonics or No Phonics," Lillian Beatrice Currier concluded: "The most important thing in reading is to hold, strengthen and develop the interest of pupils. Lead pupils to crave reading quantities of the very best material available. Choose silent reading material with care, bearing in mind the varied tastes of the pupils."[3]

In its report on "The Status of Phonics Today," the *Chicago Schools Journal* summed up the case against phonics this way:

[2] *The Pedagogical Seminary*, Vol. XXIII (1916).
[3] *Elementary School Journal*, February 1923.

Phonics is based on an imperfect conception of the "phonetic" character of the English language. It is out of harmony with what is known as the laws of learning. It develops habits counter to desirable eye movement habits. It tends to shift emphasis from meaning to pronunciation. It does not insure application of phonetic analysis to words in the context. It fails to solve several important types of difficulties in recognizing words. It does not utilize children's power to detect similarities and differences of form other than phonetic. It neglects individual differences. Its overuse is often accountable for the loss of interest in reading.[4]

Silent vs. Oral Reading

The emphasis on speed and comprehension in reading was setting off a chain of developments, among them the trend toward silent reading in the schools.

The importance of oral reading, which had been taken for granted as long as reading had been taught, was now being seriously questioned. Studies were conducted to determine the usefulness of oral reading in life after school. When it was found that the adult in our society had much more use for silent reading than for oral reading, the emphasis in the schools shifted to silent reading. When it was found that the fastest readers were often the ablest readers, speed and comprehension in silent reading was the goal toward which reading instruction was directed.

With reading speed and comprehension receiving top rating, and with the theory that the habit of "sounding out" words slowed down the reader's rate and interfered with his thinking while reading, phonics was believed to be incompatible with the new objectives in reading.

Studies of eye movements in silent reading brought into focus the incompatibility between the reader's response to the letter sounds in words and the ideas the symbols conveyed. By comparing the eye movements of good and poor readers, the correlation between the eye movements and proficiency in reading was established. When it was found that the poor reader concentrates on a word at a time, while the able reader takes in a group of words in a single eye sweep, and that the habit of looking at the individual elements in the word interferes with proper eye sweep

[4] Vol. XIII (April–May 1931).

in silent reading, the case against phonics was unquestionable. Further evidence, however, was still to come.

PSYCHOLOGICAL IMPLICATIONS AND CHILD DEVELOPMENT

The application of psychology to reading instruction and the influence of newly established principles of child development had a damaging effect on phonics. The theory that the "whole child" comes to school with varied interests, needs, and potentialities was alien to "phonetic" instruction and favored the dictum that children learn to read by reading, which was but another way of saying that instruction in phonics was unnecessary anyway. It was concluded that the emphasis on drill in phonics dulled the child's interest and enthusiasm for learning and stressed the mechanical rather than the mental and emotional aspects of reading. The practice of teaching children to "sound out" the unfamiliar words in reading was regarded as unsound, and it was thought that the methods of teaching the letter sounds in isolation violated the law of transfer of skills from phonics to reading. Little if anything at all was left to be said in favor of "phonetic" instruction in the schools.

With each additional study in educational psychology and the nature and character of the reading process, the ultimate fate of phonics became increasingly clear. Arthur I. Gates summed up the situation in a single statement when he said, "Carry-over of phonetic knowledge in reading is a clumsy and wasteful process with no certainty of results."

"PHONETIC" INSTRUCTION THREATENED WITH EXPULSION

By 1930 the mounting evidence against phonics could no longer be ignored. The philosophy of Dewey and the investigations of Thorndike, Judd, Buswell, Gates, Gray, and others left no doubt in the minds of many school administrators that henceforth phonics would have to be relegated to a minor role in reading or be ousted from the schools altogether. Directors of elementary education and supervisors of classroom instruction were adamant in their stand against the traditional methods of teaching phonics. Often with as much heat as reason! In many schools teachers were warned by their superiors against emphasizing the "phonetic" aspect of the words in reading. Meaning was to be considered the chief factor in word perception in reading, and children were to be instructed to identify the new words by "guessing from the context."

It must not be assumed, however, that "phonetic" instruction, although bitterly opposed by many, was rejected by all or that all methods of teaching phonics were opposed with equal intensity or that those who "believed" in phonics gave up without a struggle. Teachers, especially those in the primary grades, were among the most loyal supporters of phonics, and although the defenders were often outnumbered by those who opposed phonics, both groups were equally unmovable.

Educational meetings in which both schools of thought were represented were certain to be exciting. With the first mention of phonics the battle lines formed, and the fight was on.

The diehards, determined to save face, mourned their lost love in secret. The teachers who had always depended on phonics as an aid to reading were unable to see how they or their pupils were going to succeed without it. "But phonics," as one teacher later expressed it, "in our school was out, and I was scared to death to teach it!"

Others confessed that they went right on teaching phonics when no one was looking, as if on the theory that what one doesn't know doesn't hurt him. With the lesson completed, the phonic charts and cards were restored to their secret place in the closet, until the next time when no one in authority would know what the conscientious teacher was up to!

By the beginning of the 1940s enough pressure had been brought to bear by parents and teachers alike to alert the educational consciousness to the need of phonics as a means of independent word perception in reading. The failure of the unplanned hit and miss procedures in the teaching of reading, together with the inability of children to cope with the reading vocabulary in the elementary grades and high school, eventually brought down the wrath of parents. Gradually with the silencing of the opposition to phonics the once-unwanted waif was being welcomed back to the schools.

PHONICS, BY POPULAR DEMAND

After more than a decade of teaching reading with little or no systematic instruction in phonics, the parents of the pupils in the schools had become seriously disturbed, and the teachers shared the parents' distress over the children's failure in the various subjects that depended upon the ability to read.

The layman contended that if pupils were taught the sounds of the letters in the unfamiliar words instead of having to guess the words or having to rely on a picture or the sense of the sentence to help with the word, all the confusion between words like *love* and *live, stores* and *stories, contents* and *contain,* and *experiment* and *experience* would be avoided. *Mother inquired* would not be misread *Mother asked,* or *Mother announced* as *Mother said.* There would be no need for remedial reading, since every child would be "up to standard" in reading for his age and grade, thus the parents reasoned.

Primary teachers contended that it was much easier to teach children to read with the aid of phonics than without it. Teachers in the intermediate grades and in high school complained that their pupils had not the slightest idea how to attack and identify an unfamiliar word in reading. One high school teacher complained, "I'm supposed to teach Shakespeare to students who are still in the Peter Rabbit stage of handling the reading vocabulary."

Parents were urging the schools to return to systematic instruction in phonics as the cure for the children's reading ills, and the teachers were lending their wholehearted support to the parents' demands.

Slowly at first, as if unwilling to yield to public pressure, school administrators and instructors of reading in the teachers' colleges relaxed their opposition to phonics, and by the middle of the 1940s phonics was rapidly regaining its former prestige.

WITH PHONICS BACK IN THE SADDLE

No sooner was phonics again in good repute than the teachers who had been drilling their pupils in secret were "plying their trade" in the open. The old phonic charts and cards were dusted off, and the sounding out of words could again be heard in the classrooms. The hopes of those who had been willing to sacrifice "phonetic" instruction in the schools in order once and for all to be rid of the outmoded methods of sounding out words now seemed to be doomed.

Not only the old phonic charts and cards were again in evidence in the primary classrooms but the old drills, in new form, bearing up-to-date copyrights, were flooding the market. Anybody who was sufficiently well informed to know that there are twenty-six letters in the alphabet, known as vowels and consonants, considered himself competent to prepare publishable material for "phonetic" instruction in the schools.

The young teachers, who in their childhood had had little if any systematic instruction in phonics, and therefore felt insecure in having to teach phonics, welcomed the ready-made materials and often paid for them with their own earnings. Literally tons of worthless material printed on charts and cards were sold to the schools under the name of "phonics."

INSTRUCTIONAL MATERIALS IN PHONICS

With the acceptance of phonics by school administrators, directors and supervisors of elementary education, and reading specialists, the place of phonics in the total reading program was now assured. Professional textbooks, manuals, workbooks, programs, and games and devices for teaching phonics presented a variety of approaches to "phonetic" instruction in the schools.

Basic Reading Manuals and Workbooks

The basic reading systems reflected the schools' renewed interest in phonics. The publishers of basic readers announced with pride the provision for "phonetic" instruction in the teachers' manuals and in the children's workbooks that accompanied their readers.

While phonics was in ill repute little mention of phonics was made in many of the basic reading materials. Today every basic reading system provides experience in auditory and visual discrimination; recognizing the "short" and "long" vowel sounds, the diphthongs, the so-called murmur diphthongs and "digraphs," the single consonant sounds, the blends in the initial and final position in words, the substitution of vowels as in changing the word *pet* to *pat* or *barn* to *burn,* and in the substitution of consonants—changing *mouse* to *house* or *track* to *black,* for example. Practice is also provided in rhyming words, in the phonetic analysis of words, and in structural analysis, as well as in the recognition of variants formed by adding *s, es, ed, er, ing, ly,* or *tion* to known root words as in *waits, wishes, waited, waiter, waiting, gladly,* and *action* and by adding *er* and *est* to a word like *tall* in forming *taller* and *tallest.*

Rules for pronunciation and syllabication are included in the teachers' manuals and their application is provided for in the children's workbooks that accompany the basic readers.

Other Methods and Materials

The return of phonics to good standing in the nation's schools gave rise to the publication of new textbooks and workbooks in phonics and of charts, cards, and games embracing a variety of "phonetic" approaches, some of which were the work of specialists in the field of reading and phonics.

Whatever the nature of the instructional material, whether textbooks, workbooks, games, charts, or cards, the material was certain to reflect the author's philosophy in regard to the teaching of phonics. Consequently, there are about as many different approaches to the teaching of phonics on the market as there are candidates for a coveted office in an election year.

1. The system of phonics which comprises a single children's textbook, a teachers' manual, and a series of children's workbooks and is intended as a complete program of phonics is based on what is known as the initial-blend method. The authors make

it clear that the child must be taught that there is one and only one place to attack a word and that is the initial blend.

The teacher is warned never to direct the pupil's attention to the middle or the end of a word, but always to the blend of sounds at the beginning of the word. After the "short" vowels and the sound (s) have been taught, the sounds are blended to form the units *sa, si, so, se,* and *su.* After the consonant sounds (t), (b), and (n) have been learned, these beginnings can be blended with the final consonants as in *sa-t, sat; si-t, sit; so-b, sob; se-t, set;* and *su-n, sun,* for example. The children then meet their newly worked out words in simple sentences for experiences in reading.

Later the children are taught to blend two and three initial consonant sounds with known vowels and learn the diphthongs and "digraphs" and the unstressed endings in words: *ed, er, or, ing, tion,* and *sion.*

The "important letters" in unfamiliar words are printed in color as a means of directing the child's attention to the letters. For example, in the word *read,* the pupil is told that the colored letter *a* is a frog, over which he must leap in sounding the word *re-d, red.* This is one of many examples in children's books in which color is used to attract the child's attention to a certain letter or letters in identifying the word.

2. Another approach to phonics and quite different from the one we have just observed is presented in a series of workbooks for children, with a teachers' edition accompanying each of the workbooks. These books provide extensive experiences in auditory and visual discrimination, in learning the "short" and "long" vowel sounds, the "digraphs" and diphthongs, the single consonant sounds like (b), (l), (m), and (p) in the initial position in words as in *ball, leaf, men,* and *pet,* for example, and in the final position as in *crab, school, drum,* and *sheep.*

Later in their experiences with sounds pupils learn to recognize the consonant blends in familiar words as in *star, sleep, blow,* and *spring* and then in the final position as in *apple, bottle, saddle,* and *eagle,* for example.

Exercises are provided in forming new words by substituting one initial consonant or consonant blend for another, as in changing *door* into *floor*, *star* into *car*, or *duck* into *truck*, for example. Similar exercises call for the substitution of a final consonant for another as in changing *pet* into *pen*, *bed* into *beg*, *had* into *hat*, or *cup* into *cut*, for example. The newly formed word is then written in the blank space in the sentence where it belongs.

Pupils are shown how to form compound words by combining two simple words and how to divide words into syllables with the aid of the rules that govern syllabication.

The workbooks are replete with sentences bearing blanks to be filled in with the missing words, thereby providing practice in applying what has been taught in phonics.

3. Unlike either of the two approaches we have just observed is a method which, instead of using reading as its starting point, begins with the pupil's learning to write the letters that stand for the sounds in spoken English as they are combined into words. The first step, then, is spelling, not reading, the theory being that if a child can write a word he can also read it. Comprehension is developed as the new words are written in the sentences.

Formal reading, that is reading from a book, is not introduced until the pupil has mastered enough words to make comprehension of a sentence instantly possible.

This approach to phonics is obviously not intended as an aid to look-say reading, but rather as a means of teaching the basic technique of the language arts—writing, reading, speaking, and spelling (including phonics) in a single "integrated subject."

4. Among the various programs of "phonetic" instruction intended as an aid to whole-word recognition in reading is one embodied in a handbook to be used by the pupils and their teacher "from day to day." This plan of instruction is presented in four parts. Part I introduces the pupils to the single consonants in their initial position in words. In Part II the consonant blends, including the triple blends, are introduced. Part III presents the vowels, beginning with the "long" vowels. The "short" vowels are introduced as "the basic sounds of the vowels." Part IV establishes the method of dealing with the vowels, which, according to the author, is the heart of the method.

There are four steps in the child's thinking in identifying an unfamiliar word: (1) How does the word begin? (2) What are the vowels? (3) What do the vowels say? (4) What is the word? The pupil then checks the word against the context to see if it fits the sense of the sentence.

The handbook, which is not intended to replace the school's basic reading program but to go along with it, is to be used as an adjunct in the presentation of new words in each reading lesson.

5. We now come to a method of instruction known as the phonetic approach to reading, in which phonics is considered not as an aid to whole-word recognition in reading teaching and learning but as *the* method of teaching children to read and which, when incorporated in a series of readers, may serve to replace the school's basic reading system.

By the phonetic approach to reading the letters of the alphabet and their sounds are made the basis for beginning reading. Thus phonics is introduced and systematic instruction in phonics starts at the time reading instruction begins.

Beginners in school are taught to analyze and sound out words before they do any preprimer reading. As soon as the first consonant has been introduced and the "long" and "short" vowel sounds have been learned, children start sounding out the words bearing the known consonant and vowel sounds. Words which have been sounded out are then used in sentences and stories for reading.

New words in sentences are sounded out before reading takes place in order to assure mastery of the reading vocabulary. For this reason and because the sounds of the letters of the alphabet rather than reading for meaning are made the basis for beginning reading, specialists and researchers in reading view with alarm the adoption of phonics as *the* method of teaching reading in our elementary schools.

6. From the phonetic approach to reading we turn our attention to a program of teaching phonics, which, although it too begins early in the first grade, recognition of a limited number of "sight" words precedes instruction in the sounds of English. According to the authors of the method, children who have achieved reading readiness are also ready to use phonics as a reading tool.

Specific instruction, they therefore conclude, should be introduced early in the first grade.

This method of teaching phonics comprises two large pictorial charts in attractive color, one for identification of the consonant sounds and the other for the vowel sounds; a teachers' manual; and a series of books intended to help the children in mastering the "phonetic" elements largely by their own efforts, with little help from the teacher.

The plan emphasizes instruction (a) in all the initial consonant sounds; (b) in all the final consonant sounds; and (c) in the vowel sounds.

In their evaluation of the method the authors point out that a child learns the sound (s), for example, without effort, thinking he is playing a game, and can very soon, by listening to the word *see,* tell his teacher whether he hears the sound (s) at the beginning or at the end of the word, and that he will not reverse the initial and final positions of the sound nor will he be likely to confuse the voiceless (s) in words like *see* and *this* with the voiced *s* as in *runs* and *goes.*

7. Let us now consider still another plan of "phonetic" instruction in workbook form, which, according to the authors, provides a balanced program of phonics and word analysis that enables pupils to pronounce and understand new words as they meet them in reading.

The word-meaning skills include inferring meanings from context clues, matching words with pictures, classifying words according to meanings, recognizing synonyms and antonyms, studying words with more than one meaning, and practice in matching words with definitions.

The phonetic-analysis skills include recognition of the consonant sounds and blends, the "phonetic" elements like *at, ot, an, en, ay, ill, all, un,* and *old,* knowing the "long" and "short" sounds of the vowels, the various vowel combinations, and the vowels with *r* as in *er, or, ir,* and *ur.*

The word-analysis skills are intended to show the pupil to see the "base form" in the simplest derived forms as *run* in *runs,* for example, and finding a small word in a longer word.

The word-structure skills include recognizing base words in derived words, omitting a first or last letter to make a new word, recognizing compound words and contractions, and dividing words into syllables.

Word-building skills include the forming of plurals by adding *s, es,* and *ies* and adding *ing; ed, y, er, est,* and *ly* to root words.

Dictionary skills include an understanding of alphabetization, syllabication, accent, guide words, respelling of words, pronunciation keys, definitions, and multiple meanings.

8. Unlike any of the foregoing methods of teaching phonics is the plan that employs the "auditory and visual approach" to phonics in a series of workbooks for the children's use. The author of the method contends that a child should not form the habit of trying to identify a word by sounding the separate letters in the word nor by analytical pronunciation. After children have adequate "phonetic" knowledge for word analysis, they are to be trained (a) to focus the attention upon the initial letter, letter combination, or syllable, getting in mind the pronunciation of the new word; (b) to look forward to see the remaining part of the word; and (c) to return the eyes to the beginning of the word, viewing it as a whole.

In case the child does not succeed in identifying the word, it is suggested that he be asked to sound or pronounce the beginning of the word, that is, the initial consonant, consonant combination, or syllable. The author contends that too often children "tear" the word apart orally and fail in the blending process that is necessary for identification of the new word as a whole.

9. Our next program for "phonetic" instruction as an aid to reading for meaning is one that comprises a textbook and two accompanying workbooks for building word power in reading.

The program provides practice in auditory discrimination by utilizing the sound elements in the pupil's spoken vocabulary and associating the sounds with the visual form of the word. The older methods, the authors point out, translated visual forms into speech elements without the certainty that the pupil had heard the sound elements in speech, and since only words are used that are already in the child's speaking vocabulary, attention to meaning is maintained throughout at a high level of interest.

Ear training begins with children's listening for initial consonant sounds and advances to listening for initial consonant blends, final consonant sounds, and rhyming words.

Exercises in visual discrimination begin with simple matching of letters and continue through the more difficult stages of detecting differences in words that are only slightly unlike in appearance.

The workbooks that provide varied experiences in "fundamental instruction in visual and auditory perception of word elements" are not, according to the authors, to be interpreted as presenting a complete program in reading.

10. The "phonetic" program that was the outcome of a phonetic analysis of the sounds of English in the children's reading vocabulary in the first three grades and experimental research to determine when and how phonics should be taught as a functional means of independent word perception in reading comprises a series of children's textbooks for instruction in phonics, a set of workbooks that may be used with, or independently of, the children's books, a readiness book in phonics, and a teachers' manual.

The program provides (a) a period of readiness for phonics in which children learn to listen to the beginning and ending sounds in familiar words, to recognize spoken words by their beginning sounds, and to discriminate between likenesses and differences in spoken and written words; (b) for the children's discovery of the vowel and consonant sounds from known words that were learned as "sight" words in reading; and (c) for instruction in learning how to attack and identify an unfamiliar word while reading, not by sounding out the word but by associating the sounds with the letters in the word, then blending the sounds and checking the word against the context to see if it fits the sense of the sentence.

The plan further provides for the ready recognition of the most frequently occurring prefixes and suffixes, the variants formed by adding *s, es, est, ed, er, or, ar, ly, ing,* and *tion* to root

words in the children's reading vocabulary, the rules for pronunciation and syllabication, and a brief introduction to the
dictionary.

The "phonetic" program is intended as a part of the schools'
total reading program, whether it be individualized reading, or a
basal reading system that may or may not be based on the linguistic theory of learning to read.

11. Finally, there is the plan of instruction that was developed for the teaching of spelling, with the purpose of giving
the child mastery over the spelling of words, but which is also
recommended as an aid in teaching phonics and word analysis.

The program includes a chart, two attractively colored "sound
sticks," one black and the other red, and several recorded lessons.
The consonants and consonant blends that are used for the beginnings of words are on the black sound stick; those that are
needed for the endings of words are on the red sound stick. The
chart bears the vowels and combinations of vowels that are used
as the foundation letters in forming words. As the teacher pronounces a word the pupil maneuvers the colored sticks on the
chart so as to form the word the teacher pronounced.

The recorded lessons are useful in demonstrating the teaching
of the consonants, vowels, key words, blends, and the syllabication of words.

PHONICS AND THE LINGUISTS' THEORY OF READING INSTRUCTION

The proponents of the linguistic approach to reading,
which is based on the alphabet principle—the spelling patterns
of words—find "phonetic" instruction irrelevant to reading teaching and learning.

In his book *Linguistics and Reading,* Charles C. Fries states
the situation clearly when he says:

> During the practices necessary to build up automatic responses to
> the distinctive features of the letters of our alphabet in contrast
> with each other and in the contrastive sequences, there must be no
> attempt to connect these letters with sounds . . . Building a clear
> understanding of the connection of spelling-patterns with the word

patterns of the language is the most important step in learning to read.[5]

The avoidance of teaching the sounds of the letters is emphasized by Fries when he says:

> Only complete words are pronounced. The pronunciation of the "word" is thus attached to the total spelling pattern that represents that word. The spelling pattern *cat* presents the word (kæt) as pronounced. Sounds are not given to the separate letters of a spelling pattern. The understanding of the difference that any particular letter makes in the spelling pattern is built up out of the experience of pronouncing a variety of word pairs with minimum differences in their *spelling patterns*. We avoid completely such a question as "What does the letter C say?"[6]

In an article in the *Elementary English Review,* the late Leonard Bloomfield had this to say:

> The most serious drawback of all the English reading instruction known to me . . . is the drawback of the word method. . . . The chief source of difficulty in getting the content of reading is imperfect mastery of the mechanics of reading. . . . We must train the child to respond vocally to the sight of letters.
>
> The letters of the alphabet are signs which direct us to produce sounds of our language. A confused and vague appreciation of this fact has given rise to the so-called "phonic" methods of teaching children to read. These methods suffer from several serious faults.
>
> The inventors of these methods confuse writing with speech. They plan the work as though the child were being taught to pronounce—that is, as if the child were being taught to speak. . . . If a child has not learned to utter the speech-sounds of our language, the only sensible course is to postpone reading until he has learned to speak. As a matter of fact, nearly all six-year-old children have long ago learned to speak their native language; they have no need whatever of the drill which is given by phonic methods.[7]

Under the heading "Teaching Children to Read" in *Let's Read* by Leonard Bloomfield and Clarence L. Barnhart, the authors tell us:

5 (New York: Holt, Rinehart and Winston, Inc., 1963), p. 195.

6 *Ibid.*, pp. 203–204.

7 April–May 1942.

When we present a pair of words like *can* and *fan,* a child may have no notion that these words are similar in sound, or that the similar spelling indicates a similar sound. It would be a waste of time to try, as do the advocates of "phonic" methods, to explain this to him. All we do is to present such words together; the resemblance of sound and spelling will do its work without any explanation from us. Only we must remember that this takes a great deal of time and repetition.[8]

To the linguist, then, who would teach children to read by developing automatic responses to the spelling patterns of words, and to the contrastive items and sequence of items within pairs of word patterns that separate and identify each of the word patterns, phonics as an aid to reading is inapplicable.

If proof were needed to substantiate the belief that phonics is today as it has been in the past, a controversial subject among the "experts" and the would-be experts in education, one would find ample evidence in the varying approaches to reading teaching and learning, and in the widely differing methods and materials for teaching phonics in the nation's schools.

*AN INFORMAL TEST**

1. Which one of the famous Websters introduced the instruction of the "powers" of the letters of the alphabet in the schools 180 years ago?

2. Who was the distinguished educator of Massachusetts whose caustic condemnation of the alphabet method of reading instruction paved the way for the "more sensible phonetic approach" to reading, but who did not live to see the ABC method outmoded in the schools?

3. The demand for instruction in phonics in the 1880s was prompted by the dissatisfaction of which of the following methods of instruction: the word method, the phonetic approach, or the linguistic approach to reading?

4. Which method of blending the sounds in "phonetic" instruction did Rebecca Pollard contribute to the teaching of reading, the initial blend method or the "families" of sounds?

[8] (Detroit, Mich.: Wayne State University Press, 1961).

* Answers are listed under the appropriate chapter number in the Appendix.

5. Did the initial blend method of the Beacon system of phonics (a) precede or (b) follow the organized systems of phonics based on the concept of "families" of sounds?

6. Were the earliest systems of phonics synthetic or analytic in their approach?

7. Was it the alphabet-phonetic approach to reading or the ABC method of teaching reading that was superseded by the word method of reading in the middle of the 1800's at about the time the McGuffey Readers were published?

8. Was the philosophy of the founders of the progressive movement in education in harmony with, or in opposition to, the highly organized systems of phonics in relation to reading instruction in the schools?

9. Which of the following factors contributed to the discredit of "phonetic" instruction in the nation's schools a generation ago: (a) the relative importance of silent versus oral reading in life after school; (b) the damaging effect of "sounding out" words on speed and comprehension in reading; (c) the esteem in which phonics was held by certain school administrators, their teachers, and the patrons of the schools; or (d) the lack of carry-over of "phonetic" knowledge and skill to comprehension in reading?

10. In a given school in which whole-word recognition or look-say reading is the prevailing method of teaching reading, are the sounds of the letters of the alphabet likely or unlikely to be the basis of instruction in beginning reading?

11. Is the function of phonics in relation to reading viewed differently or alike by the proponents of (a) the phonetic approach to reading; (b) look-say or whole-word recognition in reading; (c) the linguistic approach to reading?

12. Is the concept of phonics as an aid to reading in harmony with or in opposition to the phonetic approach to reading?

13. Do all workbooks and other teaching materials on phonics currently in use in the schools bear evidence that the original practice of sounding out words in reading has been completely abandoned?

14. Since it has been found that the practice of teaching the sounds of the letters in isolation, that is, apart from the word whole, violates the law of transfer of skills, has the practice been discontinued in the schools?

15. When pupils who rated highest in their ability to sound out the unfamiliar words in reading consistently made the lowest scores in

speed and comprehension was that (a) necessarily the fault of phonics or (b) could the methods of teaching phonics in relation to reading have been to blame?

16. When phonics was on trial during the 1930s, who on the whole were its most ardent supporters, the educators or the parents of the children in the schools?

17. Is look-say reading associated with (a) the phonetic approach to reading or (b) the concept of phonics as an aid to whole-word recognition in reading?

18. Now that phonics is once more in good repute, is there a oneness of opinion on how and when phonics should be taught, or is phonics still a controversial subject among educators and laymen alike?

13

SPEAKING OF PHONICS

Phonics, long a controversial subject among educators, is no longer the concern solely of the schools. Editors and staff writers of lay periodicals are alerting the public to the need for more and earlier instruction in phonics as the "only means of remedying the large scale retardation in reading in the nation's schools"; and what the public wants is not always in keeping with the policies of our educational institutions.

When, how, and how early in the school life of a child phonics should be taught depends upon the educational philosophy of those who are defending their positions in regard to the teaching of phonics.

To the laymen and the educationists who would have children learn from the very beginning to recognize and recall a word not by the way the word looks and by its meaning in the sentence, but by the sounds of the letters in the word, look-say reading teaching is anathema; it must be replaced, they contend, by the phonetic approach to reading if the young people of America are to learn to read as well as the youth of other lands, notably Russia.

On the other hand are the specialists and researchers in the field of reading who value phonics not as a method of teaching reading but as one of many means of independent word perception in whole-word recognition; phonics should be utilized, this group contends, after beginners in school have developed the desire to read and have acquired the habit of reading for meaning.

To the parents of the children in the schools, phonics occupies a place apart in their hearts and minds. The average parent in speaking of phonics is all but reverent in its praise. He "believes" in phonics as the panacea for a child's reading ills, often in disregard of the nature of the difficulty or its cause. To him phonics is the unfailing means of sounding out the new words the young reader meets on the printed page; and since recognizing the words is in his judgment synonymous with knowing how to read, and since the ability to read is essential to a child's success in school, one can understand a parent's faith in the efficacy of phonics.

THE PHONETIC APPROACH TO READING

Phonics as *the* method of teaching reading, although aptly described in the following manner by Rudolph Flesch, the author of *Why Johnny Can't Read,* is not so narrowly interpreted by every advocate of the method.

> We mean phonics as a way to learn reading. We mean phonics that is taught to the child letter by letter and sound by sound until he knows it—and when he knows it he knows how to read. . . . We mean phonics as it was taught in this country until some thirty years ago and it is taught all over the world today. . . .
>
> Let's understand each other. Systematic phonics is one thing, un-systematic phonics is another. Systematic phonics is *the* way to teach reading, un-systematic phonics is nothing. . . . Phonics is *not* one of many techniques the child can use to unlock the meaning of words—phonics is simply the knowledge of the way spoken English is put on paper.[1]

Upon the completion of Flesch's four clearly defined steps of classroom procedure in teaching reading, the author points out that Johnny has learned to read and write practically all the words that follow some spelling rule.

Then, after his having also mastered the irregular spellings, words with *sion, tion; ight, ought; chief, thief;* and *break, steak,*

[1] (New York: Harper & Row, Publishers, Inc., 1955), pp. 121–122.

as well as words with silent *v, t, l,* and *g,* Johnny, according to the author, has learned to read.

It is understandable that the patrons of the schools should have found in Flesch an ardent disciple of their own beliefs in regard to the teaching of reading. The time-honored concept of sounding out the words on the printed page persists in the popular mind, if for no other reason than that the plan of beginning with the smallest elements in a word and proceeding to the larger unit, the whole word or sentence, seems so much more logical than the analytic approach of starting with the whole word and proceeding to the smaller units in the word.

It is understandable, too, that parents whose children are retarded in reading, believing that the phonetic approach to reading is but another name for phonics, welcome it as the means of teaching their children to read.

Unfortunately, the layman has little knowledge of what the phonetic approach really is. One intelligent but uninformed parent learned quite by accident what the method implies. Barbara's father was a student in college when his daughter was in the first grade. At home one evening, with her book opened before her, Barbara was sounding out every word as she came to it in the sentence she was trying to read.

"Wuh e, we; fuh ou n duh, found; a buh i guh, big; buh uh guh, bug. We found a big bug."

"What on earth are you doing?" her father asked in amazement.

"Reading!" Barbara said. "We all read that way in school."

The following morning Barbara's father was in the principal's office. "When will my daughter be taught to read?" he demanded to know. "Instead of reading the sentences, she sounds them out! Since when has this jargon taken the place of reading in the school?"

The change-over from whole-word recognition to the phonetic approach to reading was initiated by a group of parents who repeatedly had called to the attention of the board of education what they believed to be the critical need for earlier and more instruction in phonics.

It should be said in defense of the well-meaning but uninformed parents that they were wholly unaware of the gravity of the error they had initiated. They did not know that when a beginner in reading is taught the sounds of the letters before he has learned to read for meaning, the habit of concentrating on the sounds and their letters in the sentence has to be unlearned before the mind is free to comprehend what the author of the sentence is telling the reader. When wrong habits of reading have become firmly fixed in the mind of a child, it is extremely difficult to uproot them. It has been done, but not without a great deal of reteaching, and with children whose intelligence was considerably above the average. Unless Barbara is a bright child she may never become the proficient reader she might have been.

PHONICS AS AN AID TO WHOLE-WORD RECOGNITION IN READING

In the belief that reading from the primary school through the university and indeed in life after school is an intellectual activity, the real job of teaching reading is teaching pupils to think. A child's first experience with the printed page should be that of finding out what the black marks on white are telling him, the words being but the symbols by means of which the author is signaling the reader to hear what he has to say.

Whole-word recognition, then, comes first. Phonics comes later to reinforce look-say reading when the reading vocabulary becomes too diversified to be recognized and recalled on sight with only the help of an obliging context, except perhaps by the gifted in reading.

In whole-word recognition, instead of sounding out the sentence about the big bug, the beginner in school reads the line straight through, *We found a big bug,* unimpeded by the letters and their sounds while his mind is on the meaning of the sentence.

In a first-grade room where whole-word recognition is the prevailing method of teaching reading, one of the boys, after having read the sentence: "It takes a lot of courage for a man to be an astronaut," commented on the bravery our astronauts have displayed.

On another occasion after a visitor had expressed her appreciation of the visit she had enjoyed in Miss Jenkins' first-grade room, and where the children are also being taught look-say reading, one of the pupils reached for a book on the reading table with the question: "May I read something from this book, Miss Jenkins, that our visitor made me think of?" Whereupon the little fellow proceeded to read:

> And they danced and they sang,
>   and each Visitor's attitude
> Was his very best way
>   of expressing his gratitude
> To Johnny Crow and his Garden[2]

How long might it have been before this first-grade child could have interpreted the quotation as he did, had his ability to read the lines depended upon his first having to learn the sounds of the letters in the words, and then having to recognize the words by sounding them out?

It must not be assumed that look-say reading teaching and learning is for the bright child only. Children of average intelligence and below the average in mental ability are learning to read by the same method their more gifted contemporaries are enjoying, provided that the whole-word method of recognition is reinforced by effective means of word perception in reading.

When reading for meaning precedes instruction in phonics, the readiness program in phonics may run concurrently with the school's program in beginning reading. Like proficiency in reading, which is certainly not achieved by a single bound, "phonetic" skill and ability do not spring full-blown into being like Minerva from the head of Jupiter. Every primary teacher knows how gradually, sometimes almost imperceptibly, the majority of children grow into reading and phonics, often with serious handicaps to impede their progress.

DEVELOPING "PHONETIC" SKILL AND ABILITY

The ability of the young reader to listen to the sounds in spoken words, and then to be able to identify an unfamiliar word

2 From *Johnny Crow's New Garden* by L. Leslie Brooke. Used with the permission of the copyright owners, Frederick Warne & Co., Inc.

so quickly that he remains in communication with the author of the sentence as he works out the new word is the result of his having achieved several specific skills and abilities. Beginning perhaps in the kindergarten, children learn to hear like beginnings and endings in familiar words and to recognize the spoken words by their beginning sounds; later they learn the sounds of the letters in the reading vocabulary; and how to attack and identify an unfamiliar word in reading without losing contact with the author of the text, while in the process of identifying the word.

Hearing When Words Begin Alike

Being able to discriminate between the sounds in spoken words ranks high among the abilities that determine both a pupil's success in learning to read and his readiness for phonics as an aid to reading.

In their clinical studies of children's abilities in reading, Donald D. Durrell and Helen A. Murphy found that among the many factors that determine a child's success in learning to read, his ability to notice the separate sounds in spoken words is a highly important one. It was found that every child who came to the clinic with reading achievement below first-grade level had a marked inability to discriminate sounds in words.[3]

It is significant in this connection to note that English-speaking children who are not handicapped by impaired hearing have already had several years of preschool experience in hearing the sounds in English words. Thus beginners in school are ready to build on the experiences they have had since infancy in hearing sounds in spoken words. They learn through listening to hear that *mummy* and *mother* begin like *Monday, money,* and *monkey;* that *milk* begins like *mittens* and *middle;* that *mouse* begins like *mouth* and *mountain* and not like *money, milk,* or *music.*

When children are expected to hear that words begin alike because they start with the same consonant, regardless of the adjacent vowel sound, they are expected to hear that which it is almost impossible to hear.

One *hears* like beginnings in words or syllables when *both* the initial consonant and the adjacent vowel sound alike, because the vowel is invariably blended with the initial consonant

[3] *Education,* 82 (May 1962).

in the spoken word. Thus one hears a different beginning in *big, box, bunny, bounce, beautiful* (even though they all begin with the same consonant) because the vowel sounds differ at the beginning of the words. One hears (bĭ) in *big*, (bŏ) in *box*, (bŭ) in *bunny*, (bou) in *bounce*, and (bū) in *beautiful* when the words are said or sung in the English language.

It has also been found that in the functioning of phonics in word perception in reading, it is the *beginning* (vowel and consonant sound) of the unfamiliar word that gives the reader the clue to the word's identity.

"I was pretty sure that word was *mountain*," a young reader reported, "because I saw that it started with (mou). Then when the story said that it was a big hill that the boy climbed up, I knew it was *mountain*."

It was the beginning of the word—the consonant plus its vowel sounds and not the consonant by itself that gave the reader the clue to the word *mountain*. Another child had guessed that the new word in the sentence she was reading was *leaped*, "because," she said, "I saw that it started with (lea) and it told how the rabbit got over the ground."

Hearing When Words End Alike

So far we have been speaking only of the beginning sounds in words. What about the sound or sounds one hears at the end of a spoken word or syllable? The sound (g), for example, is heard at the end of the words *pi-g, do-g, fla-g, ru-g, fo-g;* the sound (sh) at the end of *di-sh, spla-sh, ru-sh;* the sounds (st) at the end of *fir-st, la-st, mu-st, ea-st, pa-st,* for example (see Chapter 3).

Discovering the Vowel and Consonant Sounds

When reading precedes instruction in phonics, children may have the creative experience of *discovering* the sounds in the reading vocabulary from words that have been learned as "sight" words in reading.

The Vowel Sounds

We observed in Chapter 3 that any known word bearing the vowel sound to be learned and which can be pictured may serve as the pupil's key or cue word for learning the sound.

In most school districts the word *bag* or *bags* is a suitable word for discovering the vowel sound (ă). In other communities the word *cat* or *bat* or even *rat* may be more meaningful to the children. The word *pig* is an excellent word for discovering the vowel sound (ĭ), except for children who have never seen a pig. They may never have seen a kid, but what American child is not thoroughly familiar with the term *kids.* The words *pin, picture,* or *pickles,* too, may serve as key or cue words for discovering the sound (ĭ). From a conceptual standpoint, the word *pistol* would leave nothing to be desired, but one would hardly use *pistol* as an appropriate word for instructing a child in phonics.

For children who are familiar with the plump, red-breasted bird, *robin* is an interesting word for discovering the vowel sound (ŏ); for others, the word *box* or *bottle* might be more meaningful. The word *nest* is generally appropriate for learning the vowel sound (ĕ). The word *bed* is equally good unless it is used for discovering the consonant sound (d). The word *bus* is a suitable word for the vowel sound (ŭ) for children who ride buses. In one school where the children had never seen a bus, the words *mud, mutt, tummy,* and even *mussed-up* and *monkey business* were suggested by the pupils as good words for the sound (ŭ).

The word *cute* was suggested by a teacher for the sound (ū). "But," she asked, "how would one picture the word *cute?*" The word *mule* is equally appropriate in some sections of the country. The word *music,* although a bit difficult to picture, is generally a suitable word for the sound (ū). The words *meat, leaf,* or *leaves* may serve as key or cue words for discovering the sound (ē). In one school a boy offered the word *fleas* instead of *leaves,* "because," he said, "fleas are alive and leaves aren't." Another child suggested the "policeman's beat" as being a good word for the sound (ē); "beetles," he added, "would be awfully good too!"

The word *cow* or *cows* is appropriate for the vowel sounds (ou) except where the children have never seen a cow. In one Midwest community a little girl who had lived on a farm suggested the word *sow* for the vowel sounds (ou) and added, "and it rhymes with *cow!*"

The Consonant Sounds

We noted in Chapter 3 that any known word bearing the consonant sound to be learned and which occurs at the end of the word where it can clearly be heard and which can be pictured may serve as the key or cue word for discovering the sound.

The word *sheep* may be an excellent word for discovering the consonant sound (p). In some school districts, the words *cap, pup,* or *mop,* or better yet *cop,* would be better known than *sheep* and would therefore be preferable to *sheep* for learning the sound (p).

The word *boat* may be a known word for discovering the sound (t) where children are familiar with boats. In some school districts it was found that *coat* or *feet* or *cat* was more meaningful than *boat* as a key or cue word for learning the sound (t). The word *cub* or *crab* or *tub* may be useful as a known word for discovering the consonant sound (b). In one school a child contributed the word *rob* as a useful word for learning the sound and told how the word could be pictured by showing an appropriate drawing for the word. In a rural community a little girl suggested *corncob* as an interesting word for the sound (b).

The word *drum* or *ice cream* is a more meaningful cue word for discovering the sound (m) than *broom,* for example. The word *gum* is frequently suggested by children as a good word for the sound. The word *bed* is a familiar word to nearly all children, although the word *God* has frequently been suggested, as well as the word *mad.* The word *ball* or *bell* is more appropriate than *doll* as a key or cue word for learning the sound (l). Where children are familiar with trains the known word *train* may serve as a key or cue word for the sound (n). In some school districts the word *clown* may be better known and is of course much more interesting to a child than *man* or *men,* and the word *gun* is not infrequently suggested by someone in the group as a good word for the sound (n). The word *dog* is a universal favorite for discovering the sound (g); *frog* is also frequently suggested as another good word for the sound (g). On one occasion when a little girl suggested the word *rag* as a cue word for the sound (g) another child offered the word *tag,* "because *tag,*" she said, "is a lot more fun than *rag.*"

The difference in ease and interest between a child's discovering the vowel and consonant sounds himself and having the sounds told to him is the difference between his enjoying a creative experience and being subjected to boredom and unnecessary hardship in learning the sounds. How exciting it is to discover the sounds in familiar words and then to find these same sounds again and again in working out new words and phrases in the reading situations; and how dull and monotonous the drill on isolated sounds! Moreover, when a child learns to associate a sound with its letter in a word whole, he is learning a skill in a situation in which the skill is to function. When he is taught the sounds in isolation he is being expected to learn them in a situation in which the skill never functions in reading. Every teacher knows that in reading the letter sounds always occur in words, never in isolation apart from the words.

After the children have learned the sounds from their key or cue words the next step is, of course, to associate the sounds with the letters in working out new words in reading as we observed in Chapter 3.

CHILDREN'S NEED
FOR WORD-PERCEPTION SKILLS

A junior high school teacher recently complained that although his students knew the sounds of all the letters in the alphabet, they had not the slightest idea how to "unlock" the unfamiliar words in their subject-matter textbooks. "If they can't guess the word," he said, "they're sunk! There's something radically wrong with the way reading is being taught down there in the grades. That's for sure!"

It is look-say reading—whole-word recognition that is being taught "down there in the grades," and it is a foregone conclusion that when students have difficulty in coping with the reading vocabulary on the higher levels of learning the blame for the difficulty is placed squarely on look-say reading in the school. It is for the prevention of conditions like the one cited by the junior high school teacher that the advocates of the phonetic approach to reading claim to have the perfect prophylaxis.

A case in point is that of a student named Helen, in whose

school look-say reading is the prevailing method of teaching reading, and who, like the junior high school students, had difficulty in identifying the vocabulary in her subject-matter textbooks, in spite of the instruction she had had in phonics.

Before Helen was seven years old she astounded her parents by her ability to read. "I can't understand how that child can know what the words are!" Helen's mother was heard to exclaim. "I've seen her time and again read a whole story by herself during the commercials on a TV show."

"I know that word," she will tell me. "That's *grandfather*. It's a lot bigger than *father* and it looks like *grandfather*. That's *circus* and that word is *clown;* and I think that word has to be *clown*. He was as funny as any clown, and made everybody laugh."

It's a mystery to me how that child can tell what the words are simply by the way they look. *School, story, baby, boys, girls, telephone, automobile, said, and, was, have, want, look, found, grasshoppers, skunks, frogs, bees, rabbits, mice*—she takes them all in stride as she reads. She doesn't pay any attention to the way the words are spelled. I don't think she even looks at the letters. She just sees the words and knows what they say in the sentence. It's really wonderful! And she's still only in the second grade.

When she was halfway through the fifth grade, Helen's father requested an interview with the school superintendent. "Will you tell me," the father asked, "what has happened to my daughter's reading? All through the first grade, she was a bluebird [the bluebirds being the ablest readers in the grade]. Even in the second grade she was a bluebird! And what is she now? A remedial reading case! A remedial reading case!" the man repeated, bringing his clenched fist down on the desk. "What happened between the second grade and now? Can you tell me?"

Helen's parents could not understand why their once able reader should now be having so much difficulty with the vocabulary in her textbooks that she was falling behind in her studies and was no longer interested in reading. The words, she complained, "kept getting her down."

In the primary grades the number of different words in the readers was still small enough to be identified on sight, so the whole-word method alone sufficed in meeting Helen's vocabulary needs. But now in the fifth grade, where the social studies—

history and geography—health, mathematics, and science were adding their own particular terminology to the total vocabulary load, there were far too many different and unfamiliar words to be identified and recalled on sight.

Does that mean that Helen should have been taught from the very beginning to recognize words by the way they sound and not by the ways the words look and by their meaning in the sentence? Helens' parents thought so. Indeed, they were sure of it. "It's that modern look-say way they now have of teaching reading," they contended, that was responsible for their daughter's plight. If the schools would go back to the phonetic way of teaching reading, they insisted, the students would know how to read and there would be no need for remedial reading.

It may seem reasonable to blame the prevailing method of teaching reading when pupils like Helen and the junior high school students did not know how to "unlock" the new words in their subject-matter textbooks. It was, however, not look-say reading that was at fault but the failure of their schools to reinforce whole-word recognition with effective techniques of word perception.

Our fifth-grade pupil and the junior high school students lacked the know-how to identify the vocabulary in their subject-matter textbooks. What they had been taught in phonics fell short of enabling them successfully to identify the reading vocabulary when it had become too diversified to be recognized and recalled on sight. These young people did not have the techniques of word perception they needed to reinforce look-say reading now that whole-word recognition *alone* was no longer adequate. Nor was this all that the students lacked. Let it be said, and emphatically, that the ability to "unlock" the unfamiliar words on the printed page is not synonymous with "knowing how to read," a fact that is often overlooked by the layman and educationalist alike.

Having worked out the unfamiliar words on the printed page, the reader still has to come to grips with what the author of the text is telling him. The reader must be able to reproduce in his mind what he would hear if the author were speaking to him. The words on the printed page are but the symbols of the author's ideas. Having the know-how to "unlock" the reading vocabulary is one thing, but knowing what the words symbolize is quite another!

It is the function of phonics to enable the young reader, in conjunction with such other means as are needed, to identify the reading vocabulary. It is not the business of phonics to instruct and inspire the reader to comprehend the meaning of the words. To expect phonics to embrace the conceptual aspects of reading is expecting the impossible.

We observed in Chapter 2 how the two boys, George and John, identified the new words in the article they had chosen to read, and to do it so quickly that they remained in communication with the author of the piece while they identified the words. The boys had learned upon encountering a new word in reading to see whether a quick look at the word as a whole with the sense of the sentence in mind would reveal the word's identity. If so, all well and good! If more help was needed, they had learned to look for a known part or component in the word for a clue to the word's identity. Recognition of the first syllable, or even the beginning (vowel and consonant) of the word, with the help of the context, may be all that is needed, provided, of course, that the reader has auditory knowledge of the word.

We noted how George, upon giving the word *capsule* "the once over," as he said, saw right away that the word started with *cap;* whereupon, and without further ado, he guessed that the word was *capsule,* "because," as he said, "it fit the sentence."

If upon meeting a new word in reading the youngster fails to find a clue that will reveal the word's identity, then what? This was John's situation when, although he had recognized the syllable *cap,* he was still unable to identify the word *capsule.* He therefore proceeded to work out the syllable *sule* by associating the sounds with the letters in the syllable; then by blending the two syllables, he recognized the word and checked it against the context to see if it fit the sense of the sentence.

Suppose that the word the child meets in reading for the first time is entirely unfamiliar. Such was the case of the little girl who in reading the story of Rumplestiltskin was for the first time confronted with the name *Nickerruckerrubblegrubb.* But having learned the sounds of the letters in the reading vocabulary and how to identify an unfamiliar word by associating the sounds with the letters in the beginning and ending of the syllables straight through the word, *Ni-ck er ru-ck er rub-ble gru-bb,* and then by blending the syllables, our young reader identified the name. And she did it almost as quickly by means of phonics as if by look-say reading had the word consisted of ten known "sight" words instead.

LOOK-SAY PHONICS IN RELATION TO READING

When phonics functions almost as readily as look-say reading, it may appropriately be called look-say phonics, which equates with look-say reading in that both are geared to speed and comprehension in reading; and both function in conjunction with the contextual clue. By look-say reading a word is identified by the way the word looks, that is, by its form and the meaning of the word in the sentence. By look-say phonics the reader identifies the new word by associating the sounds with the letters he sees in the word, and by the meaning of the word in the sentence.

The reader who with the sense of the sentence in mind identifies the words *bought, thought, brought, sought,* or *wrought* by means of comparison with the known word *ought;* or *bright, fight, fright, slight,* or *plight* with the known word *right* or *night;* or the words *bold, fold, sold, hold,* or *mold* with the known word *old* may be combining look-say phonics with look-say reading in identifying the new words.

RELATION OF THE CONTEXT TO WORD PERCEPTION IN READING

We have observed again and again how the young reader, after having worked out a new word, or the unfamiliar components in the word, checked the result against the context to see if the word "fit the sense of the sentence." If it did not, but if the reader approximated the identity of the word closely enough, he was able with the help of the context to make an "educated guess" in identifying the word.

This was the case you may recall when both George and John in Chapter 2 went astray in their attack on the new word *govern-*

ment in the article they were reading. But having approximated the word's identity and with auditory knowledge of the word the boys were able, when aided by the context, to identify the word. We noted in Chapter 2, how the context came to the rescue when the little girl, upon meeting the word *meant* in the sentence she was reading, called it (mēnt). "But that," she said, "didn't make sense, so I changed it to (mĕnt) and that was right."

Then there was the case of the young reader who called the word *bushel* (bus'hel) and then corrected his mistake because the sentence told about a bushel of ripe apples. So here, too, the context came to the rescue.

Again, what was it if not the sense of the notice posted in the coach that prompted the young passenger on the train, after his having misread the line as: "No smŏk'ing in this car," to change it to "No smōk'ing in this car"?

Is the pink bow a (bou) or a (bō) in the little girl's hair? It is said of Abraham Lincoln that he taught himself to read. Is the word (rĕd) or (rēd)? There is a sentence in a certain story that tells that the animals all sat down to dinner in a row. Did the animals sit down in a (rou) or in a (rō)? The context in which each of the words in question occurs provides the answer.

IN CONCLUSION

In a language in which the sound-to-letter and letter-to-sound relationships are as irregular as in English, the reader when engaged in identifying an English word "phonetically" may not associate the right sounds with the letters in the word.

Since phonics is dependent upon the context for its validity as a feasible means of independent word perception in the English language, one should expect no more of phonics as an aid in reading the English language than to enable the reader to approximate the word's identity so closely that with the help of the contextual clue he can guess the word.

The problem of "phonetic" instruction being inextricably interwoven in the controversy over teaching reading in the nation's schools presents three widely varying points of view. The basic educationists who would make the sounds of the letters of the alphabet the basis of reading instruction in the schools are as far apart as the poles from those who regard phonics not as *the* method of teaching reading but as an aid to whole-word recognition or look-say reading teaching. The linguists, whose theory of reading instruction is entirely different from that of either the basic educationists or the specialists in the field of reading, subscribe neither to the phonetic approach to reading nor to the use of phonics as a means of independent word perception in reading.

Finally, in respect to those who have the most at stake in the controversial subject of reading teaching and learning, namely, the children in the nation's schools, let it be said that the youngster who has learned to make a quick judgment on the best way to attack and identify a new word in reading, losing no time by trial and error methods and thus is able to remain in communication with the author of the text as he identifies the word, has something of intrinsic value to take with him into high school and college and which becomes increasingly useful as he advances through his school life.

Although reading as an intellectual activity involves much more than word perception, it is nevertheless dependent upon one's recognizing the symbols that stand for the ideas expressed on the printed page, namely, the words in the reading vocabulary. To enable the young reader successfully to identify these symbols—whether he be a slow or fast learner, underprivileged or overindulged—is the goal that independent word perception in reading is intended to achieve.

Ultimately the reading vocabulary on all levels of learning must be identified and interpreted on sight—a degree of reading proficiency it is the responsibility of the schools to develop in students. The sequential stages in learning to read then, are briefly (1) when the beginner in school recognizes and recalls the printed symbols on sight, before instruction in phonics begins; (2) when phonics reinforces whole-word recognition in independent word perception in reading; and (3) when perfect synchrony between sight and sound in word perception has been achieved and the reader recognizes the reading vocabulary on sight!

ði ɛnd.

APPENDIX

Answers to the Informal Tests, Chapters 2–12.

CHAPTER 2

1.—(b)	6.—(a)	11.—(a)	15.—(a)
2.—(a)	7.—(b)	12.—(b)	16.—(b)
3.—(b)	8.—(b)	13.—(b)	17.—(a)
4.—(a)	9.—(b)	14.—(b)	18.—(b)
5.—(b)	10.—(b)		

CHAPTER 3

1.—visual; 2.—auditory; 3.—precedes; 4.—vowel; 5.—not; 6.—sound; 7.—sound; 8.—end; 9.—sound; 10.—consonant; 11.—readiness; 12.—clue; 13.—identity; 14.—identify; 15.—beginning; 16.—isolation; 17.—skill; 18.—"long"; 19.—first; 20.—end.

CHAPTER 4

1.—Phonetics; 2.—Phonetic; 3.—sound; 4.—three; 5.—four; 6.—ʒ; 7.—dʒ; 8.—ŋ; 9.—θ; 10.—ð; 11.—ʃ; 12.—ɔ:; 13.—æ; ɪ; ʌ; 14.—schwa; 15.—diphthong; 16.—(ā); (ō); (ī); 17.—macron; breve; circumflex; tilde; 18.—Second; 19.—Third; 20.—saʊndz.

CHAPTER 5

1.—(b)	4.—(b)	7.—(b)	10.—(a)
2.—(b)	5.—(b)	8.—(a)	11.—(b)
3.—(a)	6.—(a)	9.—(a)	12.—(b)

CHAPTER 6

1.—(a)	7.—(a)
2.—(a)	8.—(a)
3.—(a)	9.—(b)
4.—(b)	10.—(b)
5.—(b)	11.—(a)
6.—(b)	12.—(b)

13.—(b)	19.—(a)
14.—(b)	20.—(b)
15.—(b)	21.—(a)
16.—(a)	22.—(b)
17.—(a)	23.—(b)
18.—(b)	24.—(b)

CHAPTER 7

1.—The consonants vary in this respect.
2.—No.
3.—in *think, thistle,* and *bath*
4.—*gr, x,* and *j*
5.—(kw) in the words *queen* and *choir*
6.—*hats* and *quartz*
7.—because in the word *accent* the two *c*'s stand for different sounds
8.—(sp) and (bl)
9.—*school* and *chorus*
10.—The first sound in the words *chair* and *chimes* is (t); and the first sound in *gem* and *jet* is (d).
11.—in the words *stiff, cough, photograph,* and *laugh*
12.—the sound ʒ

13.—The letter *n* has the sound n in the words *run, nut,* and *thin* and the sound ŋ in *think, anchor* and *stronger.*
14.—The letters *ng* stand for the sounds (ŋ) + (g) in the words *finger* and *congress.*
15.—The letter *x* stands for the voiceless blend (ks), and for the voiced blend (gz).
16.—the consonant sound ʃ
17.—the consonants *h, wh,* and *y*
18.—the consonants *m, n, p, v, z, th* and *sh*
19.—The letter *l* is "silent."
20.—The letter *p* is silent in *pneumonia* and *pseudonym;* the letter *t* is silent in *listen* and *soften;* and the letter *b* is silent in the words *debt, lamb* and *plumber.*

CHAPTER 8

1.—(b)	7.—(b)
2.—(b)	8.—(a)
3.—(a)	9.—(b)
4.—(b)	10.—(a)
5.—(a)	11.—(b)
6.—(a)	12.—(b)

13.—(b)	19.—(a)
14.—(a)	20.—(b)
15.—(b)	21.—(b)
16.—(a)	22.—(a)
17.—(b)	23.—(a)
18.—(b)	24.—(b)

CHAPTER 9

1.—(a)	6.—(b)	11.—(a)	16.—(a)
2.—(a)	7.—(a)	12.—(b)	17.—(a)
3.—(a)	8.—(b)	13.—(b)	18.—(b)
4.—(a)	9.—(a)	14.—(b)	19.—(a)
5.—(b)	10.—(b)	15.—(b)	20.—(b)

CHAPTER 10

1.—(a)	4.—(b)	7.—(a)	10.—(a)
2.—(b)	5.—(a)	8.—(b)	11.—(b)
3.—(a)	6.—(a)	9.—(b)	12.—(a)

CHAPTER 11

1.—not true; 2.—not true; 3.—true; 4.—not true; 5.—true; 6.—not true; 7.—true; 8.—true; 9.—not true; 10.—true; 11.—true; 12.—true; 13.—not true; 14.—true; 15.—true; 16;—not true; 17.—true; 18.—not true; 19.—not true; 20.—not true; 21.—true; 22.—not true.

CHAPTER 12

1.—Noah Webster
2.—Horace Mann
3.—the Word Method
4.—the "families" of sounds
5.—(b)
6.—synthetic
7.—the alphabet-phonetic approach
8.—in opposition
9.—(a), (b), and (d)
10.—unlikely
11.—differently
12.—in opposition
13.—no
14.—no
15.—(b)
16.—parents of the children
17.—(b)
18.—still a controversial subject

INDEX

INDEX